The Ethics of Assistance

As globalization has deepened worldwide economic integration, moral and political philosophers have become increasingly concerned to assess duties to help needy people in foreign countries. The chapters in this volume present the latest ideas on this important topic by authors who are leading figures in these debates. At issue are both the political responsibility of governments of affluent countries to relieve poverty abroad and the personal responsibility of individuals to assist the distant needy. The wide-ranging arguments shed light on global distributive justice, human rights and their implementation, the varieties of community and the obligations they generate, and the moral relevance of distance. This provocative and timely volume will interest scholars in ethics, political philosophy, political theory, international law and development economics, as well as policy makers, aid agencies, and general readers interested in the moral dimensions of poverty and affluence.

DEEN K. CHATTERJEE is Associate Professor of Philosophy at the University of Utah. His areas of specialization are political philosophy, applied ethics, and philosophy of religion and culture. He is co-editor of *Ethics and Foreign Intervention* (Cambridge, 2003), and *Globalization, Development and Democracy* (2004).

Cambridge Studies in Philosophy and Public Policy

General editor: Douglas MacLean, *University of North Carolina, Chapel Hill*

The Ethics of Assistance

Morality and the Distant Needy

Edited by

DEEN K. CHATTERJEE
University of Utah

CAMBRIDGE
UNIVERSITY PRESS

CAMBRIDGE UNIVERSITY PRESS
Cambridge, New York, Melbourne, Madrid, Cape Town, Singapore,
São Paulo, Delhi, Dubai, Tokyo

Cambridge University Press
The Edinburgh Building, Cambridge CB2 8RU, UK

Published in the United States of America by Cambridge University Press, New York

www.cambridge.org
Information on this title: www.cambridge.org/9780521527422

First published 2004
Fourth printing 2007

A catalogue record for this publication is available from the British Library

Library of Congress Cataloguing in Publication data
The ethics of assistance : morality and the distant needy / edited by Deen K. Chatterjee.
  p.   cm. – (Cambridge studies in philosophy and public policy)
  ISBN 0 521 82042 1 (hardback) – ISBN 0 521 52742 2 (paperback)
  1. Economic assistance – Moral and ethical aspects – Developing countries.
2. Basic needs – Moral and ethical aspects – Developing countries.   3. Poverty – Moral
  and ethical aspects.   I. Chatterjee, Deen K.   II. Series.
  HC60.E744   2004   174 – dc22   2003055817

ISBN 978-0-521-82042-4 Hardback
ISBN 978-0-521-52742-2 Paperback

Transferred to digital printing 2009

Contents

Contents

Notes on contributors

RICHARD J. ARNESON is Professor of Philosophy and former Chair of the Department of Philosophy at the University of California, San Diego. He writes on topics in moral and political philosophy, especially about how to accommodate concerns about personal responsibility within egalitarian theories of distributive justice and about how to defend consequentialist moral theory in the light of the recent criticisms it has attracted. He has published more than sixty essays in journals and collections.

CHARLES R. BEITZ is Professor of Politics at Princeton University. His main works include *Political Theory and International Relations* (revised edition, 1999) and *Political Equality* (1989) as well as articles on a variety of topics in international ethics and democratic theory. Beitz co-edited *International Ethics* (1985) and *Law, Economics, and Philosophy* (1983). His current work includes projects on the philosophy of human rights and the theory of intellectual property. He has received fellowships from the Rockefeller, MacArthur, and Guggenheim Foundations, the American Council of Learned Societies, and the American Council on Education. He is the Editor of *Philosophy & Public Affairs*.

DEEN K. CHATTERJEE is Associate Professor of Philosophy at the University of Utah. His areas of interest are political philosophy, applied ethics – especially international development ethics – and philosophy of religion and culture. His publications include *Ethics and Foreign Intervention*, co-edited with Don E. Scheid (2003) and *Globalization, Development and Democracy*, co-edited with Michael Krausz (2004). He is Advisory Editor of *The Monist* 86:3 and Managing Director of Beas Foundation (a project of Tides Corporation in Washington DC). He is currently completing a book on human rights and development assistance.

F. M. KAMM is Professor of Philosophy and Public Policy, Kennedy School of Government, and Professor of Philosophy, Harvard University. Her publications include *Creation and Abortion* (1992); *Morality, Mortality*, vols. I and II (1993, 1996); "Supererogation and Obligation," in *Journal of Philosophy* (1985); "Harming Some to Save Others," in *Philosophical Studies* (1989); "Responsibility and Collaborations," in *Philosophy & Public Affairs* (1999); and "Rescuing Ivan Ilych," in *Ethics* (2003).

ERIN KELLY is Associate Professor of Philosophy at Tufts University. Her main research interests are in moral and political philosophy. Her recent publications include a chapter titled "The Burdens of Collective Liability," in *Ethics and Foreign Intervention* (2003); several papers, including "Personal Concern," in *Canadian Journal of Philosophy* (2000); and "Habermas on Moral Justification," in *Social Theory and Practice* (2000). She is editor of John Rawls, *Justice as Fairness: A Restatement* (2001).

JUDITH LICHTENBERG teaches in the Department of Philosophy at the University of Maryland at College Park and works also at the university's Institute for Philosophy and Public Policy. She has written on international ethics, immigration, nationalism, and other issues in moral and political philosophy. She is the editor of *Democracy and the Mass Media* (1990) and coauthor (with Robert K. Fullinwider) of *Getting a Leg Up: What's Fair in College Admissions* (forthcoming).

DAVID MILLER is Professor of Political Theory at the University of Oxford and an Official Fellow of Nuffield College. Among his recent books are *On Nationality* (1995); *Principles of Social Justice* (1999); *Citizenship and National Identity* (2000) (ed. with Sohail Hashmi); *Boundaries and Justice* (2001); and *Political Philosophy: A Very Short Introduction* (2003). He is currently working on the question of national responsibility and what it means for international justice, and on the impact of multiculturalism on social justice.

RICHARD W. MILLER is Professor of Philosophy at Cornell University. His writings, in social and political philosophy, ethics, epistemology, the philosophy of science and aesthetics, include many articles and three books, *Analyzing Marx* (1984); *Fact and Method* (1987); and *Moral Differences* (1992). He is currently writing a book on global justice.

MARTHA C. NUSSBAUM is Ernst Freund Distinguished Service Professor of Law and Ethics at the University of Chicago, appointed in the Philosophy Department, the Law School, and the Divinity School. She is an Associate in the Classics Department and the Political Science Department, an Affiliate of the Committee for Southern Asian Studies, and a member of the Board of the Human Rights Program. She is the founder and coordinator of the new Center for Comparative Constitutionalism. Her publications include *Upheavals of Thought: The Intelligence of Emotions* (2001); *Women and Human Development* (2000); *Sex and Social Justice* (1998); *Cultivating Humanity: A Classical Defense of Reform in Liberal Education* (1997); *For Love of Country* (1996, 2002); *The Fragility of Goodness* (1986, 2000); and *The Quality of Life*, ed. with Amartya Sen (1993).

ONORA O'NEILL is Principal of Newnham College at Cambridge University and the author of *A Question of Trust* (2002); *Autonomy and Trust in Bioethics* (2002); *Bounds of Justice* (2000); *Constructions of Reason* (1989); *Faces of Hunger: An Essay on Poverty, Justice, and Development* (1986), and many important articles on justice, gender and international boundaries.

THOMAS W. POGGE teaches moral and political philosophy at Columbia University. His publications include *World Poverty and Human Rights* (2002); *Global Justice* (ed., 2001); "What We Can Reasonably Reject," in *NOÛS* (2002); "Can the Capability Approach be Justified?," in *Philosophical Topics* (2002); "On the Site of Distributive Justice," in *Philosophy and Public Affairs* (2000); *Realizing Rawls* (1989); and, with Sanjay Reddy, "How Not to Count the Poor" (www.socialanalysis.org). Pogge is editor for social and political philosophy for the *Stanford Encyclopedia of Philosophy* and a member of the Norwegian Academy of Science.

HENRY SHUE is Senior Research Fellow in Philosophy, Merton College, and Visiting Professor of Politics and International Relations, University of Oxford. He was a Founding Member of the Institute for Philosophy and Public Policy at the University of Maryland and the first Director of the Program on Ethics and Public Life at Cornell University. Best known for his *Basic Rights* (1980, 1996), he is also the author of many influential articles and book chapters on ethics and global affairs.

PETER SINGER is Ira W. De Camp Professor of Bioethics at Princeton University. His publications include *Pushing Time Away* (2003); *One World* (2002); *Writings on an Ethical Life* (2000); *A Darwinian Left* (1999); *How Are We to Live?* (1995); *Rethinking Life and Death* (1994); *Practical Ethics* (2nd ed., 1993); *Animal Liberation* (2nd ed., 1990); and "Famine, Affluence and Morality," in *Philosophy and Public Affairs* (1972). Blackwell Publishers' Philosophers and Their Critics series has featured *Singer and His Critics* in 1999, edited by Dale Jamieson.

Preface

The nature of international duties of assistance and the moral consequences of global interdependence have become central topics in political philosophy, ethics, and political and legal theories. Cambridge Studies in Philosophy and Public Policy address these topics in two high-profile anthologies. One is the present collection of articles on non-interventionist humanitarian assistance; the other concerns assistance in the form of humanitarian military intervention, titled *Ethics and Foreign Intervention* (eds. Deen K. Chatterjee and Don E. Scheid, 2003).

The present collection draws on nearly all of the leading figures in recent debates on transnational non-interventionist assistance. The issues discussed include the extent to which affluent countries should provide tax-financed aid to the foreign poor or otherwise bear responsibility for remedying poverty-related deprivation, and the question of individuals' personal responsibility to needy, distant strangers (for example, those they could help by giving to international charities). The contributors include established scholars from political philosophy, ethics, and political theory, working in various styles and perspectives in both the United States and the United Kingdom. Utilitarian, Kantian, Rawlsian, and feminist approaches are among their varied starting points. Some emphasize current political controversies, others general questions of how various forms of distance can affect moral duties. All chapters in this volume reflect the latest ideas of their authors. None has appeared elsewhere in the version published here, and nearly all are entirely new.

Special thanks to Hilary Gaskin of Cambridge University Press for making this volume possible through her steady support and to Rebecca Bruschek of the University of Utah for her helpful assistance in the project.

Chapter 1

Introduction

DEEN K. CHATTERJEE

This collection of chapters seeks to describe our duties to help those who are in need but who are strangers to us due to distance – physical or otherwise. If we have duties and obligations toward each other in everyday moral contexts, should these duties be extended to the distant needy? If so, what should be the nature and role of institutions implementing such duties beyond our own borders of special ties and communities? Though moral philosophers have pondered these questions in the past, such issues have recently become the focus of especially intense debate. Today we live in a world in which spheres of interaction are constantly expanding, while advanced technology makes it easy to reach the distant needy and vividly broadcast their plight to all. In parallel with the growth of these global relationships, there has been an enormous increase in ethicists' interest in questions regarding the morality of affluence in a world of poverty and the individual's response to it. In addition to creating new perspectives on individual moral obligation, this discussion is transforming political philosophy. While the initial florescence of interest in theories of justice that began with John Rawls' *A Theory of Justice* (1971) solely concerned relationships among fellow-citizens, theorists of social justice now frequently attend to issues of global inequity and institutional responses to it.

Peter Singer's seminal article "Famine, Affluence and Morality" (1972) has been a central focus of debate over the individual's obligation to respond to the distant needy. Singer argued that we are as much obliged to help a distant stranger in dire need as we are to help somebody in extreme distress who is in close proximity to us. Intuitively, we seem to have stronger moral obligations to those who are physically or affectively near than to those who are remote. Distance seems to set moral boundaries, and distant strangers are accorded minimal

1

moral concern. Singer's article questioned these intuitive assumptions, arguing that closer scrutiny of the differences between the near and the distant reveals nothing that could justify the usual deadly neglect of the distant needy.

Singer's primary concern was the duty of individuals in affluent countries to send money to overseas charities. However, there are several approaches to remedying poverty-related miseries in addition to aid of the sort that individuals can provide. They include foreign aid from governments (both unilateral and via multinational organizations), debt forgiveness, a new international economic order, more equitable trade policies, compensation for past wrongs, and help in consolidating transitions from unjust to more just forms of government. They require political and institutional directives on a wide range of issues related to poverty and deprivation. This volume puts all these strategies as well as the individual's obligation to help under the general topic of assistance. It leaves out the topic of humanitarian military intervention to assist the distant needy, which is the theme of another related volume (see Preface).

In Part I, Peter Singer, Richard Arneson, F. M. Kamm, and Judith Lichtenberg address broad questions about the moral significance of distance, primarily attending to its importance or unimportance to an individual's duty to aid others, rather than to political duties of support for institutions. Singer considers a variety of special relationships which, according to his critics, create grounds for bias in aid that would block his original arguments for an enormously demanding duty of aid to the foreign poor. While discerning impartialist reasons to give some scope to these forms of partiality, he argues that they require no substantial change in his original view. Singer also assesses John Rawls' *The Law of Peoples* and finds it inadequate in regard to assisting the poor nations in meeting the basic needs of their people. (The chapters in Part III discuss the law of peoples in greater detail.) Singer's chapter concludes with a note on human nature and the motivation to assist – an important issue that is the topic of Lichtenberg's chapter.

Arneson claims that Singer was right in 1972 when he argued that there is no morally significant difference between a drowning child nearby and a distant stranger who is in dire need. So, if we are obliged to help the child even at a considerable cost to ourselves, we have a similarly demanding duty to help distant strangers. After criticizing less demanding doctrines of duty, Arneson seeks to reduce resistance to Singer's stern demand by further specifying its subject-matter. Distance makes no difference to questions of right and wrong, but it does affect blame-worthiness and morally appropriate guilt.

Kamm argues that distance does matter morally yet she also argues that distance between aider and aidee is just part of a larger package of morally relevant spatial relationships, including, for example, closeness to the potential aider of means of aid. Her total account of the ways in which nearness is morally important allows for strong duties to aid a distant stranger while also affording nearness of aider and aidee special moral significance.

Whatever the proper moral relevance of distance, its psychological influence is widely acknowledged. But the kinds of distance that affect propensities to give and the mechanisms responsible for these connections are in need of specific, empirically informed description, if undue effects of distance are to be reduced. Lichtenberg discusses this issue of the moral psychology of distance in her chapter. She claims that people in general are not motivated to aid the distant needy even if they are in a position to do so. Accordingly, she argues, instead of engaging in the empty rhetoric of obligations to give aid, it makes more sense to see how, in a morally permissible manner, people can be made more prone to giving. This chapter illustrates and supplements the Singer problematic with which the volume begins.

The vast majority of non-philosophers believe that ties of community – political, social, or cultural – create special duties of aid. Any global impartiality will run counter to this commonly held bias toward moral closeness. The two chapters in Part II deal with alternative kinds of community and the obligations they generate. Richard Miller contends that we should balance national concerns and international needs in the political sphere. While giving a philosophical defense of our ordinary biases toward moral closeness, and arguing that equal respect needn't mean equal concern for all, Miller contends that the grounds for these biases also entail corresponding but less demanding reasons to help the foreign poor. Just citizens, he argues, have special duties to compatriots because of fellow-citizens' role in coercively imposing rules of self-advancement on one another and their just expectation of loyal allegiance to centrally important shared institutions. However, similar, though weaker considerations of coercion and loyalty currently create duties to aid poor foreigners in our global world. Duties of world community add to the force of mere humanitarian requirements even if they fall short of duties of political community. Miller's chapter provides a challenging contrast to Singer and Arneson and tries to work out a position believable to non-philosophers who may have trouble with the extent of Singer's rigorous moral demands.

David Miller explores the idea of independent political communities and their duties of international justice. He contends that because all such political communities are culturally unique, no general principle of redistribution of wealth from the rich to the poor communities will work, though rich communities have an obligation to ensure a minimum level of human well-being in poor communities. International justice must ensure that all political communities are able to determine their own future and administer justice among their members, and be held responsible for their falling below the minimum standard of well-being if their own political and social policies lead to it. Miller's view of the (often) national sources of bad development is, at the very least, in tension with Thomas Pogge's emphasis, in Part IV, on a skewed international economic system benefiting the rich countries.

The chapters in the next two groups approach questions of international assistance from perspectives sympathetic to John Rawls' liberalism, though they are sometimes critical of Rawls' specific claims concerning its international implications. In contrast to the relatively limited duties of global assistance constrained by the demands of communities, they exhibit a more impartial and demanding duty to help the distant needy, though not as demanding as the cosmopolitan claims made by Singer and Arneson in the first part.

In his ground-breaking inquiry, *A Theory of Justice* (1971), Rawls defended liberal egalitarian principles of justice among fellow-members of a single society as the social contract that would result from hypothetical deliberations in which members of a society assumed to be self-sufficient seek to pursue their individual interests in ignorance of the nature of their goals and resources. Although others have extended this conception of justice as fairness to the world at large, Rawls himself determines international justice, in *The Law of Peoples* (1999), by hypothetical deliberations between representatives of sovereign peoples, not individuals, which result in much more moderate requirements of international equality and relatively high barriers to international intervention. In Part III, Martha Nussbaum, Erin Kelly, and Charles Beitz assess Rawls' account of global justice and the duty to assist. Nussbaum holds that though Rawls is sensitive to the issues of global inequalities, especially as they affect women, he doesn't adequately deal with certain important issues in his scheme of global justice. These inadequacies point to general shortcomings in his theory that adversely affect all oppressed groups, especially women. Nussbaum specifically faults Rawls for his weak requirement for basic human rights protection, offered as accommodating decent but hierarchical societies in the society of peoples. She believes that Rawls should have applied the same person-centered principle of domestic liberal justice to the global arena because the fundamental unit of justice is the person, not sovereign peoples. Nussbaum contends that states, being the institutions of the basic structure of society, have more moral significance than groups or peoples because states have the structural mechanism for justice that allows individuals to express their autonomy. Still, Nussbaum's liberal cosmopolitanism does not find the nation-state paradigm fully adequate for global justice in today's world.

In contrast to Nussbaum, Kelly's chapter, which follows a broadly Rawlsian approach toward moral responsibility in the global community, finds the narrow construal of human rights a useful tool in framing foreign policy imperatives. She claims that the international community has a duty to assist the burdened or failed states in attaining a decent minimum, a duty she defends and specifies as the outcome of a reasonable consensus respectful of the global diversity of groups, cultures and values. All nations have a moral obligation to ensure, through their foreign policies, that no society fails to provide access to such rights for its citizens. Such a foreign policy imperative could range from non-coercive aid, development assistance, and reforming international institutions and treaties to coercive measures including military intervention in rare cases. Given the resources available to the rich and powerful countries, Kelly believes that they have a prime responsibility to assist the poor nations, within the limits of a decent minimum. This limit, which goes beyond the Rawlsian idea of assistance (helping the poor nations in attaining the institutions of liberal or decent societies) still falls far short of the more egalitarian requirements that Nussbaum, Beitz, Thomas Pogge, and others have defended, which more closely resemble Rawls' domestic model of egalitarian justice.

In his essay on the nature of human rights, Charles Beitz develops a practical and political account, as opposed to the foundational and normative account that is standard among political philosophers. Sympathetic to Rawls' emphasis on the practice of public discourse among agents with diverse perspectives, Beitz seeks to describe the nature of human rights in terms of the functions that appeals to human rights play in international justification and criticism of governments' conduct. Beitz takes this broadly Rawlsian methodology to give shape and substance to rights to subsistence that are not much discussed in Rawls' own work. In Beitz's view, the human rights illuminated by the practical approach correspond to demanding obligations, even if the remedy is not as demanding and urgent as Singer's and Arneson's arguments suggest. One question prompted by his chapter is what the proper role of normative, foundational arguments ought to be. Normative theorists regard practical consequences as essential to the evaluation of institutions, and disagreements as to what rights have the obligatory status Beitz describes may depend on normative and foundational arguments for their resolution. If this dependence is pervasive and unavoidable, the division of labor between the practical–political and normative–foundational might, in the final analysis, be close to the expectations of orthodox, foundational philosophers.

Following the lead of the authors in Part III, all three contributors in Part IV call on philosophers doing work on human rights and poverty alleviation to be more specific with respect to the assignment of duties to institutions and more knowledgeable about the empirical facts and contending policies. Henry Shue's point about applied ethics incorporating empirical understanding and operationalizing rights-respecting duties is an illustration of this move. Shue does this via a defense of a middle way between thick localism and thin universalism and a critique of Michael Walzer's and Charles Taylor's localism. Shue acknowledges localists' concern that liberal theories of rights have suffered from excessive abstraction. This he believes is due to lack of an adequate account of positive duties, which is needed to understand the implementation of any rights, positive or negative. However, Shue believes that to construe such an account one needn't go the communitarian way of thick localism – one can have a richly embedded notion of rights without being locked into any one specific culture as Walzer and Taylor suppose. Appealing to realities of current global practice, Shue emphasizes the actual vitality of cross-cultural discourse concerning human rights and the heterogeneity of religious and cultural communities such as Islam which tend to be treated as uniformly committed to restrictive views.

Like Shue, Onora O'Neill is concerned about empty rhetoric of rights. (In the first part of this anthology, Judith Lichtenberg responds to what she perceives as the empty rhetoric of obligations.) O'Neill claims that if rights are to be taken seriously – especially the rights of the poor in developing countries – then there has to be a substantive notion of obligation, based on a realistic and fair account of the agents and the agencies capable of discharging them. She believes that neither the utilitarian nor the rights-based cosmopolitan theories, both of which she labels as "abstract cosmopolitanism," have paid enough attention to the empirical details of who ought to do what for whom. When weak states cannot provide for urgent needs of their citizens, O'Neill suggests that non-state agencies such as NGOs or TNCs should be accorded a larger role in the ascription of duties of international economic justice. She claims that states or multi-governmental agencies such as the United Nations are not the only, and sometimes not the most capable, institutions for projecting economic justice into developing nations. She believes that in the absence of efficient reform of state or international institutions, which may take a long time, it is imperative to look into the prospect of NGOs and TNCs as effective international benefactors. Such supplementary strategies could make a meaningful difference by providing viable grounds for rights claims.

Thomas Pogge's chapter is about real-world mechanisms by which the poor get poor and are kept poor, and by which they can overcome their poverty. Pogge argues for more extensive measures to reduce international inequality than Rawls requires, basing this stronger egalitarianism on specific features of current international relationships rather than general principles of aid to those in need. He holds that poor countries are being harmed through an inequitable global order, continuously shaped and coercively imposed by affluent countries that benefit from the consequent inequalities. The causal and moral responsibility of rich nations for the deprivations of individuals in poor nations is endemic in the international economic order, not isolated to some specific cases of transgressions. Pogge believes that the removal of such burdens by the beneficiaries is the sort of negative duty (to stop harming) whose force is in no way mitigated by considerations of distance or culture. Conformity to this duty requires a fundamental economic and political reform in the current global order, a reform that Pogge calls "re-redistribution." Though this may sound like a tall order, Pogge believes such a reform would not unduly compromise the lifestyle of the citizens of affluent nations. He views external aid and country-specific development efforts as less important than the duty to change the international economic order.

The chapters in this collection challenge and defend assumptions about the moral importance of distance that are among the most deep-seated convictions concerning individual morality and political choice. In addition to suggesting new perspectives on aid to needy strangers, they use the current debate over the moral implications of distance to shed light on enduring questions about morality as a whole, such as the nature and limits of moral impartiality, the role of human psychology in the determination of moral duty, and the moral importance of equality. Along with providing new depth and directions to normative inquiries that add to the conceptual enrichment of the seminal issues in ethics and political philosophy, the chapters make vivid the importance of grounding claims of practical relevance in the global realities of politics and law. Applied philosophy is now being challenged to grapple with the difficult questions of justice and equality in the real-world politics of poverty, affluence, and deprivation. Whatever the outcome of the new attention to the distant as well as the near, ethics and political philosophy will never be the same.

PART I

The ethics of distance

Chapter 2

Outsiders: our obligations to those beyond our borders

PETER SINGER

In an article entitled "Famine, Affluence and Morality," first published in 1972, I argued that:

it makes no moral difference whether the person I help is a neighbor's child ten yards from me or a Bengali whose name I shall never know, ten thousand miles away[1]

As far as I am aware, no one has disputed this claim in respect of distance *per se* – that is, the difference between 10 yards and 10,000 miles. Of course, the degree of certainty that we can have that our assistance will get to the right person, and will really help that person, may be affected by distance, and that can make a difference to what we ought to do, but that will depend on the particular circumstances we find ourselves in. The aspect of my claim that has been the subject of greatest philosophical dispute is the suggestion that our obligation to help a stranger is as great as our obligation to help a neighbor's child. Several critics have claimed that we have special obligations to our family, friends, neighbors and fellow-citizens. Raymond Gastil, for example, has objected that:

There is no doctrine of nonuniversalistic obligation with which Singer seriously deals. The flatness of his map of obligation and responsibility is suggested by the remark that "... unfortunately most of the major evils – poverty, overpopulation, pollution – are problems in which everyone is almost equally involved."[2]

My aim in this paper is to restate and defend my earlier view, or at least something still recognizably related to it. Before I do so, I shall note that the issue of our obligations to strangers as compared with our obligations to our compatriots is raised not only by the issue with which

I was concerned in "Famine, Affluence and Morality" – that is, the issue of how much aid we ought to give to those in danger of starvation, malnutrition, or death from easily preventable diseases – but also in many other arenas. One prominent example is the strategy followed by the NATO powers in their 1999 intervention in Kosovo, where the restriction of intervention to aerial bombardment meant that the NATO forces suffered not a single casualty in combat, but approximately 300 Kosovar, 209 Serb and three Chinese civilians were killed.[3] Another issue that raises the relative weight we place on the interests of our own citizens and those of other nations is trade policy, a topic on which there has been heated debate since the 1999 World Trade Organization meeting in Seattle. I will not, however, have space here to pursue any of the additional ramifications of the issue of the relative weight that political leaders may give to protecting the lives and incomes of their own citizens, as compared with those of other countries. That must await another occasion.

SOME MORAL TOPOGRAPHIES

If it is supposed to be a mistake to have a map of moral obligation that is as flat as mine, then where, on a morally superior landscape, should the peaks, plateaus and escarpments be placed? Here are some examples of how people have structured the moral landscape:

(1) In Victorian England, Henry Sidgwick presented the moral topography of Victorian England as follows:

> We should all agree that each of us is bound to show kindness to his parents and spouse and children, and to other kinsmen in a less degree: and to those who have rendered services to him, and any others whom he may have admitted to his intimacy and called friends: and to neighbors and to fellow-countrymen more than others: and perhaps we may say to those of our own race more than to black or yellow men, and generally to human beings in proportion to their affinity to ourselves.[4]

(2) Paul of Tarsus, in his Epistle to the Galatians, urges:

> As we have, therefore, opportunity, let us do good unto all men, especially unto them who are of the household of faith.[5]

(3) In the following well-known passage from *The Adventures of Huckleberry Finn*, Huck explains to Aunt Sally why he was delayed:

"We blowed out a cylinder-head."
"Good gracious! anybody hurt?"
"No'm. Killed a nigger."
"Well, it's lucky; because sometimes people do get hurt."[6]

(4) Here is a more extreme statement of an essentially similar attitude:

We must be honest, decent, loyal and friendly to members of our blood and to no one else. What happens to the Russians, what happens to the Czechs, is a matter of utter indifference to me. Such good blood of our own kind as there may be among the nations we shall acquire for ourselves, if necessary by taking away the children and bringing them up among us. Whether the other races live in comfort or perish of hunger interests me only in so far as we need them as slaves for our culture; apart from that it does not interest me. Whether or not 10,000 Russian women collapse from exhaustion while digging a tank ditch interests me only in so far as the tank ditch is completed for Germany.[7]

(5) Alasdair MacIntyre offers us a contemporary version of Sidgwick's outline of relationships:

I am someone's son or daughter, someone else's cousin or uncle; I am a citizen of this or that city, a member of this or that guild or profession; I belong to this tribe, that clan, this nation. Hence what is good for me has to be what is good for one who inhabits these roles. As such, I inherit from the past of my family, my city, my tribe, my nation, a variety of debts, inheritances, rightful expectations and obligations. These constitute the given of my life, my moral starting point. This is part of what gives my life its moral particularity.[8]

(6) In the course of a recent defense of human dominion over other animals, Lewis Petrinovich claims that ". . . certain biologically instated [sic] moral boundaries are imperatives." He gives as examples "children, kin, neighbors, and species."[9]

THE IMPARTIAL JUSTIFICATION OF PARTIALITY

This grab-bag of alternatives to a flat moral landscape reminds us that the categories to which people give moral significance vary over time and place. For reasons that I shall discuss shortly, this is not true of all such categories. It is significant, though, that whereas it is easy to find thinkers from different times and places to whom it is intuitively obvious that we have special obligations to those of our own religion, race, or ethnic affiliation, this does not seem so obvious to contemporary ethicists and political theorists. If the strength of intuitions favoring special obligations based on racial and religious affinity is not sufficient grounds for accepting them, then the strength of our intuitions about, say, special obligations based on fellow-citizenship, should also not be sufficient reason for accepting them. Instead, we need another test of whether they should be accepted. I propose that the test should be whether accepting the idea of having these special duties can itself be justified from an impartial perspective. The remainder of this paper is an attempt to work out the implications of this proposal and defend it against some recent objections and alternative views.

The proposal itself is anything but novel; indeed we are re-entering a debate that goes back two hundred years to William Godwin, perhaps the first notorious champion of impartiality. Godwin asserted that if Archbishop Fénelon, whose writings have brought happiness and consolation to thousands, should be trapped in a burning building together with your mother, and there is no time to rescue both, it is the celebrated Archbishop whom you should save.[10]

Godwin's view was highly controversial in his own time. Some of the most trenchant criticism came from the clergyman Samuel Parr, who preached a sermon against Godwin's "universal philanthropy." Parr argues against impartialism in ethics on the grounds that it takes an unrealistic view of human nature. Our real desires, our lasting and strongest passions, are not for the good of our species as a whole, but, at best, for the good of those who are close to us, and we should not demand of men something that they cannot give.[11] Godwin subsequently, perhaps influenced by his wife Mary Wollstonecraft, accepted some elements of Parr's argument and sought to make room within his universalist view for natural feelings like love for one's parents or children.[12]

The contemporary debate on this issue is not all that different from that which took place between Godwin and Parr. Today the critics of impartialism argue that an advocate of an impartial ethic such as utilitarianism would make a poor parent, neighbor or friend, because the very idea of such personal relationships involves being partial toward the other person with whom one is in the relationship. This means giving more consideration to the interests of your child, neighbor or friend than you give to strangers, and from the standpoint of an impartial ethic this seems wrong. Consequentialists have responded to these objections by claiming that their position does not require that we should be impartial in every aspect of our lives. Rather, there must be an impartial justification for accepting areas of our lives in which we may act partially. R. M. Hare, for example, has developed a two-level version of utilitarianism. He argues that in everyday life it will often be too difficult to work out the consequences of every decision we make, and if we were to try to do so, we would risk getting it wrong because of our personal involvement, and the pressures of the situation. For guiding our everyday conduct, he therefore suggests that we need a set of principles that should become something that we know intuitively, without a lot of reflection. In a calmer or more philosophical moment, on the other hand, we can reflect on the nature of our moral intuitions, and ask whether we have developed the right ones, that is, the ones that will lead to the greatest good, impartially considered. When we engage in this reflection, we are moving to the critical level of morality.[13]

Do any of the special obligations suggested by the passages quoted above survive Hare's demand for impartial justification, and if so, which ones? If we subject our intuitions about the preferences we should give to the interests of different groups of people to a test of this kind, I think we will find that the first set of preferences mentioned by Sidgwick – family, friends, those who have "rendered services" to us, and neighbors – stands up quite well. The love of parents for their children, and the desire of parents to give preference to their children over the children of strangers is, as the experience of utopian social experiments has shown, highly resistant to change.[14] Here Petrinovich's reference to the "evolutionary imperative" is at its most plausible. Not, of course, that we can deduce moral imperatives from evolutionary theory, as Petrinovich appears to do – that would involve an indefensible crossing of the gap between "is" and "ought" – but evolutionary theory can make a contribution to this debate. It offers us reasons for believing that some of our emotional attachments are deeply rooted in our nature as intelligent, long-lived primates, or even in our nature as social mammals. These attachments are therefore likely to be common, if not quite universal, in all human cultures. Even if we were to decide that these attachments are undesirable, we would find them very difficult to eradicate, and any attempt to do so would have high costs and would require constant supervision or coercion to ensure that people did not act on the attachments in question. Unless we are willing to engage in an all-out campaign of intense moral pressure, backed up with coercive measures and draconian sanctions, to suppress parental bias, we are bound to find that most parents constantly favor their children in ways that cannot be directly justified on the basis of equal consideration of interests. If we do engage in such a campaign, our only achievement may well be that we have brought about guilt and anxiety in parents who want to do things for their children that society now regards as wrong. This is not mere speculation. In the early days of the Israeli *kibbutzim*, or socialist collectives, the more radical *kibbutzim* sought to equalize the upbringing of children by having all children born to members of the *kibbutz* brought up communally, in a special children's house. For parents to show particular love and affection for their own child was frowned upon. Nevertheless, mothers used to sneak into the communal nursery at night to kiss and hold their sleeping children, presumably, if they shared the ideals of the *kibbutz*, feeling guilt for doing so. Such guilt will itself be a source of much unhappiness. Will the gains of diminishing partiality for one's own children outweigh this? That seems unlikely, because for the children themselves, the care of loving parents is likely to be better than the care of paid employees, no matter how benevolent they may be, or how professionally skilled in carrying out their duties. There is evidence, too, that children are more likely to be abused when brought up by people who are not their biological parents.[15] Given the unavoidable constraints of human nature and the importance of bringing children up in loving homes, then, there is an impartial justification for approving of social practices that presuppose that parents will usually be partial towards their own children.

It is even easier to find an impartial reason for accepting love and friendship. If loving relationships, and relationships of friendship, are necessarily partial, they are also, for most people, at the core of anything that can approximate to a good life. Very few human beings can live happy and fulfilled lives without being attached to particular other human beings. To suppress these partial affections would destroy something of great value, and therefore cannot be justified from an impartial perspective.

Bernard Williams has claimed that this defense of love and friendship demands "one thought too many."[16] We should, he says, visit our sick friend in hospital because he is our friend and is in hospital, not because we have calculated that visiting sick friends is a more efficient way of maximizing utility than anything else we could do with our time. This objection would be valid if pressed against those who claim that we should be thinking about the impartial justification of love or friendship at the time when we are deciding whether to visit our sick friend; but it is precisely the point of two-level utilitarianism to explain why we *should* have an extra thought when we are thinking at the critical level, but not at the level of everyday moral decision-making.

Consider the idea supported, to varying degrees, in the passages I have quoted from Sidgwick, Twain, and Himmler, to the effect that, say, whites should care more for, and give priority to, the interests of other whites, or that "Aryans" should give priority to the interests of others "of their blood." These ideas have had, in their time, an intuitive appeal very similar to the intuitive appeal of the idea that we have obligations to favor family and friends. But racist views have contributed to the worst crimes of our century, and it is not easy to see that they have done much good, certainly not good that can compensate for the misery to which they have led. Moreover, though the suppression of racism is difficult, it is not impossible, as the existence of genuinely multi-racial societies, and even the history of desegregation in the American South, shows. White people in the South no longer think twice about sharing a bus seat with an African American, and even those who fought to defend segregation have, by and large, come to accept that they were wrong. Taking an impartial perspective shows that partialism along racial lines is something that we can, and should, oppose, because our opposition can be effective in preventing great harm being done to innocent people.

Thus we can turn Williams' aphorism against him: philosophers who take his view have one thought too few. To be sure, to think *always* as a philosopher would mean that, in our roles as parents, spouse, lover, and friend, we would indeed have one thought too many. But Williams *is* a philosopher, and there are times when he should be prepared to reflect critically on his intuitions – and not only philosophers, but all thoughtful people, should do this. If we were all simply to accept our feelings without the kind of extra reflection we have just been engaged in, we would not be able to decide which of our intuitive inclinations to endorse and support, and which to oppose. As the quotations with which I began indicate, the fact that intuitive responses are widely held is not evidence that they are justified. They are not rational insights into a realm of moral truth. Some of them – roughly, those that we share with others of our species, irrespective of their cultural background – are responses that, for most of our evolutionary history, have been well suited to the survival and reproduction of beings like us. Others – roughly, those that we do not share with humans from different cultures – we have because of our particular cultural history. Neither the biological nor the cultural basis of our intuitive responses provides us with a sound reason for taking them as the basis of morality.

Compare the passages I have quoted above from Sidgwick and MacIntyre. The most curious aspect of MacIntyre's list is race, which reminds me of "the curious incident of the dog in the night-time" to which Sherlock Holmes once directed Dr Watson's attention.[17] The dog, of course, did nothing in the night, and MacIntyre's list, though it appears to mention every other association that comes to his mind, says nothing about the racial basis of fellow-feeling that has been so great a force in the world over the past two hundred years and more. Why does MacIntyre include such groupings as "my clan, my tribe, my nation" but not "my race"? Because, I would suggest, in the light of the crimes committed by those who follow their racial feelings, it would be impossible for MacIntyre to recognize its existence while continuing to deny the need for critical evaluation of the "debts, inheritances, rightful expectations and obligations" that we inherit from our past and which give our lives their "moral particularity." That critical evaluation, however, requires us to take a standpoint that transcends our particularity, a possibility that MacIntyre is reluctant to accept.

Let us return to the issue of partiality for family, lovers, and friends. We have seen that there are impartial reasons for accepting some degree of partiality here. But how much? In broad terms, as much as is necessary to promote the goods mentioned above, but no more. Thus the partiality of parents for their children must extend to providing them with the necessities of life, and also their more important wants, and must allow them to feel loved and protected; but there is no requirement to satisfy every desire a child expresses, and many reasons why we should not do so. In a society like America, we should bring up our children, both for their own good and for those of others, to know that others are in much greater need, and to be aware of the possibility of helping them, if unnecessary spending is reduced. They should also learn to think critically about the forces that lead to high levels of consumption, and to be aware of the environmental costs of this way of living. With lovers and friends, something similar applies: the relationships require partiality, but they are stronger where there are shared values, or at least respect for the values that each holds. Where the values shared include concern for the welfare of others, irrespective of whether they are friends or strangers, then the partiality demanded by friendship or love will not be so great as to interfere in a serious way with the capacity for helping those in great need.

What of the other categories on Sidgwick's list of those to whom we are under a special obligation to show kindness: parents, kin, "those who have rendered services," "neighbors" and "fellow-countrymen"? Can all of these categories be justified from an impartial perspective? The inclusion of "those who have rendered services" is seen by ethicists who rely on intuition to be a straightforward case of the obligation of gratitude.[18] From a two-level perspective, however, the intuition that we have a duty of gratitude can be seen not as an insight into some independent moral truth, but something desirable because it helps to encourage reciprocity, which makes cooperation, and all its benefits, possible. Here too, evolutionary theory can help us to see why reciprocity, and with it the sense of gratitude, should have evolved. Reciprocal relationships are common among primates and in some other social mammals. They have been studied extensively by anthropologists, ethologists and game theorists, and shown to be highly advantageous for those who participate in them. Moreover the rewarding of cooperative behavior has benefits for the society as a whole, and not only for those who are cooperating. If one agent makes a cooperative move, for example, sharing food when she has more than someone else, then the recipient has a choice between reciprocating when she has more, or cheating, by not sharing when she has more. If cooperative moves are usually reciprocated, cooperators will do well and cooperation will thrive; if cooperative moves are rarely reciprocated, cheats will do better than cooperators, and cooperation will decline. Since both being cheated and guarding against being cheated have costs, everyone is better off if society recognizes a general duty of gratitude – and a duty of retribution against those who do cheat. That is, in some form or other, a universal norm in all human societies.[19]

Once a duty of gratitude is recognized, it is impossible to exclude parents from the circle of those to whom a special duty of kindness is owed. For since parents have generally "rendered services" by the million to their children, we can hardly subscribe to a general principle of gratitude without recognizing a duty of children towards their parents. The exception here would be the case of children who have been maltreated or abandoned by their parents – and it is the exception that proves the rule, in the sense that it proves that our common moral consciousness sees the obligation largely as one of gratitude, rather than one based on blood relationships.

Another of Sidgwick's categories, that of our neighbors, can be handled in the same way. It is not so much the fact of geographical proximity that makes it good for us to be especially concerned about our neighbors, but rather that this proximity means that we have many opportunities to enter into relationships with them of various kinds, but especially those of friendship and mutually beneficial reciprocity. Of course, increasing mobility and communication has, over the course of the past century, eroded the extent to which neighbors are important to us. We can talk to our friends wherever they live, and in large cities we can visit them without taking much more trouble than is involved in visiting a neighbor. Hence the common phenomenon of living in suburbs with neighbors one sees frequently, but barely speaks to. In these circumstances, it becomes doubtful if we have special duties of kindness to our neighbors at all, apart from, perhaps, the things that only a neighbor can do, like calling the police if one sees someone trying to break into the house while the neighbor is on vacation.

This leaves, of Sidgwick's list, only "kin" and "fellow-countrymen." "Kin" is an expression that ranges from the sibling with whom you shared your childhood, and with whom you may later share the task of caring for your parents, to the distant cousin you have not heard from for decades. The extent to which we have a special obligation to our kin should vary accordingly. Kin networks can be important sources of love, friendship, and mutual support, and then they will generate impartially justifiable reasons for promoting these goods. But if that distant cousin you have not heard from for decades suddenly asks for a loan because she wants to buy a new house, is there an impartially defensible ground for believing that you are under a greater obligation to help her than you would be to help an unrelated equally distant acquaintance? That would seem to depend on whether there is a recognized system of cooperation among relatives. In rural areas of India, for example, such relationships between relatives can play an important role in providing assistance when needed.[20] Under these circumstances there is an impartial reason for recognizing and supporting this practice: in the absence of any such system, there is not.

Finally, then, what impartial reasons can there be for giving preference to one's compatriots over foreigners?

HELPING OUR OWN FIRST: THE EFFICIENCY ARGUMENT

Robert Goodin defends a system of special obligations to our compatriots "merely as an administrative device for discharging our general duties more efficiently."[21] If you are sick and in hospital, Goodin argues, it is best to have a particular doctor made responsible for your care, rather than leaving it up to all of the hospital doctors in general; so too, he says, it is best to have one state that is clearly responsible for protecting and promoting the interests of every individual within its territory. There is no doubt something in this, but it is an argument with very limited application in the real world. Goodin recognizes this, saying:

> If there has been a misallocation of some sort, so that some states have been assigned care of many more people than they have been assigned resources to care for them, then a reallocation is called for.[22]

Evidently, our world suffers from very grave misallocations, for some nations have abundant resources, and others far too few. But while we wait for the required reallocation to occur, what should ordinary citizens do? Although Goodin starts his essay by inquiring into the special duties that "we have toward particular individuals because they stand in some special relation to us,"[23] by the end of his essay he writes of the duties of the state, rather than of the duties that "we" have to other individuals. Arguably, though, it would follow from Goodin's view that individuals should do what they can, using the resources under their own control, to remedy the misallocation of resources between states. While it may, in general, be more efficient for states to look after their own citizens, in the real world, this is not so if we are living in one of the countries that has more than its fair share of resources to protect and promote the interests of its citizens. Then we can use our resources far more efficiently by assisting people in countries where $1,000 is three times the average annual income, than we can in our own country, where that amount would barely keep a family for a month. Hence the argument from efficiency, far from being a defense of special duties towards our compatriots, provides grounds for holding that any such duties are overwhelmed by the much greater good that we can do abroad.

WELLMAN'S IMPARTIAL REASONS FOR PREVENTING INEQUALITY WITHIN A SOCIETY RATHER THAN BETWEEN SOCIETIES

Christopher Wellman has recently suggested three other impartial reasons for thinking that it may be particularly important to prevent economic inequality from becoming too great *within* a society, rather than *between* societies. These reasons would therefore, if valid, give grounds for some degree of preference for one's compatriots. The first is that political equality within a society may be adversely affected by economic inequality within a society, but is not adversely affected by economic inequality between societies; the second is that inequality is not something that is bad in itself, but rather something that is bad in so far as it leads to oppressive relationships, and hence we are right to be more concerned about inequality among fellow-citizens than we are about inequality between foreigners who are not in a meaningful relationship with each other; and the third is a point about the comparative nature of wealth and poverty.[24] The classic expression of this last point is by Karl Marx:

A house may be large or small; as long as the surrounding houses are equally small it satisfies all social demands for a dwelling. But let a palace arise beside the little house, and it shrinks from a little house to a hut . . . however high it may shoot up in the course of civilization, if the neighboring palace grows to an equal or even greater extent, the occupant of the relatively small house will feel more and more uncomfortable, dissatisfied and cramped with its four walls.[25]

These three points have some weight when they are brought against the strong claim that it is *no* less desirable to eliminate marked economic inequality between any of the world's inhabitants than it is to eliminate it within a single society. But the weight we should give them is limited, and subject to particular circumstances. In regard to the third point, for example, it is a mistake to think that people compare themselves only with their fellow-citizens, and with all their fellow-citizens. Inhabitants of rural Mississippi, for example, probably do not compare themselves with New Yorkers, or at least not in regard to income. Their lifestyle is so different that income is merely one element in a whole package. On the other hand, many Mexicans living in Tijuana obviously do look longingly north of the border, and think how much better off they would be if they could live in the United States. That is shown by the attempts that many of them make to get there. And the same can be true of people who are not in close geographical proximity, as we can see from the desperate attempts of Chinese to travel illegally to countries like the United States and Australia, not because they are being politically persecuted, but because they will have a better life.

Despite these qualifications, let us grant that there are some reasons for thinking that we should place a higher priority on avoiding marked economic inequality within a given society than on avoiding it across the entire range of the planet's inhabitants. Even so, Wellman would, I think, agree that in the present situation, we may have duties to foreigners that override duties to our fellow-citizens. For even if inequality is often relative, there is also a state known as absolute poverty, that is, poverty that is not relative to someone else's wealth. Absolute poverty has been described as:

a condition of life so characterized by malnutrition, illiteracy, disease, squalid surroundings, high infant mortality and low life expectancy as to be beneath any reasonable definition of human decency.[26]

Reducing the number of human beings living in absolute poverty is surely a more urgent priority than reducing the relative poverty caused by some people living in palaces while others live in houses that are merely adequate. Here Sidgwick's account of the common moral consciousness of his time is in agreement; for after giving the list of special obligations I quoted above, he continues:

And to all men with whom we may be brought into relation we are held to owe slight services, and such as may be rendered without inconvenience: but those who are in distress or urgent need have a claim on us for special kindness.

There can be no doubt that those living in absolute poverty are in distress and in urgent need.

RAWLS AND *THE LAW OF PEOPLES*

If efficiency arguments do not justify much in the way of preference for our compatriots, what of social contract arguments? I shall not attempt to cover the entire range of arguments that might be derived from the various ideas about social contract that are currently circulating in political philosophy. That would be too large a task for this paper, and it is in any case a task that would take us too far from my original claim about our obligations to aid distant strangers. Social contract theory is generally, though not invariably, addressed to the question of what kind of principles a society should adopt, rather than what our personal obligations may be. Nevertheless, in view of the recent publication of John Rawls' *The Law of Peoples*, a work that is sure to influence discussions of what different "peoples" owe one another in the way of assistance, I cannot refrain from making a few comments on the arguments of that book.

When I first read *A Theory of Justice* I was astonished that a book of nearly 600 pages with that title could fail even to tackle the injustice of unequal wealth between different societies. That omission cries out for explanation, so I will offer one. Rawls' method is to seek principles of justice by asking what principles persons in the original position would choose, if they were choosing behind a veil of ignorance that concealed from them certain facts about themselves. If we apply this method globally, rather than for a given society, it is obvious that one fact the veil of ignorance should conceal would be whether one is a citizen of a developed nation like the United States, or a less developed nation like Haiti, Bangladesh or Mozambique. Given a veil of ignorance that concealed nationality, Rawls' arguments for the choice of a principle that maximizes the prospects of the least-advantaged would immediately be transformed into an argument for maximising the prospects of the worst-off people in the world. This means that the argument would lead to conclusions that are in direct and deep conflict with our settled intuitions about what we owe people from other countries. But for Rawls, a sound theory of justice ought to be able to match our settled intuitions in a state of reflective equilibrium. To apply Rawls' methods globally would therefore imperil his entire project, for it would lead to the conclusion that the foundation of the theory – choice behind the veil of ignorance – is in irreconcilable conflict with our settled intuitions. We would have to throw out either the foundation or the intuitions, and once we did that, anything could emerge, perhaps something quite different from the ethical theory that Rawls was defending.[27]

With the publication of *The Law of Peoples* Rawls has at last addressed himself to the issue of justice beyond the borders of our own society. Consistently with what I have argued in the preceding paragraph, he does so in a manner that does not disturb conventional moral views about what we owe to those who are not our compatriots. But to do so, he has to use arguments that are sharply at odds with positions he took in his earlier work.

Here is one example. Rawls asks us to consider a world in which there are two societies, each of which satisfies internally the two principles of justice in *A Theory of Justice*, and in which the worst-off representative person in the first society is worse off than the worst-off representative person in the second. He then supposes that it were possible to arrange a global redistribution that would improve the lot of the worst-off representative person in the first society, while allowing both societies to continue to satisfy the two principles of justice internally. Should we prefer that redistribution to the original one? No, Rawls says, "The Law of Peoples is indifferent between the two distributions."[28]

How does an advocate of a system of justice in which "no one is advantaged or disadvantaged in the choice of principles by the outcome of natural chance or the contingency of social circumstances"[29] reach a position of *indifference* to consequences of something as contingent as which side of a national border one happens to live? The answer lies in Rawls' abandonment of the methodology of argument used in *A Theory of Justice*. In contrast to the "original position" in that work, in which the deliberating parties weigh up alternative principles of justice, such as classical utilitarianism and moral perfectionism, in the second "original position," to decide on a framework for international relationships, in *The Law of Peoples* the deliberating parties do not even consider classical utilitarianism as a possible principle by which they might regulate the way in which peoples behave towards each other. This is because, Rawls tells us:

a classical, or average, utilitarian principle would not be accepted by peoples, since no people organized by its government is prepared to count, *as a first principle*, the benefits for another people as outweighing the hardships imposed on itself.[30]

Clearly, here the descriptive truth – if it is a truth – that no people *is* prepared to count the benefits for another people as outweighing the hardships imposed on itself serves Rawls as a conclusive reason for ruling out of consideration any possibility that they *would* choose to accept this principle, if they were choosing in the original position. And from there, of course, it is a short step to the moral claim that they *ought* not to accept it. But why should we accept what governments are now prepared to accept as decisive about what they would accept, if they were choosing impartially? In contrast to the case I defended before regarding parents' attitudes towards their children, we do not know how difficult it might be to persuade people to give more weight to benefits to other peoples. We have scarcely begun the task of educating people towards taking a larger and more generous perspective.

Another strange aspect of *The Law of Peoples* is Rawls' readiness to invoke, against the idea of economic redistribution between nations, arguments that could easily be brought against economic redistribution between individuals or families *within* the same nation. Thus he invites us to consider an example of two countries that are at the same level of wealth, and have the same size population. The first decides to industrialize while the second, which prefers a more pastoral and leisurely society, does not. Decades later, the first is twice as wealthy as the second. Assuming that both societies freely made their own decisions, Rawls asks whether the industrializing society should be taxed to give funds to the pastoral one. That, he says, "seems unacceptable,"[31] But if Rawls finds this unacceptable, how does he answer the critics of his position in *A Theory of Justice* who find it unacceptable for a person who has worked hard and achieved wealth to be taxed in order to support someone who has led a more relaxed life and so is now among the worst-off members of society?

Rawls does, in *The Law of Peoples*, urge that "well-ordered peoples have a *duty* to assist burdened societies," that is, those societies that "lack the political and cultural traditions, the human capital and knowhow, and, often, the material and technological resources needed to be well-ordered."[32] The duty extends, however, only to the requirement of assistance to help the societies to become "well-ordered"[33], and for this purpose Rawls places emphasis on the need for societies to develop a suitable culture, for he conjectures "that there is no society anywhere in the world – except for marginal cases – with resources so scarce that it could not, were it reasonably and rationally organized and governed, become well-ordered."[34] This conjecture may or may not be correct, but it leaves untouched the plight of individuals who are dying from starvation, malnutrition, or easily preventable diseases, in countries that presently lack the capacity to provide for the needs of all their citizens. The same is true of Rawls' further discussion, a few pages later, of the reasons for reducing inequalities in the domestic situation and between peoples:

In itself, it doesn't matter how great the gap between rich and poor may be. What matters are the consequences. In a liberal democratic society that gap cannot be wider than the criterion of reciprocity allows, so that the least advantaged (as the third liberal principle requires) have sufficient all-purpose means to make intelligent and effective use of their freedoms and to lead reasonable and worthwhile lives. When that situation exists, there is no further need to narrow the gap. Similarly, in the basic structure of the Society of Peoples, once the duty of assistance is satisfied and all peoples have a working liberal or decent government, there is again no reason to narrow the gap between the average wealth of different peoples.[35]

Rawls does say, in the course of discussing contrary views of international justice by Charles Beitz and Thomas Pogge, that he shares their goals "of attaining liberal or decent institutions, securing human rights and meeting basic needs," and he believes that these goals "are covered by the duty of assistance."[36] But he nowhere suggests that wealthy nations ought to try to assist poor nations to meet the basic needs of their citizens, except in so far as this is part of a much broader project of helping those peoples to attain liberal or decent institutions. The probability that, in the real world in which we live, tens of millions will starve or die from easily preventable illnesses before such institutions are attained, is not something to which Rawls directs his attention.

THE PROBLEM OF MOTIVATION

In conclusion, I want to return to the objection urged by Samuel Parr against William Godwin's "universal philanthropy." If Parr were alive today he might well point to modern evolutionary psychology as explaining and underpinning his observation that our lasting and strongest passions are for the good of those who are close to us, not for the good of the species as whole. Contemporary writers have echoed Parr's point. David Miller, for example, says that "universalism rests upon an implausible account of ethical motivation . . . For the mass of mankind, ethical life must be a social institution whose principles must accommodate natural sentiments towards relatives, colleagues, and so forth . . ."[37] I do not challenge this general account of what human nature is like, on the whole – subject to the usual qualifications demanded by the range of human variation. I would, though, question two possible implications that have been drawn from this account of human nature. The first dubious implication is that we are somehow motivated to assist our compatriots to a much more significant degree than we are to assist foreigners. Arguably, wartime and other national crises apart, the requirement to assist our compatriots, simply because they are our compatriots, is already beyond the motivation of most human beings. Especially where there is ethnic diversity, or great disparity of wealth, it is hard to believe that the bond between compatriots is based on any kind of natural love and affection that makes it different in kind from that between members of different countries. If the motivational claim defeats arguments for an obligation to assist strangers in other countries, then, it also defeats arguments for an obligation to assist anyone other than one's family, friends and some other relatives.

I do not, however, accept that this account of human nature shows that impartialism in ethics is untenable. Parr asserts that "the moral obligations of men cannot be stretched beyond their physical powers."[38] but impartialism is not beyond our physical powers. It is not even, strictly speaking, beyond our moral powers. Each of us, individually, is *capable* of acting impartially, even if most of us, most of the time, choose not to do so. That is true, too, of Miller's "mass of mankind." "Ought" implies "can," not "is likely to." Impartialists would be relying upon "an implausible theory of human motivation" only if they expected most people to act impartially. But they need not do so. There is nothing contradictory or incoherent in saying: "Everyone ought to do X" and "It is certain that most people will not do X."

Still, it might be argued that it is poor policy to advocate a morality that most people will not follow. If we come to believe that we are doing wrong when we do not give nearly all we have to assist those who are starving, then our response, following the maxim of "damned for a penny, damned for a pound," may be, not to give more, but to be less observant of other moral rules that we had previously followed. Thus making morality so demanding threatens to bring the whole of morality into disrepute.

Once the objection shifts to become a point of policy, rather than principle, however, the nature of the question changes. It is again a matter of what policy will produce the best consequences. If it is true that advocating a highly demanding morality will lead to worse consequences, for all those affected, than advocating a less demanding morality, then indeed we ought to advocate a less demanding morality – even though, at the level of critical thinking, we will know that impartialism is sound. Here Sidgwick's point holds good: there is a distinction between "what it may be right to do, and privately recommend," and "what it would not be right to advocate openly."[39] Some philosophers reject this distinction, claiming that there is a "publicity requirement" for moral judgments. We can, if we wish, define an institution such that no rule in that institution can be valid unless it can be publicly advocated. We can even specify that we will call that institution "morality." To do so achieves very little, however, for now any reflective person will have to ask why, in our own conduct and our private recommendations, we should do what "morality," as now defined, demands, when doing something else will have better consequences for all concerned. The answer "because you cannot publicly advocate the course of action that will have the best consequences" does not seem very convincing, if we didn't intend to advocate it publicly anyway.

Finally, what about the *ad hominem* objection that impartialism is too demanding even for its most unflinching proponents? Would William Godwin really have left his mother in the burning building while he rescued the noble archbishop? He was never put to the test; I have, however, been judged to have failed a similar challenge. My critics have claimed that, by paying for home care for my mother after she began to suffer from dementia, I have violated the standard of impartiality that I advocate.[40] R. M. Hare has suggested that because I know my mother well, and can see that the money being spent on her care does mean that she gets excellent care, and does not suffer, the money is well-spent[41] He may be right. Suppose, however, that it were crystal clear that the money could do more good elsewhere. Then I would be doing wrong in spending it on my mother, just as I do wrong when I spend, on myself or my family, money that could do more good if donated to an organization that helps people in much greater need than we are. I freely admit to not doing all that I should do; but I could do it, and the fact that I do not do it does not vitiate the claim that it is what I should do. This leads, of course, to the further question of whether it makes sense to ask why we should act morally, and if it does, what kind of an answer it is possible to give; but that is another topic, on which I have written elsewhere.[42]

NOTES

I have learned much from discussing the subject of this chapter with Paula Casal, Thomas Pogge, and Dale Jamieson; the first two of these also kindly read, and suggested valuable improvements to an earlier draft. A different version of this essay appears in Peter Singer, *One World: The Ethics of Globalization* (New Haven: Yale University Press, 2002).

1 "Famine, Affluence and Morality," *Philosophy & Public Affairs*, 1:2 (1972), 231–2.
2 Raymond D. Gastil, "Beyond a Theory of Justice," *Ethics*, 85:3 (1975), 185; cf. Samuel Scheffler, "Relationships and Responsibilities," *Philosophy & Public Affairs*, 26 (1997), 189–209.
3 See "Civilian Deaths in the NATO Campaign," *Human Rights Watch*, 12 (1), available at www.hrw.org/reports/2000/nato. I thank Aaron Jackson for his assistance with this research.
4 Henry Sidgwick, *The Methods of Ethics*, 7th edn. (London: Macmillan, 1907), p. 246. Note that Sidgwick is here merely setting out the moral sense of Victorian England in order to examine to what extent it is coherent and defensible; he does not take it as a standard of what is right.
5 *Galatians* vi, 10.

6 Mark Twain, *The Adventures of Huckleberry Finn*, ch. 32. [1885] various editions.

7 Heinrich Himmler, Speech to SS leaders in Poznan, Poland, October 4, 1943; cited from www.historyplace.com/worldwar2/timeline/Poznan.htm.

8 Alasdair MacIntyre, *After Virtue* (Notre Dame: University of Notre Dame Press, 1984), p. 220.

9 Lewis Petrinovich, *Darwinian Dominion: Animal Welfare and Human Interests* (Cambridge, Mass.; London, England: MIT Press, 1999), p. 29.

10 William Godwin, *An Enquiry Concerning Political Justice and its Influence on General Virtue and Happiness* [1793], ed. and abr. Raymond Preston (New York, 1926), pp. 41–2.

11 Samuel Parr, *A Spital Sermon Preached at Christ Church upon Easter Tuesday, April 15, 1800, to which are added notes* (London, 1801), p. 4.

12 For a more detailed discussion of Godwin's views on impartiality, see Peter Singer, Leslie Cannold, and Helga Kuhse, "William Godwin and the Defence of Impartialist Ethics," *Utilitas*, 7 (1995), 67–86.

13 R. M. Hare, *Moral Thinking: Its Levels, Method and Point* (Oxford: Clarendon Press, 1981), pt. I.

14 Perhaps the most revealing and best documented of these experiments in collective child-rearing is the Israeli kibbutz movement. See Yonina Talmon, *Family and Community in the Kibbutz* (Cambridge, Mass.: Harvard University Press, 1972), pp. 3–34.

15 See Martin Daly and Margo Wilson, *The Truth About Cinderella: A Darwinian View of Parental Love*, (London: Weidenfeld and Nicolson, 1998).

16 Bernard Williams, "Persons, Character and Morality," in Bernard Williams, *Moral Luck* (Cambridge: Cambridge University Press, 1981), p. 18.

17 A. Conan Doyle, "Silver Blaze," in *The Memoirs of Sherlock Holmes*, [1894] various editions.

18 See, for example, W. D. Ross, *The Right and the Good* (Oxford: Clarendon Press, 1930), p. 21.

19 See Alvin Gouldner, "The Norm of Reciprocity," *American Sociological Review*, 25 (1960), 171; Peter Singer, *How Are We to Live?* (Oxford: Oxford University Press, 1997), ch.7.

20 M. Rosenzweig, "Risk, implicit contracts and the family in rural areas of low-income countries", *Economic Journal*, 98 (1988), 1148–70; M. Rosenzweig and O. Stark, "Consumption smoothing, migration and marriage: Evidence from rural India," *Journal of Political Economy*, 97 (4) (1989), 905–26. I am grateful to Thomas Pogge for this information.

21 Robert Goodin, "What is so special about our fellow countrymen?" *Ethics*, 98 (1988), 663–86, and reprinted in Robert Goodin, *Utilitarianism as a Public Philosophy*, (Cambridge: Cambridge University Press, 1995), p. 286. I was reminded of this quotation by Christopher Wellman, "Relational Facts in Liberal Political Theory: Is there Magic in the Pronoun 'My,'" *Ethics*, April

2000. I thank Christopher Wellman for sending me this paper prior to publication.

22 Goodin, *Utilitarianism as a Public Philosophy*, p. 286.

23 Ibid., p. 265.

24 Christopher Wellman, "Relational Facts"; this third point is also made by David Miller, *Principles of Social Justice* (Cambridge, Mass.: Harvard University Press, 1999), p. 18.

25 Karl Marx, *Wage Labour and Capital*, in David McLellan (ed.) *Karl Marx: Selected Writings* (Oxford: Oxford University Press, 1977), p. 259.

26 Robert McNamara in World Bank, *World Development Report, 1978* (New York: World Bank 1978), p. iii.

27 See John Rawls, *A Theory of Justice* (Oxford: Oxford University Press, 1971). The objection to Rawls that I have put here was made by Brian Barry in *The Liberal Theory of Justice* (Oxford: Oxford University Press, 1973), pp. 129–30. See also the same author's *Theories of Justice* (Berkeley: University of California Press, 1989). Other arguments to the same end have been pressed by Charles Beitz, *Political Theory and International Relations* (Princeton: Princeton University Press, 1979), and "Social and Cosmopolitan Liberalism", *International Affairs*, 75: 3 (1999), 515–29; and by Thomas Pogge, *Realizing Rawls* (Ithaca, NY: Cornell University Press, 1989), and "An Egalitarian Law of Peoples," *Philosophy and Public Affairs*, 23: 3 (Summer 1994).

28 John Rawls, *The Law of Peoples* (Cambridge, Mass.: Harvard University Press, 2001) p. 120.

29 John Rawls, *A Theory of Justice* (Oxford: Oxford University Press, 1971), p. 12; see also p. 100.

30 John Rawls, *The Law of Peoples*, p. 40.

31 Ibid., p. 117.

32 Ibid., p. 106.

33 For Rawls, a society is "well-ordered" when it is designed to advance the good of its members and effectively regulated by a public conception of justice. For further details, see *A Theory of Justice*, pp. 4f, 453f.

34 Rawls, *The Law of Peoples*, p. 108.

35 Ibid., p. 114.

36 Ibid., p. 116.

37 David Miller, *On Nationality* (Oxford: Oxford University Press, 1995), pp. 57–8; quoted by Wellman, pp. 555–56.

38 Samuel Parr, *A Spital Sermon*, p. 4.

39 Henry Sidgwick, *The Methods of Ethics*, pp. 489–90.

40 See Michael Specter, "The Dangerous Philosopher," *The New Yorker*, September 6 (1999), 46–55; Sharon Churcher, "Philosopher Peter Singer believes that the terminally ill and severely handicapped have less right to life than animals . . . but what will he do now that his own elderly mother is dying of

Alzheimer's disease?", *Mail on Sunday* (London) September 12 (1999), 54–5; Peter Berkowitz, "Other People's Mothers: The Utilitarian Horrors of Peter Singer", *The New Republic*, January 10 (2000), 27–37.

41 R. M. Hare, personal communication, September 23, 1999.

42 See *Practical Ethics*, 2nd edn. (Cambridge: Cambridge University Press, 1993), ch. 12; *How Are We to Live?* (Amherst, NY: Prometheus, 1995).

Chapter 3

Moral limits on the demands of beneficence?

RICHARD J. ARNESON

If you came upon a small child drowning in a pond, you ought to save the child even at considerable cost and risk to yourself. In 1972 Peter Singer observed that inhabitants of affluent industrialized societies stand in exactly the same relationship to the millions of poor inhabitants of poor undeveloped societies that you would stand to the small child drowning in the example just given. Given that you ought to help the drowning child, by parity of reasoning we ought to help the impoverished needy persons around the globe. To capture this intuition Singer proposed this principle of benevolence: If one can prevent some significant bad from occurring, without sacrificing anything of comparable moral importance, one ought morally to do so.[1] Premature death caused by preventable disease, injury, and poverty is uncontroversially a significant bad. Donations to charitable organizations such as Oxfam can prevent many of these deaths around the world, so Singer's principle holds that we ought to donate (or take some action that is comparably efficient at saving lives).

But this principle of benevolence is far more stringent than commonsense opinion, for even after one has donated most of one's income each month to world poverty relief, one could still donate more, and should do so according to the principle. For after all, the further reduction in one's available spending money does not incur anything that is comparable in badness to the loss that occurs to those in need of charitable relief if one's extra monthly donation is not forthcoming. The Singer Principle thus entails that one should continue to give until the point at which the marginal value of the next bit of money one might give would do equal good as famine relief and as an increment to one's available spending money. Very few inhabitants of affluent industrialized societies today act as though they believe that the morality of benevolence is anywhere near this demanding. Hence the puzzle: what distinguishes the case of the drowning child nearby from the case of the distant starving stranger?

This chapter considers three strategies of argument that aim to set moral limits on the requirements of beneficence. In the end none of these strategies proves viable, so the Singer Principle is embraced. But of course from the fact that some arguments for rejecting a moral principle are unsuccessful it does not follow that the principle is correct. My aim is limited to showing that it is harder than one might think to translate our intuitive revulsion against some implications of broadly consequentialist principles of beneficence such as the Singer Principle into a theoretically satisfying rationale for rejecting the lot. Still, the revulsion persists. Toward the end of this essay I attempt to lessen the counterintuitive sting of consequentialist beneficence principles by distinguishing between what one morally ought to do and what one is morally obligated to do and should be punished in some way for failing to do.

The Singer Principle is a close cousin to act-consequentialism, the doctrine that one morally ought always to do an act whose consequences are not less good than those of any available alternative. The difference is that whereas act-consequentialism denies the existence both of deontological constraints and of morally permitted options, the Singer Principle denies options but not constraints. It would be consistent with the Singer Principle to deny that one should provide aid to many distant strangers whose lives are at risk if the only effective way to provide help would involve violating a moral constraint against deliberately inflicting harm on some innocent by-stander. In this essay I want to examine the merits of act-consequentialism while bracketing the issue of constraints. This amounts to an assessment of the Singer Principle.

The worry that consequentialism is too demanding proceeds from the assumption that the scope of moral demands is limited and that while respecting these demands an individual is (except perhaps in unusual extreme circumstances) free to lead her life as she chooses in any of a wide variety of ways. But if morality requires that one always should do what will produce the best, one is only free to choose among those actions whose outcomes are tied for best. The moral freedom to live as one pleases drastically shrinks on this conception of morality.

Actually we should distinguish several different ways in which a morality might be thought to impose requirements on conduct that are too demanding.

(1) One is that the morality unduly limits moral freedom as just char-
    acterized.
    Here are some others:
(2) The morality imposes requirements that in many circumstances will
    turn out to be strongly opposed by the desires and inclinations that
    agents come to have, so it is psychologically difficult and burden-
    some to comply with these requirements.
(3) The morality imposes requirements that are strongly in conflict with
    what is in the self-interest of the agent. Any morality will impose
    requirements that conflict with the course of action that would be to
    the maximal advantage of the agent in many circumstances and with
    a course of action necessary to avoid disaster for the agent in extreme
    circumstances. But a morality will seem excessively demanding if
    its requirements standardly require an agent to act in ways that are
    enormously to her disadvantage.
(4) The morality imposes requirements that give no special weight to
    the personal concerns of the agent, the concerns that especially mat-
    ter to that agent, with the result that doing what morality requires
    standardly and enormously conflicts with doing what would pro-
    mote the agent's personal concerns. Here we suppose that an agent's
    personal concerns might not be exclusively self-interested, so de-
    mandingness (3) is not the same as demandingness (4).

When we characterize a morality as excessively demanding, we are
at least implicitly comparing it to another morality that seems more
plausible in part because it is less demanding either in the terms of limits
on moral freedom, opposition to inclinations, conflict with self-interest,
or conflict with personal concerns.

FAIRNESS AS CONSTRAINT ON REQUIRED BENEVOLENCE

Liam Murphy explores the interesting suggestion that what is most
problematic about the consequentialist account of the moral wrongness
of failing to provide aid when doing so would produce the best outcome
is that the requirement of beneficence that falls on the individual may
increase in virtue of the failure of others to do their part. To avoid this
result, which he finds unpalatable, Murphy introduces a "Compliance
Condition: a principle of beneficence should not increase its demands
on agents as expected compliance with the principle by other agents

decreases."[2] This Compliance Condition is satisfied by a principle of beneficence that fixes the upper bound of what is required of any individual by the cost the individual would have to undergo if there were full compliance by all agents with the principle in question. In this spirit Murphy proposes a Cooperative Principle of beneficence:

Each agent is required to act optimally – to perform the action that makes the outcome best – except in situations of partial compliance with this principle. In situations of partial compliance it is permissible to act optimally, but the sacrifice each agent is required to make is limited to the level of sacrifice that would be optimal if the situation were one of full compliance; of the actions that require no more than this level of sacrifice, agents are required to perform the action that makes the outcome best.[3]

Murphy's Cooperative Principle gives a straightforward response to the problem of distinguishing the case of helping a drowning child close at hand and providing lifesaving aid to needy persons threatened with premature death around the globe. We assume I face the drowning child alone, so one should do the optimal,[4] helping act. But many people are in a position to help the global needy, and according to the Cooperative Principle, the requirements on an individual to offer aid do not increase because others are not doing their share. One is required to give aid at the level that would produce the best outcome if everyone complied with moral requirements, no more and no less.[5]

Notice first of all that Murphy's Cooperative Principle renders a person's obligations of beneficence constant in the face of changes in the ratio of the cost she must suffer if she gives aid to the benefit that others will gain if the aid is forthcoming (so long as the required act is optimal in consequences). Suppose a famine is in progress and can be interrupted, with a consequent reduction in the misery of the famine victims that just barely outweighs the losses that aid-givers must incur to produce this result. If famine relief, though barely worth its costs, yields the best outcome that can be reached, and an optimal arrangement is set in place, with everyone doing his part, then the agent in turn must do her assigned part in the aid scheme, even if the good she would do by her contribution just barely exceeds the good she could do by going to the movies instead. In this scenario, the Cooperative Principle requires the agent to contribute to the famine relief scheme.

In contrast, consider a case in which others are not doing their part in what would be the optimal arrangement for bringing about the best outcome, but the cost to the agent/gain to beneficiaries ratio is extremely favorable if the agent provides aid above the level of sacrifice she would have to incur if all had done their part. Suppose a thousand people have fallen off a ship and are in danger of drowning. One hundred persons including the agent are standing on the deck and could save lives by tossing life preservers to the drowning. If the hundred were to divide the lifesaving effort in an optimal fashion, each would incur a trivial cost, say of one dime's worth of inconvenience, and 1,000 lives would be saved. Unfortunately, apart from the agent, none of the hundred persons standing on the deck is fulfilling the obligation to aid, but nonetheless the agent could undertake the entire lifesaving operation herself, undergoing, let us say, eleven dollar's worth of inconvenience to save 1,000 lives. Here act-consequentialism yields the plausible verdict that the agent should undertake the entire rescue operation and save 1,000 lives at small cost of inconvenience to herself. Murphy's Cooperative Principle yields the distinctly implausible verdict that the agent is required to do no more than act in an optimal way to save lives up to the level of sacrifice she would have sustained had there been full compliance. The agent under the Cooperative Principle is then required to undertake a dime's worth of sacrifice that saves ten lives, leaving 990 persons to perish who could have been saved at very modest cost to the agent.

This result to my mind shows that the Cooperative Principle is unacceptable. The mere fact of non-compliance by some does not automatically set an upper limit on the amount of sacrifice it is reasonable to demand of others who can provide cost-effective aid.

My route to this conclusion may be wayward. At any rate, there is a flaw in the example of the 1,000 lives at risk that I used to illustrate the unpalatable implications of the Cooperative Principle. An example of a case in which some can rescue others near at hand at severe risk of death or injury tends to elicit from ordinary common sense the judgment that the obligation to effect easy rescue is stringent. But rescue cases elicit the response that help is obligatory even from people who do not think there is any stringent duty to provide assistance to needy distant strangers. The salience of the imagined fact that in rescue cases the person in distress is about to perish in one's sight and that one could easily prevent this catastrophe distorts ordinary judgment. If one redescribes the case so that physical proximity does not seem to put the person at risk and the potential rescuer into an I–Thou relationship, the strong judgment that aid must be forthcoming tends to evaporate.[6]

My response is that noting this psychological proclivity regarding easy rescue does nothing to diminish the unattractiveness of the Co-operative Principle. Let it be specified that in the 1,000-person example described three paragraphs back, potential rescuers and rescuees are temporally and physically distant from each other. Let the personal identity of the victims be unknown so that no vivid and evocative description of the plight of those who might be helped is possible. I say none of this should matter. The point I insisted on still holds.

In many situations, it will turn out to be the case that when the most efficient scheme would be for many to offer aid, but some members of this optimal group of cooperators fail to do their part, the cost-of-giving / gain-from-receiving ratio that would characterize action by the remaining faithful cooperators that takes up this slack would significantly increase. But I submit that when this is so, it is this unfavorable shift in the relevant ratio of cost to benefit that renders it at least somewhat plausible to hold that the moral obligation to sacrifice for the benefit of others gives out. What does not seem even initially plausible is that the sheer fact of non-compliance with the optimal scheme by some (yielding increased costs to be incurred by the rest) lessens the level of sacrifice that morality demands of potential cooperators.

Notice that there can be cases in which some are not cooperating with the optimal scheme for provision of aid, so the Cooperation Principle triggers an absolute permission not to aid, but a subset of potential cooperators has made significant sacrifices that will bear no fruit unless the agent cooperates. In such cases, fairness to a subset of potential cooperators who are actually cooperating is ignored by the Cooperative Principle, which registers a fairness concern only among all potential cooperators. One might also object to the Cooperative Principle on the ground that in many cases considerations of fairness to the potential beneficiaries of our cooperative acts should outweigh any countervailing considerations of fairness among the set of potential cooperators. The Cooperative Principle takes account only of a limited aspect of the fairness considerations that bear on the determination of what I ought to do and ignores the rest.

The ratio of the cost-to-the-agent-from-giving to the-net-gains-that-the-beneficiaries-obtain is an important determinant of the moral obligation to give aid on any plausible view that denies that agents are always obligated to do whatever will bring about the best outcome at least in situations in which deontological constraints are not in play. Of course, this cost to benefit ratio cannot be the entire story about permissible departures from consequentialist beneficence. After all, this cost to benefit ratio might be extremely favorable in a case in which only piddling amounts of good are at stake. Perhaps in some set of circumstances by raising my left eyebrow slightly at absolutely trivial cost to myself I could bring about an ever so slight feeling of comfort in someone who is staring at me. The relevant cost to benefit ratio is overwhelmingly favorable but the total gain if I undertake this act of beneficence is so slight that if I am ever morally at liberty to deviate in my conduct from optimal action, I must be morally at liberty so to deviate in this sort of case.

A similar point might hold when the cost to the agent of helping becomes extremely high. Imagine a science fiction scenario in which subjecting myself to a long life of utter hell or intense continuous suffering that is not offset by any compensating goods at all, a life that is far worse than instant death, would somehow bring it about that huge numbers of people threatened with hellish lives come to have excellent lives. One might take the line that no matter how favorable the cost to benefit ratio, if the gain to others consequent on giving is too small, the agent must be permitted not to give, and if the cost to the agent of giving is too large, the agent must also be permitted not to give.

Against Murphy, I have urged that the proper limits of the moral requirements of beneficence must depend on the ratio of the cost to the agent / gains to the potential beneficiaries. The Cooperative Principle entirely ignores this factor, so it is unacceptable. Later in this essay, discussing Samuel Scheffler's agent-centered prerogative, I deny that this cost/benefit ratio does constrain the requirements of beneficence, so it might seem my argument undermines itself. Not so. Against Murphy I hold that IF there are moral limits on beneficence, they must be set or at least significantly partly determined by the moral cost/benefit ratio. Against Scheffler I deny the antecedent of this conditional.

SELF-INTEREST AS CONSTRAINT ON PERMISSIBLE SELF-SACRIFICE

Up to this point we have been reviewing a proposal to limit the extent of morally required optimal beneficence. Jean Hampton interestingly suggests a far more radical proposal that asserts stringent limits on the extent of morally permissible beneficence (whether optimal or not).[7] Hampton's account turns the problem that the Singer Principle raises on its head: The needs of the self and of those loved by the self take strict priority over the needs of mere strangers, so the question, what stops the needs of strangers from dominating the appropriate choices of how to live, is just a non-starter.

Hampton imagines an agent, Terry, who sacrifices her own interests for the sake of the interest of her family members. She does so in a lop-sided fashion, preferring to sacrifice her own important interests even with respect to such basics as good health in order to achieve trivial advantages for her family members. Terry believes in a rigid division of labor between men and women such that childrearing and homemaking are the responsibilities of the wife and mother, and these responsibilities must be fulfilled even at great cost to oneself. Hampton rather plausi-bly suggests that as described, Terry's self-abnegating behavior seems morally wrong. The moral of the story drawn by Hampton is that many views of morality construe it as concerned with requiring individuals to cater to the well-being and freedom of other persons, but this undue emphasis on what we owe to others tends to obscure the issue of what each of us owes, as a matter of morality, to herself.

Focusing on the self-regarding aspect of morality, Hampton finds its demands to be stringent, amounting almost to morally compulsory ego-ism. The story she tells is complex. Its upshot is that altruistic behavior is morally wrong when it conflicts with the requirements of self-respect, which include valuing oneself as a human being of equal worth and tak-ing care that one flourishes as a human being and as a particular human being. The latter involves self-authorship, which one achieves by devel-oping preferences and aims that are genuinely one's own, defined by oneself, and having content that does not "conflict with what is required to meet the person's objective needs as a human being."[8] Choosing to help others at cost to oneself is only compatible with the requirements of self-respect and hence morally permissible if it is "authentic and done out of love."[9] An authentic choice is autonomous, and proceeds from a self-authored preference. Choices are done out of love when the do-ers conceive themselves as "so unified with those whom their acts are attempting to benefit that what they regard as good for themselves is what will be good for those with whom they are united."[10] It might seem then that true self-sacrifice is ruled out and egoism is morally oblig-atory, on Hampton's analysis. Altruism that involves "self-sacrifice" and is morally permissible gives to another whose interests are fused with one's own interests, so that what might seem self-sacrifice really redounds to one's own interest. But this is not quite correct. Hampton is prepared to acknowledge that there might be authentic altruistic choices done from love that benefit the helper to some extent, because to some extent a gain for the helped is a gain for the helper, but overall the helper predictably ends up worse off from the altruistic act, because the gain from fused interests is overbalanced by loss to the giver. Hampton gives the example of a woman who must choose either to care for her ailing alcoholic father, whom she loves, or to pursue an independent life that develops her talents, when she cannot do both. In such a case, really sacrificing oneself for the sake of another might be morally permissible, Hampton allows.

The main argument that Hampton offers to motivate this elaborate structure of moral constraints on self-sacrificing beneficence is the case of Terry. For the moment let us accept, what seems at least somewhat plausible, that Hampton is right to judge that Terry acts wrongly in sacrificing herself. What might explain this judgment? Hampton leaps to a position that is very near to moral egoism to explain the wrongness of what Terry does. There are other possible explanations that she neglects to consider:

(1) In the example Terry sacrifices a lot of her own well-being or utility in order to gain a very little well-being for her close relatives. A straight utilitarian morality condemns this self-abnegating altruism, which we will construe as sacrificing one's own interests to benefit others when the benefits are worth less than the costs to self as assessed by impartial moral standards.

(2) Perhaps the most salient ground for thinking that Terry acts wrongly is that she lets down the side. By accepting an arrangement with her husband in which he gets the lion's share of benefits and the squirrel's share of burdens and she gets the squirrel's share of benefits and the lion's share of burdens, she contributes to the poor bargaining position of many other women struggling for fair terms in their relationships with male husbands and boy friends. Moreover, in acting out the terms of this grotesquely lopsided bargain in daily family life, she trains her children to accept inferior caste status for women as morally appropriate. In these ways she behaves unfairly to women who continue to suffer from social norms, sustained by widespread beliefs and expectations, that put women at a disadvantage in dealings with men.

This line of thought is especially interesting but raises issues that are tangential to the concerns of this paper, so I shall ignore it.

(3) Terry's behavior would also be condemned by a moral principle that was advanced by C. D. Broad under the label "self-regarding altruism."[11] According to this view, one ought to act so as to maximize a function of human good that gives special weight to advancing the good of those people to whom one is connected by ties of affection and involvement. That is to say, one should give special weight to advancing the good of those who are near and dear to us. The person to whom one is most near and dear is oneself, so each of us should put ourselves first. The good of mere strangers should count in these calculations, but at a discount compared to the good of those to whom we have close ties. Self-regarding altruism would approve Terry's giving priority to helping her own family members rather than to attending to the needs of strangers but would disapprove her putting the good of family members above her own good in the manner of self-abnegating altruism.

My first claim about Hampton's argument then is that each of these three explanations of why Terry's conduct as described is morally wrong is initially more plausible than Hampton's postulated near-egoism. They at least deserve a careful hearing. So even if Hampton had guessed right in her account of what makes Terry's conduct wrong, Hampton would not be entitled to claim her account is correct, in the absence of any careful assessment of the obvious alternative accounts.

But is Terry's conduct morally wrong? If it is not, Hampton is providing an explanation of a nonfact. A plausible line of thought leads to the conclusion that the answer is No, Terry's conduct is permissible. Before tracing this line of thought, I want to register some doubts about Hampton's account of the moral priority of helping oneself before helping others. (I should note that I ultimately will hold that Terry's conduct as described is morally wrong because it violates the Singer Principle and act-consequentialism.)

Some of Hampton's restrictions on beneficence seem too stringent. Consider the requirement that altruistic self-sacrifice, if it is to be morally permissible, must proceed from a love that connects the person aiding and the person aided so that, from the standpoint of the aiding person, their interests are unified. If it is the case that most humans are capable of summoning up such love only for their kin and friends and close associates, then for most of us Hampton's rules straightaway forbid any significant self-sacrifice for the sake of distant strangers. This conclusion looks to be implausible on its face, and since she does not provide any argument that might mitigate this initial impression, the impression stands.

The requirement that the choice to sacrifice oneself for the sake of others must be authentic, meaning in part that it must proceed from a self-authored preference, seems to rule out as impermissible all altruism chosen by those who through bad luck or their own fault have failed to develop self-authored altruism. When Sidney Carton, the wastrel character in the novel by Charles Dickens, says, "It is a far, far better thing that I do, than I have ever done," he may well be speaking truly, and his act of self-sacrifice might be motivated in part by inchoate guilt and feelings of low self-esteem.[12] Yet his act might be reasonable and morally permissible even if he cannot summon up the will to do the act just because he perceives it to be right, and even if he is motivated in part by considerations that are nonauthentic. The act might still be the one he ought to do, and a fortiori morally permissible, even if his doing it lacks moral worth.

Hampton starts from the insistence that the agent must respect himself in the sense of regarding himself as a human being and so possessing the equal worth that all humans share. But in a world where natural and human evils bring it about that many of these equally morally worthy humans will not have the opportunity to satisfy their basic needs, why must the agent who recognizes he is equal in moral worth to any other person give priority to bringing about the satisfaction of his own basic needs when he could produce a better outcome by sacrificing his needs so that others can flourish? The transition in Hampton's argument from the assertion of Kantian moral equality of persons to the presumption in favor of oneself is obscure.

Let's return to the question: is Terry's conduct morally wrong? Suppose one holds that favoring oneself over the interests of other persons in deciding what to do is not morally required, as Hampton urges, but is at least morally permissible. Terry then is allowed to deviate from doing what would bring about best consequences as impartially assessed by giving special weight to her own personal needs and interests. She is morally permitted to pursue her own lesser good instead of the greater good of others. But if she is permitted to favor herself over others, counting a gain in her own utility (avoidance of utility loss) as more valuable than a same-sized utility gain (or avoidance of loss) for others, why should she not equally be morally at liberty to give the same greater weight to the good of any other person rather than to her own good? This is exactly what she does. If favoring self is morally permissible, then favoring anyone else other than the self should be equally morally permissible, and then the ground for condemning Terry's conduct slips away beneath our feet.

THE AGENT-CENTERED PREROGATIVE

The idea that the moral limit of required benevolence is set by the comparison between the cost of benevolence to the agent and the gain to others it would bring about is the basis of an appealing proposal developed by Samuel Scheffler. Scheffler suggests that one is morally permitted to deviate from acting as act-consequentialism would dictate according to what he calls an "agent-centered prerogative."[13] This allows one to give greater weight to one's own personal concerns in deciding what to do than the weight that would be accorded those concerns in an agent-neutral consequentialist calculation. Each of us has a personal perspective and cares about things in a certain way from that perspective. What makes no difference at all from the impartial perspective makes all the difference from my individual partial perspective. It is entirely natural and understandable that each of us in deciding what to do gives weight to her own perspective in assessing the consequences of actions she might take.

Scheffler asserts that an agent is always permitted to do a less than optimal act just in case the loss to him if he were to do any act available to him whose outcome is superior, as assessed by impartial calculation, instead of this less than optimal act is less than M times greater than the loss to others as assessed by impartial calculation if he were to do the impartially superior act instead.[14] The multiplier M registers the disproportionate weight the agent is allowed by the agent-centered prerogative to give to her own projects and plans in deciding what to do. The agent is always permitted to do the optimal act if she chooses, but she is also free to choose any less than optimal act whose benefit to her (compared to what would ensue for her if she did any alternative impartially superior act) when multiplied by the factor M is greater than the loss to others consequent on her doing her preferred less than optimal act.

The agent-centered prerogative provides a partial but appealing resolution of the puzzle about beneficence introduced by Singer. When the agent faces the drowning child in the pond, the impartial value of avoiding the child's premature death outweighs the value of avoidance of minor inconvenience (mud-stained pants) even when the agent's presumed personal concern for his personal convenience is given extra weight according to the prerogative. But when we imagine the agent being asked to give more and more of his monthly income to save the lives of needy persons around the globe, at some point the disvalue to the agent of his lost income outweighs the great impartial good of saving more lives in a calculation in which the agent's personal concerns are given extra weight by the prerogative. What is appealing about this sketch of a resolution is that we preserve the intuitively attractive judgments that the agent must help the child and need not help the distant strangers. (If the agent happens to have a special personal concern to help those needy strangers near at hand and vividly present to her mind, that personal concern gives extra weight to choosing to help the drowning child, so it might well be permissible to save the drowning child even when the impartially best outcome the agent could produce would be to abandon the child and use the extra resources saved to help a greater number of needy distant strangers.)

The match of common-sense moral judgment and the recommendations dictated by the agent-centered prerogative is not complete. If the impartial good the agent could gain by ever greater contributions to the project of helping distant needy strangers is sufficiently large, then a prerogative with a reasonable multiplier would require the agent to sacrifice her personal concerns to the impartial good to an enormous extent. An alternative related possibility is that if the prerogative is set with a multiplier large enough to allow the agent to pursue her own personal concerns in the face of enormous impartial good to distant strangers that tending her own private garden forgoes, this prerogative will give so much weight to the agent's own personal concerns that it allows her to let the drowning child sink to the bottom of the pond with the result that her concern to avoid muddying her pants is satisfied. But the agent-centered prerogative makes it possible to develop moral judgments about beneficence far more in line with ordinary moral opinion than the Singer Principle and act-consequentialist moralities.

Most of the critical response to Scheffler's proposal centers on the fact that it draws no distinction between options and constraints.[15] If it would be acceptable for me to act to get myself a benefit of a certain size, which imposes costs totalling C on other agents by way of neglecting to act to help them, it would be equally acceptable for me to get a benefit for myself of that same size by doing an act that violates a moral constraint against harming others and imposes in this way costs on others totalling C. The critics claim that any multiplier stipulated by the agent-centered

prerogative that is large enough to give an agent an intuitively satisfying range of options would yield counterintuitive recommendations
when the agent-centered prerogative is applied to choices in which an
agent would suffer loss to self consequent on obeying some significant
moral constraint against harming other people in some specified way.
This issue is beyond the scope of this essay, and so not our concern
here.

My worry is different. The Scheffler proposal yields implausible recommendations that are flawed in essentially the same way that the
Hampton proposal was found to be. Scheffler's agent-centered prerogative makes the permissibility of acting to promote a concern depend on
whether or not it is mine. For example, suppose the prerogative would
have it that I am permitted to give medicine to my sick father rather than
do any of the alternative acts available to me that would bring about a
better outcome as impartially assessed. In the same circumstances the
prerogative would not permit me to give the same medicine to someone
else's equally sick father even though the gain to him would be identical to the benefit my father would gain and the act of helping someone
else's father would produce an outcome that is just as good as assessed
from an impartial perspective as the outcome that would result from the
act of helping my own father. In other words, the Scheffler prerogative
supposes that there is moral magic in the pronoun "my." My concerns,
my projects and plans are given special extra weight in moral calculation
that determines what it is permissible for me to do, whereas exactly similar concerns, plans, and projects that are other people's rather than my
own do not generate special moral license to act to fulfill those equally
morally worthy matters.

For another example, consider the act of buying for my own consumption a giant hot fudge sundae instead of performing some act with
an outcome that is superior according to impartial assessment. The costs
and benefits to self and others are such that the prerogative gives me
permission to do the self-favoring act. Now suppose that on a whim I
decide instead to buy for someone else's consumption the same giant
hot fudge sundae instead of performing some act with an outcome that
is superior according to impartial assessment. We suppose the beneficiary of my whimsical largesse would derive just as much pleasure and
nutritional gain and other benefits from eating the sundae as I would if
I ate it myself. The agent-centered prerogative gives no extra weight to
gains to this beneficiary, so it could well happen that doing the nonoptimal act that benefits another person but not me is forbidden by the

agent-centered prerogative. This result strikes me as arbitrary, just as arbitrary as the judgment by Hampton that whereas it would be perfectly morally acceptable for Terry to act so as to favor herself over others, it would be morally unacceptable for Terry to favor others over herself.

It might be supposed that I am misinterpreting Scheffler in an obvious way. If I choose to benefit another person rather than myself, then it follows that I have some personal concern, plan or project to benefit that other person. So if the prerogative gives enough weight to my personal concerns to render it permissible for me to donate resources to my sick father rather than use them to secure some impartially better outcome, then if I choose to aid someone else's similarly situated father instead, then doing that must be my personal concern, so the prerogative kicks in, and renders the decision to favor others just as permissible as the decision to favor myself. And the same goes for the permissibility of the choices canvassed in the giant hot fudge sundae example.

This suggestion is incorrect. It is true that the personal concerns that are given extra weight in calculation of morally permissible action according to Scheffler's prerogative need not be personal concerns to benefit myself. I might have a personal concern to pursue some cause, or be nice to animals, or follow any of myriad interests. But the Scheffler construction supposes one can distinguish matters that are for an agent matters of her personal concern from matters that are for that agent not matters of personal concern. The prerogative gives permissibility-enhancing weight only to the agent's personal concerns, the things she cares about, whatever they might be. But it is not taken to be necessarily or even just contingently true that each agent always acts only to further her own personal concerns. Scheffler's construction supposes that an agent in given circumstances might instead of acting to promote her personal concerns choose instead to do what is best as assessed from an impartial perspective. The agent can choose to act to promote her personal concerns or decline to do so. And just as the agent can choose to promote the impartial good instead of her personal concerns, the agent equally might choose to promote concerns of some other people rather than either her personal concerns or the dictates of impartial good. It is possible to do this, but Scheffler's agent-centered prerogative says it is wrong to do so.

My objection could be met by amending Scheffler's prerogative so that it would allow an agent to give disproportionate weight to the satisfaction of anybody's personal interests of her choosing beyond the value

that would be accorded these interests by impartially neutral calculation. The prerogative allows the individual to count the satisfaction of
these selected interests as M times more valuable than the satisfaction of
other interests in deciding what to do. Severed from the idea that people
should be free to pursue their own projects and plans to a greater extent than act-consequentialist calculation or the Singer Principle would
allow them to do, the prerogative may now look just bizarre. But there
are reasons for devising a prerogative that does not rely on the claimed
moral reasonableness of deference to personal concern. Moreover, what
we might call the *bare prerogative* has some appeal.

The Scheffler agent-centered prerogative attempts to blend together
two different lines of objection to act-consequentialism and provide a
single solution that is responsive to both objections. On the one hand,
act-consequentialism is too demanding in that in many circumstances
it would force an agent to sacrifice the pursuit of her own personal concerns to an excessive extent. On the other hand, act-consequentialism is
too demanding in that it is too restrictive of the agent's moral freedom of
choice. That these are quite different objections pulling in different directions is immediately obvious. Acceptance of act-egoism would fully satisfy the first objection but do nothing to ameliorate the second difficulty.
The second difficulty could be satisfied by a satisficing consequentialism which selects among the options of acts available to an agent those
that are "good enough" in their consequences as ranked by an impartial
consequentialist standard. The agent is then free to do any of the acts
selected as "good enough" in their consequences. Provided the bar of
"good enough" consequences is set sufficiently low, satisficing consequentialism in many circumstances would not select one act as morally
required to do but would rather give the agent a wide range of morally
permissible choices. But all of these choices might still be disastrous for
the agent's own personal concerns. Hence satisficing consequentialism
might be subject to the first objection but not the second.

Once these two strains of thought are separated, each taken separately looks problematic. Take the imperative of restricting the demands
of morality to allow the individual to pursue her own personal concerns
even if these are not weighty when viewed from the impartial perspective. Hampton's Terry case shows that it is not plausible to hold that
morality requires one to give priority to one's own personal concerns in
deciding what to do. If it would be acceptable for Terry to give special
weight beyond what impartial rankings of consequences would allow
to her own rational self-interest, then it should be acceptable for her to

give comparable extra weight to her non-self-interested personal concerns. Morality does not command that one act egoistically. Nor does morality command that one act in a way that gives special priority to the things one happens to care about. But then if it is acceptable for Terry to give special weight to the interests of Fred, for whom she has personal concern, why would it not be equally acceptable for her to give similar priority to the interests of Samantha, a stranger for whom she has no such personal concern. After all, what is morally special about the things I happen to care about?

Of course there may be answers to this sort of question from the standpoint of impartial rankings of consequences. But these answers are irrelevant in this context. For example, it may be impartially desirable that friends be true to friends, so the world in which one friend is nice to another is a better world than another otherwise identical except that the friend is nice instead to a random stranger. Relationships of parent to child might beget similar special values that are realized when parents help their own children (and that are not realized when parents give similar help to other people's children). But these considerations so regarded will affect the impartial rankings of consequences and hence the determination of what it is best from the impartial consequentialist standpoint for an agent to do in given circumstances. Our concern is different. We are concerned with cases in which the consequentialist rankings of states and affairs and acts that might produce them brings it about that it would be optimific for the agent to act in some way that is too demanding.

Consider this formulation of Scheffler's objection against act-consequentialism: By requiring us always to do what brings about what is impersonally best, consequentialism alienates us from our personal concerns. In this sense it threatens integrity. Is acting with integrity then what we morally may do or morally must do? Scheffler's position represents a compromise. According to his agent-centered prerogative, an agent is always morally at liberty to do either (1) the impersonally best act or (2) any act that brings about an outcome that advances one's own personal concerns (multiplied by the prerogative) by comparison with the benchmark level of advance of one's personal concerns that the impersonally best outcome would have achieved by an amount no less than the amount of loss of impersonal good that would be occasioned by doing this act rather than what is impersonally best. This means one is morally at liberty according to the prerogative to do an act that advances one's personal concerns less than one could permissibly attain according to the prerogative so long as the constraint just described is still satisfied. The agent-centered prerogative then gives one permission to stray from what is impersonally best only in the direction of what is better from the standpoint of one's personal concerns, but this act need not be the one that does the best one permissibly can do from the standpoint of one's personal concerns.

A limit case of acting from one's personal concerns would be acting to satisfy a momentary desire or whim. Imagine that the Schefflerian agent-centered prerogative allows me to satisfy my whim to bequeath my wealth to a random person whose physical attractiveness I fancy now in Grand Central Station rather than to bequeath to my expectable heirs, which would best satisfy my long-run overall, personal concerns, or to do what is impartially best. But since I happen not to have the momentary desire of bequeathing my wealth to a random person whose physical attractiveness I do not fancy now in Grand Central Station, that choice would be morally impermissible. Too much here seems to hang on too little. If maximal fulfillment of one's overall personal concerns is of great moral significance, and trumps any requirement to do what is impartially best, why is acting from integrity in this sense not morally required if one is going to do what is not impartially best? On the other hand, if having wide moral liberty to do as one chooses is of great moral significance, why is this moral liberty limited at all by the shape of one's actual personal concerns?

If one responds to this last question by opting for wide moral liberty over personal concerns, one then ends up with the revision of Scheffler's proposal that I have called the bare prerogative. The agent-centered prerogative then becomes a blanket permission to give special weight to any interests, above the weight these interests would get in an impartial consequentialist ranking. These interests need not be special concerns of the agent. When we press on the idea that morality allows each of us to give special weight to his own personal concerns in deciding what to do, we end up leaving the idea of the agent's own personal concerns behind. What we end up with is essentially the claim that agents should be granted wide moral freedom, should be morally permitted to act in a wide variety of ways on most occasions of choice. The question then arises why this ideal of moral freedom should be thought to be compelling. Why is this the key determinant of the limits of what we owe to distant strangers? Moral freedom in and of itself seems a bloodless and abstract matter. Imagine cases in which the agent herself has no special concern for moral freedom and takes no interest in it. The position we are considering says that even here preserving the agent's moral freedom is of great moral importance. Maybe so; but there is room for doubt.

Another source of doubt insinuates itself into the story when we ask how much weight the prerogative should give to the interests that are to receive extra weight above what impartial ranking would give them? What is supposed to determine a correct answer to this question? I find I cannot get a grip on these questions.

The proposed elaborations of the thought that act-consequentialism is too demanding (the Scheffler prerogative and the bare prerogative) are neither of them as plausible as the initial claim.

WHAT IS MORALLY RIGHT IS NOT MORALLY OBLIGATORY

I propose a way of dealing with the puzzles of benevolence discussed by Singer, Murphy, Hampton, and Scheffler that holds on to the act-consequentialist claim that one morally ought always to do the act of the available alternatives that would produce the best consequences as impartially assessed.[16]

In response to the claim that affluent people should entirely devote their lives to the relief of the suffering and crippling poverty of the worst-off persons on the globe, one's initial response is not so much that this claim is unjustified as that affluent people cannot be blamed for failing to live up to this austere ideal of self-sacrifice. Given human nature, which strongly inclines us to put ourselves and those near and dear to us first in our priorities when we decide how to act, it would be at the least extremely difficult for people to adhere to the Singer Principle, and given the great difficulty of complying with this code, it is no great sin that we do not, and priggish to act as though it were. There is the further consideration that people are not trained to accept anything close to the demands of the Singer Principle, so their intuitive responses instilled by processes of socialization pull against acceptance of it and compliance with it. So we should sharply distinguish what it is right and wrong to do and what we should be praised and blamed for doing and not doing. It is morally right to do the optimal act and morally wrong to do anything else, but in many circumstances including the context in which issues of famine relief and relief of global poverty arise, one is not (or hardly at all) blameworthy for failing to do what is morally right.

One might resist this easy division of responses to the global poverty puzzle by asserting that doing right and wrong and being subject to praise and blame are conceptually connected, so the proposal to separate them is incoherent. John Stuart Mill clearly expressed the claim that there is a conceptual connection between an act's being morally wrong and being fit for punishment. He writes, "We do not call an act wrong unless we mean to imply that a person ought to be punished in some way or other for doing it – if not by law, by the opinion of his fellow creatures; if not by opinion, by the reproaches of his own conscience."[17]

I disagree. What is morally right and wrong to do is established by the decisive balance of reasons for and against various courses of action, on the assumption that moral reasons are trumping considerations or perhaps all things considered considerations, which incorporate and assign the correct weight to all nonmoral reasons that bear on the choice of action. What is morally right is what there is most reason to do, and the other act alternatives one might do instead are morally wrong. On the act-consequentialist analysis, the act that there is most reason to do is identified with the optimal act, that act the doing of which would produce best consequences as impartially assessed. On each occasion of choice, the alternative acts one might do that are not optimal are morally wrong.[18] Nothing in the story so far says or implies anything about blame or punishment.

Shouldn't we feel guilty if we do what is morally wrong? Not necessarily. From a consequentialist standpoint, whether someone should be punished for doing or refraining from doing some act depends on what the consequences would be of performing that act of punishment. Even the punishment of guilt feelings that spontaneously well up in the consciousness of the wrongdoer can be regarded as to some extent the outcome of a mechanism that is set in place by prior human acts – acts of socialization by others and acts of self-culture or character building by the agent herself. The consequentialist evaluation of this psychic mechanism that induces guilt in a person can be traced to the assessment of the acts that combine with circumstances and the person's innate dispositions to produce the mechanism.

Let us say that an act is *obligatory* just in case one should be punished (at the minimum, by guilt or self-blame) for failure to do it. If it were the case that a person should always be punished on each occasion that she fails to do whatever is optimific, then the category of *action it would be morally wrong not to do* and the category of *obligatory action* would always coincide. But it is a common observation in discussions of consequentialist morality that failure to do what is optimific often does not render one fit for punishment in the sense that punishing one would have consequences better than any alternative. Failure to distinguish what is right and wrong from what is obligatory and forbidden renders act-consequentialism formulated in terms of the former contrast a less plausible-sounding doctrine than it should seem.

The same analysis can apply to decision problems in which one can accomplish significant good for the wretched of the earth by significant self-sacrifice. In the cases of global famine and poverty relief described by Singer, it is stipulated that doing the benevolent and self-sacrificing act produces best consequences and there is nothing morally to be said against this benevolent choice other than that it involves real self-sacrifice. Is doing the benevolent act in these circumstances the morally right act, and failure to do it morally wrong? The act-consequentialist replies resoundingly in the affirmative. Is the failure to be benevolent at significant cost to oneself a violation of moral obligation, for which one should be punished? From the act-consequentialist standpoint, the answer to this question may be very uncertain, because it is unclear, human nature being what it is, whether punishing such humdrum selfish acts would have good or bad consequences. To this extent the act-consequentialist position, in this context identical to the Singer Principle, does a good job both in matching our considered moral responses and explaining them. I am envisaging that the morally perceptive affluent person, munching his croissants and fingering the keys to his fancy car, does not hold that it is morally justified that he enjoys the good life at the moral cost that others live avoidably wretched lives. His position is, "Can you blame me?"

Raising the level of moral obligation will generally tend to produce two effects that pull in opposite directions. Setting the level higher will tend to improve the outcomes of the actions of those people who conscientiously strive to comply with the higher norm. But setting the level higher, above some point,[19] will also tend to reduce the numbers of people who conscientiously strive to comply with moral requirements. As the level of requirements becomes ever more demanding, more people will tend to become alienated from the enterprise of morality and to become less disposed to carry out even its minimal requirements. At some level of obligation these two effects balance, so that any raising or lowering of the level of obligation would produce worse consequences overall; at this point the level of obligation is optimal. But there is no particular reason to think the optimal level of obligation will hold that people are always morally obligated to do what according to act-consequentialism is morally right.

Distinguishing what is morally right and wrong from what is morally obligatory and forbidden helps make sense of intuitive puzzles about the morality of beneficence and the difficulty of coming to a stable view about the moral limits on the extent to which beneficence, when optimal, is required. If the agent is not a saint, she will be strongly motivated to give special priority to promoting her personal projects and concerns by her actions, and choosing acts that cater to these concerns that are subjectively important to her rather than choosing the available act whose consequences are ranked best from the impartial standpoint. If the agent chooses acts that cater to her personal concerns, there will virtually always be a strong excuse for her choosing to do that rather than what is impartially best. Hence blame for such cases would often be misplaced. This across the board presumption that the agent should be excused for failing to do what is optimal because she is subject to strong motives to cater to her personal concerns does not come into play if the agent acts in a way that is nonoptimal and that also does not further her own personal concerns but rather any concerns selected randomly or capriciously at the moment of choice.

I have urged that there is no more justification for acting to further one's own personal concerns than acting to further anyone else's concerns instead of doing what would produce best consequences impartially assessed. So if acting nonoptimally to further personal concerns is justified, acting nonoptimally to advance any comparable concerns not one's own is also justified. But it is odd that personal concerns and what matters from the personal point of view drop out of consideration in this way. But if we switch from thinking in terms of justification to thinking in terms of excuses and the conditions under which blame is inapplicable, the banished but seemingly sensible idea of deferring to the agent's personal concern returns and falls into place naturally. In the types of case in which we are intuitively inclined to say that act-consequentialism along with its cousin the Singer principle are too demanding in the requirements of beneficence they impose, we should instead say that these are cases where, although one should always do what would produce the best consequences, when doing so pulls sharply against one's personal concerns, the agent is not to be blamed for acting nonoptimally.

One difficulty with my proposal is that it might seem to leave unanswered the concern that act-consequentialist morality is too demanding in the sense that its dictates leave the individual choosing what to do too little moral freedom to choose among a wide range of alternative courses of action and ways of life.

My response is that once the idea of what is morally right and wrong is separated from the idea of what is morally obligatory and forbidden, with phenomena of guilt, blame, and punishment linked to violation of what is morally obligatory, the moral freedom concern becomes less urgent. The mere fact that I am not morally free to do anything except the available act on each occasion of choice that would produce consequences no worse than the consequences of any alternative I might choose is simply not in and of itself a severe restriction on my effective freedom to live as I choose. My effective freedom in a situation of choice is constituted by the options such that if I were to choose them, I would get them. Lack of opportunities and resources and lack of abilities restrict my effective freedom. If I am not morally free to choose X, that only means that I morally ought not to choose it. This is fully consistent with its being the case that I am effectively free to X – if I choose it, my choice will be effective.

More should be said to clarify the idea of an act's being fit for punishment that determines the idea of an obligation in my proposed usage. We can distinguish being obligated and feeling oneself to be obligated. Whether or not one is obligated depends on whether or not one ought to be punished for omitting to do the obligatory thing. Whether or not one feels obligated or experiences a sense of obligation depends on how one has been socialized, what norms are current in one's society, one's innate dispositions, and the current state of one's moral thinking.

We can also distinguish being ideally and pragmatically fit for punishment. The distinction turns on the degree to which the context in which the action occurs is taken for granted. In the ideal sense, an act is fit for punishment just in case a society like the actual society in which the act occurs except that it is ideally regulated by act-consequentialist principle would establish practices of socialization, social norms of conduct, and institutions of punishment that would bring it about that acts of this type would incur punishment. In the pragmatic sense, an act is fit for punishment just in case it would be optimal (produce best consequences) in the circumstances in which the act occurs that it incur punishment. Corrresponding to these two senses of being fit for punishment we can identify two different notions of being morally obligatory.

The ideal sense of obligation gives us a way of characterizing what people morally ought to do and are obligated to do under conditions that are as favorable as we could hope for the production of impartially good consequences. In the context of considering moral duties and obligations to contribute to the alleviation of avoidable global poverty and misery, the relevant society to consider would be a single world society ideally regulated by consequentialist principle. This regulatory regime will compromise with human nature rather than wage war against it. Suppose that you and I are impoverished, disease-plagued, jobless and homeless members of this society, and that many of its members are affluent to the degree that they could contribute significantly to the improvement of the quality of life of people such as you and I at a cost of self-sacrifice that is such that act-consequentialism (the Singer Principle) would endorse these possible acts of beneficence by the affluent. But in fact the affluent do not make these contributions and the social norms, socialization practices, and punishment practices of the society do not sanction their failure to help. What gives? Should not society be reformed so the affluent well off people are made to help us? If the society is ideally regulated by consequentialist principle, the following answer can be made: It is true that the affluent act morally wrongly in failing to give to help alleviate your plight. They do what is wrong. But they do not violate any moral obligation in the ideal sense. Since the order of society as it is is optimific, any attempt to sanction the affluent or alter institutions or practices in any way in order to bring it about that your and my lives are improved would bring it about that some people with (in the aggregate) greater moral claims to improved quality of life than you and I now have would be made worse off.

For all that has been said, it might well be that the widespread failure of well-off persons in affluent societies to contribute enormously more than they do at present to the relief of global poverty and misery and premature death is not only morally wrong by act-consequentialist standards but also a violation of obligation in the pragmatic sense as well as in the ideal sense. In this case, even if we do not feel guilty and blame ourselves for failure to contribute at a decent level, we should. My task in this essay is not to insulate the comfortable from blame but to indicate that an act-consequentialist morality can generate a nuanced analysis of this situation that is not obviously at variance with our reflective judgments after critical scrutiny. Moreover, achieving a reflective equilibrium among our moral judgments in this domain is not easy. If act-consequentialism and the Singer principle do poorly on this test, Murphy's Cooperative Principle, Hampton's espousal of strict requirements for permissible altruism, and Scheffler's agent-centered prerogative all score worse.

NOTES

1 Peter Singer, "Famine, Affluence, and Morality," *Philosophy and Public Affairs*, 1 (Spring, 1972), 229–43. For criticism from a deontological perspective, see Frances M. Kamm, "Famine Ethics: The Problem of Distance in Morality and Singer's Ethical Theory," in Dale Jamieson, ed., *Singer and His Critics* (Oxford: Blackwell, 1999), pp. 162–208. For elaboration of a morality of beneficence (inter alia) from a virtue ethics perspective, see Michael Slote, "The Justice of Caring," *Social Philosophy and Policy*, 15: 1 (Winter, 1998), 171–95; also Slote, *From Morality to Virtue* (Oxford: Oxford University Press, 1995).

2 Liam Murphy, "The Demands of Beneficence," *Philosophy and Public Affairs*, 22: 4 (Fall, 1993), 267–92; see p. 278. For further discussion, see Murphy, *Moral Demands in Nonideal Theory* (Oxford: Oxford University Press, 2000).

3 Ibid., p. 280.

4 Here and subsequently in this essay I use "optimal" as Murphy does: An optimal act is one that would bring about the best consequences as impartially assessed. This usage should not be confused with the entirely different idea that a situation is Pareto optimal if any alteration from it to make someone better off would make someone worse off.

5 One may wonder about how to interpret the Cooperative Principle. Are its requirements timeless, so that one is required by morality to do what would produce optimal results if everyone at all times had acted optimally? Or do we interpret the Principle as limiting the requirements of beneficence only by the level of activity that would produce optimal results if everyone now fully complied with the principle? If we accepted the Cooperative Principle, we would have to solve these problems about its interpretation, but I shall argue the Principle is unacceptable for reasons that are independent of the answers to the questions just raised. For further discussion of the Cooperative Principle see Tim Mulgan, "Two Conceptions of Benevolence," *Philosophy and Public Affairs*, 26: 1 (Winter, 1997), 62–79; also Liam B. Murphy, "A Relatively Plausible Principle of Beneficence: Reply to Mulgan," *Philosophy and Public Affairs*, 26: 1 (Winter, 1997), 80–6.

6 See Murphy, *Moral Demands in Nonideal theory*, pp. 127–33; also Peter Unger, *Living High and Letting Die* (Oxford and New York: Oxford University Press, 1996).

7 Jean Hampton, "Selflessness and the Loss of Self," *Social Philosophy and Policy* (December, 1993), 135–65.

8 Ibid., p. 152.

9 Ibid., p. 157.

10 Ibid., p. 158.

11 C. D. Broad, "Self and Others," in *Broad's Critical Essays in Moral Philosophy*, ed. D. Cheney (London: George Allen and Unwin, 1971). I owe this reference to David Brink.

12 Charles Dickens, *A Tale of Two Cities*, in *The Oxford Illustrated Dickens* (Oxford: Oxford University Press, 1949), p. 358. The novel was first published in 1859. Actually the quoted words are Carton's unspoken thoughts just before he is guillotined. I have a memory of Carton uttering the words, but this must be derived from seeing a movie version of the book or reading the *Classics Comics* summary. My suggestion in the text probably twists the meaning of the novel. Dickens, not averse to bathos, paints Carton's act of self-sacrifice as self-constituting, self-redemptive, done from love, and thoroughly authentic.

13 Samuel Scheffler, *The Rejection of Consequentialism*, revised edn. (Oxford: Clarendon Press, 1994), p. viii. This book was originally published in 1982.

14 Here I am interpreting Scheffler, *Rejection*, p. 20. Shelly Kagan finds the quoted lines from Scheffler hard to construe, and I agree. See Kagan, "Does Consequentialism Demand Too Much? Recent Work on the Limits of Obligation," *Philosophy and Public Affairs*, 13: 3 (Summer, 1984), 239–54. I am not entirely sure that the interpretation I give in the text, following Kagan, fully captures what Scheffler has in mind.

15 See for example, Kagan, "Does Consequentialism Demand Too Much? Recent Work on the Limits of Obligation"; also Frances Kamm, "Supererogation and Obligation," *Journal of Philosophy*, 82: (1985), pp. 118–38. Scheffler replies in "Prerogatives without Restrictions," reprinted in the revised edition of *The Rejection of Consequentialism*, pp. 167–92.

16 The two-level approach that I sketch here owes a lot to the two-level theory of morality proposed by R. M. Hare in *Moral Thinking: Its Method, Levels, and Point* (Oxford: Oxford University Press, 1980).

17 John Stuart Mill, *Utilitarianism*, ed. George Sher (Indianapolis: Hackett Publishing, 1979), chap. 5, p. 47. (*Utilitarianism* was originally published in 1861.)

18 One might, following Mill's suggestion (*Utilitarianism*, ch. 2, p. 7), soften the rigor of this stark division of acts by holding that the more an act diverges in its consequences from what is optimal, the more wrong it is. All the non-optimal acts are wrong, but some are "wronger" than others.

19 One might speculate that below some point, lowering the standard of obligation further would tend to increase alienation from morality among people who become disgusted at what morality countenances. The broad-stroke empirical speculation in the text just indicates the character of the cost-benefit calculation a social planner would need to undertake in order to determine how altering the current standard of obligation might promote or dampen the production of best outcomes.

Chapter 4

The new problem of distance in morality

F. M. KAMM

What is the problem of distance in morality?[1] The Standard View holds that this is the problem of whether we have a stronger duty to aid strangers who are physically near to us just because they are physically near than we have to aid strangers who are not physically near (that is, who are far), all other things being equal. A Standard Claim concerning this problem is that to say distance is morally relevant implies that our duty to aid a near stranger would be stronger than our duty to aid a far one.

Notice that the Standard View about the problem of distance in morality concerns only aiding strangers. It is not thought to be a problem of whether we have stronger duties, in general, to those who are physically near. So, for example, the duties not to harm strangers or to keep promises to aid non-strangers are not thought to be stronger to those who are near than to those who are far.

I maintain that the Standard View is not an accurate description of the problem of distance in morality. Why is the Standard View of the problem incorrect? The Standard View conceives of the possibly morally relevant feature of distance as the distance between an agent who can aid and a stranger who needs help. But agents can be near to or far from entities other than a stranger in need of help. For example, an agent could be physically near something (e.g., a missile) that presents a threat to some stranger who is far away from the agent (Agent Near Threat Case). If distance were morally relevant, this would imply that we have a stronger duty to deal with a threat to which we are near rather than one from which we are far, even though in both cases the stranger who is threatened is far. Hence, the *New* Problem of Distance in Morality (PDM) is whether distance is ever morally relevant in any context, not just between agents and strangers. Furthermore, the Standard Claim – if distance matters morally, we have a stronger duty to aid a near stranger than a far stranger – is also not correct. For if distance itself matters morally and we are near the threat to a far stranger, we might have as strong a duty to aid a far stranger as to aid a near one. Hence, the New PDM shows us, surprisingly, that if distance matters, it is because it does that we could have as strong a duty to aid the far as to aid the near.

SOME CASES CONCERNING DISTANCE

Consider some other entities between which distance could vary. (1) An agent's means of aiding a stranger could be near to or far from the stranger, even when the agent is far from the stranger. Would the agent have a stronger duty to let the means be used when it is near the stranger (Means Near Stranger Case) than when it is far? If distance mattered, he might. (2) An agent's means of helping a stranger might be near to or far from the agent. If distance matters, he might only have a duty to use the means near him (Means Near Agent Case) but not those far away. (3) An agent's means might be near a threat to a stranger, even when the agent is far and when the means and the agent are far from the stranger (Means Near Threat Case). If distance were morally relevant, then an agent might have a duty to allow his means near the threat to be used, but not the means far from the threat.

All these cases ask us how our duties might vary depending on the distance that now holds between agents or their means and threats or strangers. But it is also possible that the distance that *did hold* at a previous time (or *will* hold in the future) might affect what duties we now have. For example, suppose that at an earlier time I was near someone who was drowning and could have helped, but I did not know of his condition. Now I and my means (which are near me) are far from the stranger. But I am told that I could still help him. If what the distance *was* were morally relevant, then I might have a stronger duty to help the distant stranger I was previously near than the distant stranger I was not near.

This selection of cases is by no means exhaustive; it is only a sample. The fact that if distance mattered, it could matter in all these ways implies that those who reject the moral importance of distance will be committed to rejecting much more than just the claim that our duty to aid strangers could depend on the distance between them and us (unless they can show why distance could matter in all types of cases except the latter).

INTUITIVE JUDGMENTS AND THE NEW PDM

So far, I have said that *if* distance were morally relevant, our duties in different cases might differ, but not simply because an agent is near to rather than far from a stranger. I have done this to show that the Standard View of the problem and the Standard Claim are not accurate ways of conceiving of either the PDM or the implications of distance having moral relevance. But how could we show whether or not distance has moral relevance? One method is to reverse the order of argument. Rather than go from the moral relevance of distance to a difference in required behavior in different cases, we can see whether our *intuitive judgments* about cases reveal that we have stronger duties when distance varies. We can then use these intuitive judgments to argue that distance is indeed morally relevant.

If we are going to use intuitive judgments about cases to test the thesis that distance is morally relevant, we can learn from the use of this method when it is applied to deciding whether the difference between harming and not aiding (or killing and letting die) is morally relevant.[2] In that context, we learned that we must construct perfectly *equalized* cases. That is, in order to see whether one variable (near/far, kill/let die) makes a moral difference, we must compare two cases that differ only with respect to this variable.

Some cases that have been presented by others to compare the near with the far do not satisfy the equalization condition. For example, consider a variant of Peter Singer's cases:[3]

Pond Case: I am walking past a shallow pond and see a child drowning in it. If I wade in and pull the child out, my $500 suit will be ruined. Intuitively, I ought to wade in to save him.

Overseas Case: I know that there is a child starving to death overseas. To save him, I must send $500. Intuitively, I am not obligated to do so.

These two cases are not equalized. For example, in the Pond Case, the child who is near has had an accident, but the need of the child who is far in the Overseas Case is not due to an accident, but perhaps due to the absence of basic social justice. The Overseas Case child is not a fellow citizen or a member of the community of those who would be called on to aid; the Pond Case child probably is. In the Pond Case, the ruined suit occurs as a side effect of someone doing something minor to aid; in the Overseas Case, the monetary loss is the means to aid. In the Pond Case, the child is seen by and perhaps sees the person who would help (and who may be the only one who can help). None of these conditions are likely to be present in the far case. The far child in need is probably one of many; the near child is unique.

As an example of how to remedy some of these contextual inequalities, we could construct the following two cases:

Near Alone Case: I am walking past a pond (screened by bushes) in a foreign country that I am visiting. I *alone* learn that many children are drowning in it and I *alone* can save one of them. To save him, I must put the $500 I have in my pocket into a machine that then triggers (via electric current) rescue machinery that will certainly scoop him out.

Far Alone Case: I *alone* learn that in a distant part of a foreign country that I am visiting, many children are drowning and I *alone* can save one of them. To save him, all I must do is put the $500 I carry in my pocket into a machine that then triggers (via electric current) rescue machinery that will certainly scoop him out.

My sense is that I have a stronger duty to the near child than to the far child, and this could be due to distance.

What conclusion could we draw if we found *one* set of equalized cases in which our intuitive judgment is that a difference in distance from two strangers makes no moral difference? The following might be such a set of cases:[4]

Near Costless Case: Everything is the same as in the Near Alone Case, except that all I must do is flip a switch right next to me to save the child.

Far Costless Case: Everything is the same as in the Far Alone Case, except that all I must do is flip a switch right next to me to save the child.

We cannot conclude that distance is *never* morally relevant by showing that one time or even sometimes it makes no difference to the strength of a duty in equalized cases. This is because a property that makes no moral difference in some contexts may make a difference in other contexts. I call this the Principle of Contextual Interaction. For example, in a context where the cost of aid to the agent is low and the effects of not aiding are great to a stranger, the duty to aid a stranger who is near and the duty to aid a stranger who is far may be equally strong. Indeed, it is the point of some contexts to make distance a morally irrelevant feature. So if we are government officials who must aid citizens, the fact that one citizen is near and another is far is irrelevant. The role of government officials and the status of citizen is intended to make some other sorts of considerations (e.g., distance) irrelevant.

By contrast, we can show that distance *is* morally relevant by showing that it matters sometimes – even one time – even if it does not always make a difference. Hence, when someone argues that distance could make a moral difference, he is not committed to saying that it often or always does. For example, we may see the difference that distance can make only as we vary the size of the cost required to aid and the seriousness to an individual of not being aided (as in the two sets of cases immediately above). It may be that high costs must be borne in near cases but not in far cases, and less significant problems must be taken care of in near cases but not in far ones. (And remember as well that different things may stand in the near/far relation, as described earlier.) So an expensive means that is near to an agent (e.g., $500 cash on hand) may have to be used, but the same expensive means that is far may not need to be made available (e.g., $500 cash in a bank).

When people say that distance is less morally relevant in the modern world than in past ages, they may have in mind that when it is quite costless (in time and effort) to reach others (i.e., be near them) and to help others, distance is not relevant. They may also have in mind that when people are involved with others who are far (via economic and communicative relations), distance becomes irrelevant as a factor with respect to whom we should aid. However, when they put these points of interdependence or ease of access by saying "no one is far from any-one anymore," they thereby unwittingly give credence to the view that nearness does indeed matter.[5] Hence, interdependence and ease could be relevant, and distance can still be morally relevant. For example, when costs to reach or to aid are high or people with whom one is not interdependent ("strangers") are involved, we may have a duty to pay the costs only for those who are near.

In evaluating our intuitive judgments in a variety of equalized cases, we should consider two additional possibilities. First, nearness in the relation between some entities may be more important than nearness in the relation between other entities. If an agent is near stranger 1 (but not near the threat to him) and also near a threat to stranger 2 (but not near to stranger 2), and all else is equal, is the duty to aid stronger to stranger 1 than to stranger 2? In order to answer this question, we need to determine whether nearness to people who are strangers is more important than nearness to a threat to a distant stranger.

Second, we should consider whether in cases where nearness relates multiple sets of entities, the effects are reinforced. For example, is the duty to help someone who is near us avoid a threat to which we are near when our means are near to both of us greater than the duty to help someone who is near us avoid a threat that is distant from us when our means are distant from us, the stranger, and the threat?

DISTANCE VERSUS RELATIVE DISTANCE

What if there were no equalized pair of cases in which intuitive judgments suggested that nearness in some way made the duty to aid stronger? Even this result might be consistent with distance having moral relevance sometimes. This can be shown by considering single cases in which near and far are combined. For example:

Near/Far Case: I learn that in a distant part of a foreign country that I am visiting, a child is drowning. Someone else is near him and also knows of his plight. Either one of us could successfully help by depositing $500 in a device that will trigger a machine that will scoop the child out.

Who has a stronger obligation to help in the Near/Far Case? In the Far Alone Case, the only person who can help is far. Suppose, contrary to what I have suggested, it were true that in the Far Alone Case, one has as strong a duty to help, even at great cost, as one would have in the Near Alone Case. This would be consistent with the person who is near in the Near/Far Case having a stronger duty to aid than the person who is far in that very case has. (This would be comparable to a brother having as strong an obligation to take care of his deceased sister's child as he has to take care of his own child, but having a much weaker obligation to take care of her child if his sister is still alive to take care of it.)

However, the Near/Far Case may only measure the importance of *relative* distance. That is, when one person is nearer than another, other things being equal, the duty to aid of the nearer may be greater, at least sometimes. This leaves it open that the physically nearer person could be far away in (more) absolute terms and still have as strong a duty to aid as a physically nearer person in another case who was near in (more) absolute terms. It would be an interesting result in itself to show that *relative nearness* matters morally, at least sometimes, but this is still not the same as showing that absolute nearness matters.[6]

If we are still concerned to determine whether nearness itself (and not relative nearness) matters morally, we could try proceeding as follows: (1) Show that a far person, when no one is near, would have a weaker duty than a near one would have had when no one was far. It would then be the case that *distance per se* rather than *relative distance* has moral significance. (2) If, contrary to my suggestion, (1) does not succeed, we could use (a) a Near/Far Case in which distances of agents from a victim were all far in an absolute sense, but differed relatively, and (b) a Near/Far Case in which distances of agents from a victim were all near in an absolute sense but different relatively. If the difference in the individual cases (especially in (a)) make no difference to duties, then we would have evidence that relative distance is not a factor.[7] (3) That evidence in (2) would suggest that in a Near/Far Case where one agent is near in absolute terms and the other far in absolute terms, it would be nearness, not relative nearness, that causes a difference in duty. Such a difference in duty would indicate that nearness per se matters, even if the duties of the near and far were the same (contrary to my suggestion) when no one is near, as in the Far Alone Case. It turns out, then, that it could be very important to run the test in (2), and that even uniformly negative results in Near Alone and Far Alone types of cases would not settle the question about the moral relevance of distance.[8]

DUTY AND DISTANCE

Suppose that there is sometimes a duty to help those who are near but not a comparable duty to help those who are far. Surprisingly enough, this does not necessarily imply, I think, that we have a duty to help those who are near rather than those who are far. That is, it might be morally permissible (even if not required) to do what is not our duty rather than do what is strictly our duty. Hence, "our duty" should not be thought of as what we must do.

This point is obvious in other cases that do not turn on the relevance of distance. For example, I have promised to meet someone for lunch, so I have a duty to keep my promise. On the way, I see someone drowning, but to save him I would have to take a big risk of drowning myself. I am willing to take the risk, but it is supererogatory (and, thus, not a duty). Nevertheless, I may do the supererogatory act instead of doing my duty (that is, keep my promise).[9]

In this case, we do more good if we save a life than if we go to lunch. But in some cases, even if we would do no greater good, we may do what it is not our duty to do rather than our duty. For example, society may have a right to require us to go to work on any day but the Sabbath. Nevertheless, we could work on the Sabbath day instead of a weekday if we chose to do so.

Duties may be seen as minimum requirements in areas where our conduct is subject to dictate by others. Though people may not have the moral authority to require us to do other acts, we might nevertheless permissibly choose to do those other acts instead of performing our duties, at least sometimes. Hence, it is possible that I may permissibly choose to save a distant stranger from a distant threat with means distant from both me and the stranger rather than save someone who is near. But the permissibility of doing this would not show that I had a stronger or equally strong duty to help the distant stranger.

AGENT-CENTEREDNESS AND THE MORAL RELEVANCE OF DISTANCE

I have suggested that our intuitive judgments about properly constructed cases could provide us with evidence of whether we *think* that distance can make a moral difference and also evidence for whether distance *really does* make a moral difference. But we cannot, I think, truly justify the moral relevance of distance in some contexts without a theory explaining why this factor should have relevance. Such a justification could involve connecting distance up with some notions that clearly have moral significance.

One suggestion is that being responsible for what (whether people or threats) is physically near us or our means is an implication of what is referred to as an agent-centered prerogative. That is, individuals have a moral prerogative not to maximize overall good; they can instead focus on projects of more personal interest. If they adopt this approach to life, it may be that they also have *responsibilities* that are agent-centered. Ordinarily, these responsibilities are for the people or projects they have voluntarily adopted. But it may be that, as locatable beings taking the agent-centered perspective, people's special responsibilities also relate to the physical area around them.

In the absence of a clear justification linking distance with notions having clear moral significance, intuitive judgments that support the moral relevance of distance in some cases might be subject to debunking explanations. Debunking explanations explain away rather than justify our intuitive judgments. For example, it might be said that, traditionally, people to whom we are strongly connected and to whom we, therefore, have greater responsibilities tend to live physically close to us. We then mistakenly invert these factors and think that when people are physically close to us, we have greater responsibilities to them.

But this debunking theory cannot explain the cases in which we intuitively think that we have a duty to deal with a *threat* that is near us and will affect a distant person, but not to deal with a threat that is far from us and will affect a distant person. Is there an independent account of threats with which we must deal, such that so described these threats also tend to be close? Do we then invert these factors, saying that the close threats are the ones with which we must deal? I cannot think of a characteristic of threats (only) to others that would account for our duty to deal with them that also coincides with closeness to us. If we not only provide a positive theory of why distance matters sometimes, but also show that debunking theories are incorrect, we would further support the occasional moral relevance of distance.

A CHALLENGE AND SOME REPLIES

An alternative explanation of some of the cases I have described, one which denies that distance per se is of moral significance at least sometimes, is offered by Violetta Igneski.[10] She argues that in those situations where distance seems to matter, it is not really distance that is driving our intuitions. Rather, what she calls "the moral determinateness" of the situation in which we find ourselves accounts for our intuitions. She says that a situation has moral determinateness when the following is true of it: (1) a specific agent (2) must do a specific act (3) for a specific person (4) in order to immediately bring peril to an end. She further claims that when these characteristics obtain, an agent cannot choose among various options as to how to help, when to help, or whom to help. When the four characteristics are present, we are in a "rescue situation," according to Igneski. Nearness will seem to matter, she claims, only when it coincides with a morally determinate (rescue) situation.

By contrast, a situation is morally indeterminate when we have the option of how to satisfy the duty to help people. In such situations, we can choose how, when, and whom to help; in such situations, it could also be true that *which* agent must act to help a specific victim is not determinate.

Let us now try to get clearer about the distinction between morally determinate and indeterminate situations by examining the Joe Case. Suppose that I find myself in a situation where only I can save only Joe and I can only do so by throwing him a raft precisely at t_1. If I have no other duties, I *must* throw Joe the raft. Notice that there are two different sorts of "must" involved here. One sense is purely instrumental: *if* I am to save Joe, I must throw the raft at t_1, as nothing else will cause him to be saved. This makes the means determinate, and we can say that it makes the situation "instrumentally determinate," because a specific agent has no choice about how or when to act if he is to save a specific victim. But this alone does not imply that I must save Joe in a second, normative sense of "must," according to which I have a duty to throw Joe the raft because I have a duty to save him. I believe that Igneski is employing the normative "must" when she says that a situation is morally determinate, that is, that there is a very particular thing that an agent is morally obligated to do.

In the Joe Case, I have deliberately asked us to imagine a morally determinate situation where there are no other duties I have besides throwing the raft. This is because I believe that the best way to get clear about the distinction between morally determinate and indeterminate situations is, at least to begin with, to think of the duty to throw the raft as a pro tanto duty. That is, barring the presence of other duties I have, there is something very specific that I am morally obligated to do.

By contrast, consider a morally indeterminate situation. In the absence of other duties, the duty of helping people gives me *a duty that still includes options*. I may help now, or at any one of many later times, and any one of a number of different people in any one of a number of ways. Furthermore, the people I can help can also be helped by other people; each of the many situations calls on no specific agent. So *instrumentally*, there are many ways to pursue the duty of helping people and morally I am not obligated to pursue any one way in particular; though morally I must do something to aid.

I shall now pose some questions and problems with the distinction between "determinate" and "indeterminate" situations and duties as I have described them.

(1) Is it urgency that determines whether the duty of rescue is present rather than a duty of ordinary aid, because urgency tracks determinateness? Igneski says that in a rescue situation "an agent is bound to

some specific act to immediately end peril."[11] This, however, is not the same as "something we (in the instrumental sense) must immediately do can end peril." Determinateness, as she describes it, seems compatible with, for example, only I being able to rescue only Joe immediately using only a raft at a *specific time a month from now.* Here too there is no choice as to when to save, but it would not be described as urgent because it is not something I must immediately do. Nevertheless, there will eventually be a duty to rescue. By contrast, in indeterminate situations, while it is true that different agents have a choice among many different people and among many different times and among many different means, it is also true that for some person who needs help, it may be only immediately, and only in one way, that he can be helped. If he is not helped now in that way, then *he* will be lost. Hence, it is urgent for him to be aided. Yet there is no duty of rescue since there will still be others to be helped by any agent. I conclude that urgency need not be present in determinate situations and can be present in indeterminate ones.

(2) Is it true that rescue situations must involve determinate pro tanto duties, as Igneski claims? Consider the Indeterminate Rescue Case: Three people are near a pond where A, B, and C are drowning. A raft, a boat, and a life preserver are available to save them, and there are ten minutes in which to save all the people. Given where they are in the water, not everyone can be saved at once. Hence each agent must choose *a* person, *a* device, and *a* time at which to save, but not any particular person, device, or time. This situation does not meet Igneski's criteria for a determinate situation, but it seems to be a rescue situation with a strong duty to aid someone nonetheless. Perhaps this is because nearness is involved. But then this would mean that nearness might matter even when the situation is *not* determinate, contrary to what Igneski claims.[12]

Suppose that we have a Far Case that is indeterminate in the same way as the Indeterminate Rescue Case. My claim is not that the duty to aid someone could not be as strong in the Far Case as in the Near Case. For example, if the cost of aid was low, there could be a strong duty in the Far Case to do one of the acts. Hence, even in Far Cases, indeterminateness does not correlate with the absence of a strong duty to rescue. As the cost goes up, however, the duty in the Far Case might be defeated, unlike the duty in the Indeterminate Rescue Case, I suggest.

In some types of near and far indeterminate cases, we may know in advance that the options will extend over long periods of time. (This is what Jesus referred to when he said that the poor will always be with you.) Given that one need not always be aiding someone, one may put off even the first *near* attempt to aid, let alone the first far one, and give aid later when one would not have been obligated to aid had one aided at an earlier time.

(3) What if one has an instrumentally determinate far case? Would it be pro tanto morally determinate? I agree that it could be, as in the case presented above where the cost to aid is very low. In a case of a distant person in need, when there is some particular agent whose act would be instrumentally determinate to ending peril, my claim is not that the agent has no (pro tanto) duty to act. One of my claims is just that as the costs involved in acting go up, a duty to aid a distant person may be defeated whereas a duty to aid a near person would not be. But even in a near case with instrumental determinateness, there may not be pro tanto moral determinateness. For example, if giving up one's life is physically necessary to save a particular victim at a particular time, there may be no duty to perform such an action.

(4) Is it true that cases I have used imply that determinacy matters? Igneski says that "Kamm redefines what it means to be close" (p. 614) because "all the cases that Kamm counts as near are also cases where the solution is specific enough to ground a duty to do some particular act of rescue and the cases that she counts as far are cases where the situation is not specific enough to ground duty of rescue." (p. 613) I think this is wrong. I do not believe I changed our notion of being close in any of the articles Igneski discusses; I specifically gave the Far Alone Case, where there is also a specific determinate act the agent instrumentally must do though he is far, not near. Suppose someone managed to pair each needy person in the world, who had to be rescued at a certain time and in a certain way, with a particular distant agent who alone could aid. If distance were morally irrelevant, then each such agent would have a duty to expend as much to aid as a near agent would have to expend if someone paired him with a person in need of determinate aid. I doubt that this is true.

Furthermore, all the cases I presented involving nearness to victim or nearness to threat could be altered so that they involve a choice of types of acts to do, choices among victims to rescue (as Near Alone already does) and choices among threats from which to save victims. I do not think the intuitive judgments will change.

(5) Suppose that it is true that there is only one kind of act I *instrumentally* must do in the determinate situation, and not only one kind

of act I *instrumentally* must do in the indeterminate situation to help someone. Suppose also that there is one kind of act I *morally* must do in the morally determinate situation *when there are no other duties I have.* It is a mistake to think that this *proves* that in the determinate situation "the agent is morally bound to fulfill her obligation in a very specific way,"[13] if this is taken to mean that I morally must perform the determinate pro tanto duty rather than one of the options I have as part of my indeterminate pro tanto duty. After all, the world could be such that I have both determinate and indeterminate pro tanto duties at a given time. Indeed, one of the people I have an option of helping under a pro tanto indeterminate duty may only be relieved from peril if I aid now instead of performing the pro tanto determinate duty. Is it clear that I may not perform the indeterminate duty to aid him?

Igneski believes that the pro tanto morally determinate duty is a perfect duty and the pro tanto morally indeterminate duty is an imperfect duty. Kantians commonly hold that when there is a conflict between perfect and imperfect duties, the perfect duties take precedence. This may be why she thinks that the pro tanto determinate duty takes precedence over the pro tanto indeterminate duty. Suppose it were true that perfect duties take precedence over imperfect duties. If the pro tanto determinate duty does not always win out in conflicts with the pro tanto indeterminate duty, this will be evidence that it is wrong to think that a pro tanto determinate duty is equivalent to a perfect duty. It seems clear that I have a perfect duty not to kill someone by throwing him in the water to make a human life preserver. But suppose that the only way to fulfill my pro tanto morally determinate duty to save two people is to throw someone else into the water, making him a human life preserver and thereby killing him. It is clear that I must let the two drown rather than do what is necessary to save them. Is this a conflict between *two* perfect duties, as Igneski's view implies, one of which is *more* stringent than the other? Rather, it may be that the duty which dominates is the perfect duty, and even a pro tanto morally determinate duty to aid is an imperfect duty. In any case, the fact that a pro tanto morally determinate duty can be dominated by a perfect duty suggests that it may not have the immediate dominance over imperfect duties that a perfect duty is said to have.

Perhaps the pro tanto determinate duty to aid *is* morally overriding, that is, it has moral precedence over one of the options of the pro tanto indeterminate duty to aid. However, it is not clear that this is implied just by the ideas of these two types of situations/duties. Such an implication must be argued for, and Igneski does not do this. That a situation is pro tanto morally determinate does not show that it is *overridingly* morally determinate when there is an indeterminate duty with which it conflicts. Could it have precedence because if we do not do it when it must be done, someone will perish, but we can act on an option in the indeterminate duty at any time? The problem with this, though, is that at least one of the options in the indeterminate duty may also not be available at another time (i.e., some particular person will perish far away because we did not aid at a particular time). So why may we not select one of those options instead of the pro tanto determinate rescue?

Hence, once we are in a world where there *is* a pro tanto indeterminate duty as well as a pro tanto determinate one, the overall situation may become morally indeterminate, for all that Igneski has said.[14] It seems, though, that if one bypassed the pro tanto morally determinate duty in order to perform one of the options in the pro tanto indeterminate duty, one could no longer treat the latter as a mere option. That is, one *has* to be saving someone at a given time if one is not performing the pro tanto determinate rescue at that time. By contrast, if one is not performing one option of an indeterminate duty at a certain time, one need not be fulfilling another duty.

In sum, I have argued that a situation need not be determinate to involve the duty of rescue (as opposed to ordinary aid), determinacy and indeterminacy may be true of situations involving near and far, but the duty to aid when far may be defeated by certain factors that do not defeat the duty to aid when near. I have also argued that the duty in a determinate situation is not necessarily perfect.

(6) Recall that I claim above that the thesis that nearness matters morally could be defended even if an agent who is near and an agent who is far *when no one is near in an absolute sense* always have the same duties. For suppose that when someone is far there is also someone who is near and the latter has priority to perform rescues, other things being equal. This would be enough to show that nearness mattered in some way. This bears on the issue of determinate versus indeterminate cases in the following way. Suppose that in State 1, the world is such that only those who are near are able to provide aid. Many of these aid situations may be determinate, and then according to Igneski, there are perfect duties to aid. In State 2, the world has changed, so that for each of those previously determinate situations, many other people who are far away are able to aid in many different ways. All the determinate aiding opportunities then become indeterminate from the point

of view of both those who are near and those who are far. This opens up the possibility that some people who would have been helped previously will not be helped since helping them is now one option among many for everyone. If the near person had the strongest duty because he was near, this problem would be less likely to arise. (It would still arise to some degree if a duty did not always take precedence over a nonduty.)

NOTES

The first part of this chapter draws on my earlier discussion of distance in "Peter Singer's Ethical Theory and the Problem of Distance in Morality" in *Singer and His Critics*, ed. D. Jamieson (Oxford: Blackwell, 2000); and "Does Distance Matter Morally to the Duty to Rescue," *Law and Philosophy* 19: 6 (November 2000), 655–81. This article was prepared while the author was a fellow at the Center for Advanced Study in the Behavioral Sciences, Stanford. I am grateful for the financial support provided by the Andrew W. Mellon Foundation (grant no. 29806639) and an AHRQ/NEH Fellowship (grant no. FA-36625-01).

1 I originally referred to this as the "problem of moral distance," but I became convinced that this term suggested something different (e.g., the difference in people's moral systems or moral relations).

2 For details, see my *Morality, Mortality, Vol. II* (New York: Oxford University Press, 1996). For a shorter description, see my "Nonconsequentialism," in *The Blackwell Guide to Ethical Theory*, ed. Hugh LaFollette (Oxford: Blackwell, 2000).

3 See Peter Singer, "Famine, Affluence, and Morality," *Philosophy & Public Affairs* (1971).

4 As suggested by Connie Rosa.

5 They also introduce a debatable notion of what it is to be distant, for example, if it takes a short time to get to a place, that place is near. But that may not be true. For more on this issue, see my "Peter Singer's Ethical Theory and the Problem of Distance in Morality."

6 I owe this point to Mathew Niece. Even here, there is an ambiguity, for is it possible that relative nearness matters at some distances and not at others?

7 I say "especially in (a)" since if relative distance mattered only within absolute nearness, it would still be true that absolute, not relative, nearness stands in contrast to being far.

8 There is, of course, another way than in the Near/Far Case of combining near and far in the same case. Rather than have one victim with a near agent and a far agent, we could have one victim far from, and one victim near to, one agent. We then ask, for example, whom he has a duty to help if he cannot help both. The problem with this test, however, is that we are not always obligated to do our duty before doing a non-duty. Hence, if we did not have a duty to

help the near victim rather than the far one, this would not show that there was no duty to the near victim that was stronger than any duty to the far one. (I shall discuss this issue more in the following section.)

9 For more on this, see my "Supererogation and Obligation," *Journal of Philosophy* 82: 3 (March 1985), 118–38; and chapter 12 of *Morality, Mortality, Vol. II*.

10 Violetta Igneski, "Distance, Determinacy and the Duty to Aid: A Reply to Kamm," *Law and Philosophy*, 20 (2001), 605–16.

11 Ibid., 611.

12 When several people are near and only one is needed to aid (another indeterminate situation), it is still the duty of each to be sure someone else will aid before she walks away. Is the same true in a comparable case where one is far from the person needing aid? In both situations, if one could not "walk away" if one were the only person, one would have to be sure someone else had picked up the slack, I think.

13 Igneski, "Distance, Determinacy and the Duty to Aid," 612.

14 This dovetails with my view that the duty to those who are near may not necessarily take precedence over helping, even supererogatorily, those who are far.

Chapter 5

Absence and the unfond heart: why people are less giving than they might be

JUDITH LICHTENBERG

It was with the publication, in 1972, of Peter Singer's seminal essay "Famine, Affluence, and Morality" that contemporary philosophers begin to think hard about crushing world poverty and the radically unequal distribution of global resources, and about the moral obligations they impose on affluent people.[1] Singer stopped readers short not only because he raised the question as it had not been raised before – certainly not by philosophers – but also because he offered an uncompromising answer. We are obligated to give aid, Singer argued, until giving any more would hurt ourselves more than it would help recipients. (Singer also provided a more moderate conclusion for the faint of heart, although it was clear he thought the uncompromising answer came nearer the truth.) Singer recently restated this view in less abstract terms: "for a household bringing in $50,000 a year, donations to help the world's poor should be as close as possible to $20,000 . . . a household making $100,000 could cut a yearly check for $70,000. Again, the formula is simple: whatever money you're spending on luxuries, not necessities, should be given away."[2]

If we judge an argument's power by whether it propels hearers to act on its conclusions, Singer's project would have to be deemed a failure; those possessing the degree of moral commitment his view demands are few and far between.[3] But that lapse has itself contributed to important turns in the philosophical debate. What is the relationship between reason and motivation: does believing that one ought to do X entail that one is moved to do X? What is the role of intuitions in moral reasoning: does the fact that Singer's conclusion conflicts with common sense mean that common sense is wrong, or that Singer is wrong? Along with these metaethical questions remains the pressing substantive, practical one with which Singer began: what in the way of humanitarian assistance do people who have enough, and more, owe to those who do not?

The question looms largest for contemporary utilitarians, who generally argue that we ought to maximize utility, and thus have to explain why we should not spend every spare minute and every spare dollar doing good (or preventing harm).[4] But it also confronts moral philosophers of other persuasions. There is nothing inherent in the notions of deontological rightness or virtue-ethical goodness that limits the sacrifices we have to make to prevent human suffering; it all depends on the particular deontological or virtue-ethical view one holds.

It would be a mistake to conclude that the contemporary philosophical preoccupation with these questions should be attributed to Singer alone. Singer's essay appeared just when Anglo-American ethics and political philosophy were awakening from a long slumber during which metaethics and conceptual analysis dominated. The publication of John Rawls' *A Theory of Justice* in 1971 and the birth of the journal *Philosophy & Public Affairs* the same year signaled an interest in substantive moral and political questions that has only intensified in the ensuing decades.

Several broader historical and social factors coalesced in the second half of the twentieth century, I believe, to propel the preoccupation with the sorts of questions Singer has raised. They can be captured under several headings: affluence, awareness, power, and egalitarianism.

Affluence. Although there have always been affluent people in the world, by any standards there is a growing number of them, concentrated mainly in a few industrialized countries. I shall not try to define "affluence"; I mean to include not simply the very rich but all those with a relatively high standard of living who enjoy luxuries.

Awareness. Technological advances in telecommunications and transportation mean that the affluent are conscious as they never had to be before of the condition of poor people around the world. Equally important, poor people perceive as never before alternatives to the material conditions in which they find themselves.

Power. Technological advances in health care, agriculture, and other fields also mean that the condition of poor people is in principle more remediable than ever before. We are in a position to affect living conditions to an unprecedented degree. (Unlike the other factors, power in this sense is not a property of individuals but applies to states of technological development. But it affects individuals' perceptions of the possibilities of change.)

Egalitarianism. Finally, the growth of liberalism and egalitarianism, I believe, has rendered the condition of poor people and the glaring gap between the haves and have-nots increasingly painful to both. As the belief that each person is born to a certain station and must submit to his fate recedes into the past, we find less tolerable the knowledge that some people are fortunate enough to be able to fulfill their potential while others are not.

So there are a variety of good reasons for an increasing concern with global poverty and inequality. Moral philosophers, among others, *are* preoccupied with Singer's problem. But do they behave any differently from their predecessors, or from contemporaries who do not think about these questions for a living? There is no evidence that they do. (Remember, even Singer falls far short of his ideal.) Of course, there is no necessary inconsistency here. Singer's argument stimulated discussion, but that is not to say it produced agreement. A good deal of the reaction, predictably, consisted of attempts to show why Singer must be wrong.

This is not difficult, it turns out. However compelling Singer's argument might appear to some, it is simple to knock down. Everything hangs on the premise that "if it is in our power to prevent something bad from happening, without thereby sacrificing anything of comparable moral importance, we ought, morally, to do it."[5] The opponent may argue that what we would have to sacrifice (our "projects," the ability to lead our lives, within certain limits, pretty much as we choose) is "of comparable moral importance." Or, alternatively, she may simply point out that the premise, which appeared at first so innocuous, is upon closer inspection highly controversial.

Many people, philosophers and non-philosophers alike, want to knock down Singer's argument. They want not to believe it, because living in accordance with its dictates would require radical reductions in their living standards. Among the thousands, perhaps hundreds of thousands of students who have been exposed to Singer's views, my sense is that the reaction of most students is generally unbelief – that we definitely do not have a moral obligation to help to any great degree, if at all.

There is also more concrete evidence for our resistance to Singer's message. Although charitable giving in the United States increased in 1999 by nine percent over the previous year, to $143.7 billion, these figures amount, for individuals, to only 1.8 percent of personal income.[6] More important, since 1960, charitable giving has declined as a percentage of per capita income: "Total giving by living individuals as a fraction of national income fell from 2.26 percent in 1964 to 1.61 percent in 1998, a relative fall of 29 percent. In 1960 we gave away about $1 for every $2 we spent on recreation; in 1997 we gave away less than $.50 for every $2 we spent on recreation."[7]

These figures fall far short not only of Singer's recommendations but even of the more modest 10 percent – the tithe – traditionally recommended by the Christian and Jewish religions. The tithe may be traditional, but it is by no means ordinary. By the standards of what most people actually do, giving ten percent of one's income is a great deal.

We can also look at these matters collectively. According to an analysis by the Center on Budget and Policy Priorities of United States Office of Management and Budget Data, in 1999, development, humanitarian, and economic aid to other countries comprised 0.56 percent of the federal budget (0.11 percent of GDP), down from 3.06 percent in 1962. The United States "ranks the lowest of all twenty-one OECD countries examined in the share of national resources devoted to development aid for poor countries."[8] As Jeffrey Sachs of Harvard puts it: "Each year the average American is asked to pay a grand total of $4 in taxes toward helping the world's poorest 600 million people."[9]

The discrepancy between what we know about the extent of global poverty and suffering, and how most of us live our lives, is at the very least curious; many of us find it troubling. I speak of "the discrepancy" in order not to beg the question of what our obligations are. (Every argument for higher levels of assistance risks sounding sanctimonious, every argument against it invites the accusations of smugness and rationalization.) Indeed, I shall address that question only indirectly here, for reasons that will become clear in the next section. My main interest is in the gap between what we could and perhaps should do and what we in fact do, and how that gap might be bridged.

JUSTICE, CHARITY, AND MORAL OBLIGATION

Almost everyone believes it is a very bad thing that hundreds of millions of people in the world suffer from crushing poverty, malnutrition, disease, and lack of education. The question is what these bad states of affairs imply for those in a position to relieve them. Philosophers have framed the issue in different ways. Mainly they have distinguished between justice and charity, and between obligation and supererogation.

Do we have a moral *duty* or *obligation* to help distant strangers in need, or are such actions morally *optional*, however desirable they might be? Does justice require that the rich assist the poor, or is assistance a matter of charity? These questions are not necessarily identical, but for many purposes they are equivalent.

How you answer these questions depends in part on how you think the current distribution of wealth and poverty came about. If you think the poor are poor in part because of what the rich have done, or if you think the rich are rich because of what they have done to the poor, or if you think that rich and poor are in any case entangled in a set of significant economic or other relationships, then you are likely to say that the rich should help the poor as a matter of justice, and that they are under an obligation to do something.[10]

Suppose, however, that the poverty of the poor has no causal connection with the affluence of the rich. Determining causal connections and the truth of counterfactuals is often difficult, which is one reason those who advocate aid may prefer not to rely on them. On the other side, the argument that you should help because you are at least partly at fault possesses a certain compelling quality that an argument not dependent on fault lacks. Some will conclude that if the rich had no part in making the poor poor and if the poor had no part in making the rich rich, then the rich are under no obligation to help the poor, however much we might hope that they would help and praise them if they did.[11] Perhaps we should even condemn them if they do not help; still, on this view, we must resist saying they are under an obligation to help. Not acting may be indecent, Thomson would say, but it violates no obligation.

Whether we agree with this view or not, years of observing student reactions to Singer-inspired examples prove its appeal is undeniable. It's the idea of *obligation* that sticks in people's craw. There is a deep libertarian strain in our thinking – perhaps this is characteristically *American* thinking? – according to which you do not have positive obligations to do things unless you have in some way contracted them by previous agreements or actions.

The conclusion is not, of course, inevitable. Singer relies on no causal claims about how poverty or other suffering came about, yet he nevertheless concludes that the haves are obligated to help the have-nots. Although he does not speak in terms of justice, he clearly believes that giving aid is not morally optional.

English usage is fuzzy here. "Charity" suggests to many people the optional and the supererogatory, yet the religious injunction to tithe suggests otherwise. The Hebrew word *tzedeka* is often translated as "charity," but literally means "justice" or "righteousness."[12] Of course, if charity is not optional, the apparent moral contrast between charity and justice may be illusory. But in English, at least, "charity" seems to many people to have that ring: something it is good to do, but that one should not be criticized for not doing.[13]

Whether we use the terms "charity" or "justice," we may think that the important question is whether giving aid is morally optional or morally necessary – whether we should be congratulated for giving it or blamed for not giving it. Yet on reflection it is not clear what it means for something to be morally optional or morally necessary, or how such matters can be determined.

G. E. M. Anscombe's classic article "Modern Moral Philosophy" sheds some light on the issue. Anscombe argues that the concept of moral obligation makes no sense outside a legal or juridical framework.[14] Terms like "obligation," "is required to," and even the moral "ought," she says, come from Christianity, which has a *"law* conception of ethics" deriving from the Torah.[15] She contrasts Aristotle's conception of ethics.

Why does Anscombe believe this? She thinks terms like "obligation" imply a lawgiver who imposes the obligation or moral requirement, and metes out punishment for disobedience. If God is not at the helm, these concepts no longer make sense. Secular philosophers may find Anscombe's claim unconvincing, either because they accept Kant's view that the rational individual can replace God as the lawgiver, or because they understand the moral requiredness of an act to mean simply that not performing it would be wrong.

Nevertheless, there is something important in Anscombe's argument. I find two strands that can be drawn from her discussion. First, to speak of moral obligation is to speak of moral necessity. The implication is that you must act (or not act), *or else*. Or else what? Or else you will be punished; or else there will be consequences. In the case of most standardly accepted moral obligations – not to kill or to torture or to take what is not yours – there are external consequences of transgression in the way of legal punishment and/or social disapproval, as well as internal effects such as guilt and self-recrimination.

But suppose there are none of these. We are to imagine that Jane has a moral obligation to do something, but that she will not be punished if she fails to act, she will not be the object of strong social disapproval, and she will feel no guilt. In this case, the *or else* condition of moral obligation seems to be unmet.

In our society (perhaps in most societies) the "or elses" that normally accompany moral obligation are lacking in the case of charitable giving. There are no legal consequences; social disapproval is largely absent; and few people feel much guilt about not giving more (for reasons I shall pursue shortly). For these reasons we must be skeptical of the assertion that people have such moral obligations.

The secular philosopher who rejects Anscombe's theistic framework may have an answer to the "or else" question: or else you will be a bad person, a person below the moral minimum. But however common and tempting a reply it is (and I've made it myself many times), it is not very satisfactory. And this brings us to the second theme that can be drawn out of Anscombe's argument. Although Anscombe does not put it in precisely these terms, to explain to someone who is not already convinced that she has a moral obligation to make substantial sacrifices in order to help the poor requires a moral theory of which that is the conclusion.

Not all moral concepts are equally theory-dependent, but the concept of moral obligation is especially so. It cries out for explanation, justification. That is why it is intuitively plausible to say, as Thomson does, that one who doesn't help when he easily could is "indecent" (or, alternatively, a jerk) – less theory-dependent ideas – while at the same time denying that he violates a moral obligation. The claim of moral obligation demands a more robust account. The most popular account is probably a contractual/libertarian one according to which positive obligations arise only from agreements, implicit or explicit.

The theistic views that Anscombe describes contain robust theories of the appropriate kind. But which secular moral theory is it that entails a strong moral obligation to assist the world's poor? Some interpretations of consequentialism or utilitarianism (such as Singer's) may imply such an obligation, but others do not. Some deontological views may, but others do not. Some virtue theories may demand significant sacrifices of the good person, but – depending on their particular conception of virtue – others do not.

So to establish that people have strong moral obligations to help the world's poor, we would have to settle on an acceptable moral theory. The search to establish one is certainly a legitimate enterprise, but it is not one that interests everyone. One may be skeptical of such theorizing because one believes it misguided in one way or another – because one does not believe that the construction and development of moral theories, as these are usually understood, is the most useful way to reflect on and understand moral matters. One may also be impatient with such theorizing because of a concern to reform our practices and a belief that theorizing of this kind does not help us in this endeavor.

I am skeptical and impatient in both these ways. I believe that the assumptions needed to make plausible the importance of increased giving are minimal; they do not require robust moral theories. If some people have less than enough to lead decent lives and others have much more, that is a strong prima facie reason for thinking that transfers of goods ought to take place. The problem with those who claim we have extensive moral obligations to give is not with their sentiments or the direction their views would take us; it is with the language of duty and obligation. The consequences requisite for obligation – punishment, whether legal or social, and personal guilt – do not exist in our society to a sufficient degree. And the claim of obligation implies agreement to a moral theory. No such consensus exists.

At least as important is that the claim of obligation is likely to be counterproductive. It tends to produce resentment rather than increased levels of giving. Both for this reason, and because of doubts of the kind I have expressed about the utility of philosophical theorizing on this matter, we should think about what stands in the way of people giving more, and how best to overcome these obstacles, instead of arguing about the limits of our obligations to give aid. I turn now to these questions.

ABSTRACTNESS

Other people's suffering is almost always abstract. It's hard to appreciate the pain of a friend's backache, let alone the hunger of distant peoples. A few years ago, I suffered for several weeks from a painful case of bursitis in my left hip. Having never experienced significant pain before (except for childbirth) lasting more than very briefly, I found the experience illuminating. So this is what other people with back conditions or migraines (or other worse things) endured! Other people's suffering became vivid to me in a way it hadn't been before.[16]

But we have to work to keep the vividness before us, and most of the time we are happy to let the images fade. Few people like to think about unpleasant things, partly because they are unpleasant and also because when they do not take action to alleviate them they may feel guilty, which is also unpleasant. It is especially easy not to think about suffering when (to put it in psychological jargon) the stimuli are not salient and those suffering are strangers – not just people whom we do not know but whom we have never seen, who lack names and faces, and with whom we have little in common. In these cases it is not painful to do nothing, as it would be to watch a child drown or an accident victim bleed to death. Just don't think about it, and – for your own practical purposes – it does not exist.

The suffering of strangers is not always abstract, of course. You see the homeless person on the street (or, as is becoming increasingly common, beside your car as you wait for the light to change); you drive through a run-down neighborhood on your way to a nice restaurant; you visit India or Mexico and encounter appalling squalor right in front of your eyes. It's not as if in these cases, where suffering is palpable, people immediately divest themselves of all but the bare necessities in order to help those they see in need. Indeed, it is often said that in societies where desperate poverty is common, people quickly get used to it. (Many of us now regularly see such things on television, which, although not the same as experiencing them in person, does impart a visceralness and a sense of reality that might otherwise be lacking. Or does it? The debate has not been resolved: do these virtual experiences heighten our sensitivity, or do they desensitize us by their relentlessness and their virtuality?)

Various psychological mechanisms allow people to go on as usual even in the face of immediate suffering. When bad things happen to apparently good people, observers find ways to cope. The most striking way is documented by social psychologist Melvin Lerner, whose many experiments support the thesis that most people adjust to the existence of suffering by believing in a "just world."[17] What this means is that when confronted with the suffering of innocent victims, most people will conclude that the victim deserves his fate. Bad things don't really happen to good people.

Lerner's account helps explain the exceptional cases when people do experience strangers' pain. Even Americans who knew none of the victims personally grieved deeply for those who died in the terrorist attacks of September 11. It was impossible for most people to rationalize what happened by convincing themselves that the victims deserved their fate. But some – and perhaps a great deal – of the suffering we experienced must be attributed to fear and to the sense that it could have happened to us. There is certainly a large element of this kind of self-concern in the trait we call sympathy.

Aside from believing in a just world, observers adjust in other ways as well. They withdraw from the scene of suffering, they deny that bad things are happening, they underestimate the badness. So, for example, even when the victim's plight is grave, he is usually not dying before our eyes. And it is easy to tell ourselves he is not dying at all. His plight is not *so* serious, we think; however serious it is, some other individual or some social institution, or simple luck, will intervene to save him. By contrast, the drowning child the philosopher imagines, as well as many of the social psychologists' experimental cases,[18] involve acute and imminent threats to life or health. And they involve situations that can be alleviated by a single action.

But the suffering of other people – even strangers or non-intimates – is not always abstract and easy to ignore. Several years ago, I lived with my family for a year in downtown New Haven, Connecticut. One day soon after we moved in a man who appeared to be in his thirties rang our bell and asked if we had any work for him. We gave him a few odd jobs, and over the next months he would occasionally come by, tell us about his problems, and ask us for work and money. We gave him some of each, realizing that it might well be a mistake to encourage him. On his behalf we got in touch with several social service agencies; once we invited him in and gave him lunch. One night at 3 a.m. he called us on the phone – and kept calling and calling – begging for money. He showed up at our house shortly thereafter, pounding on the door, his drug dealer in the shadows not far off. When the police arrived after we called, they warned us never to have anything to do with him again. That was the last we saw of him.

Some examples involve such chance encounters, others old friends or acquaintances whose lives have not, for one reason or another, gone well. Our experiences of this kind have had several things in common. In each case, we found ourselves drawn into another person's difficulties, and spent a significant amount of time and money trying to help. What was especially striking in the cases that arose from chance meetings was that the relationship was so contingent: we happened to meet or re-meet someone, whose situation was no different from that of many others, and something sparked our involvement. Even at the time I was struck by the contingency of it – how did it happen that *we* came to be involved with *him*, or *her*? – and the thought that there were many others like them that we were "ignoring."[19] Clearly something about the concreteness of the encounters led us to get involved.

THE SENSE OF FUTILITY AND INEFFECTIVENESS

Another typical feature of many such cases – one we would rather not acknowledge – is their recalcitrance. It is harder to help people than we may at first believe. One reason (there are others as well) is that the external problems people suffer from – poverty, lack of education, ill-health – often cause internal, psychological problems that make it even more difficult to extricate from adversity than it would otherwise be. Sometimes internal, psychological problems are responsible for the external problems. Often it's hard to know which came first. So the well-meaning thought that "if one only did this . . ." then someone's problems would be solved is overly optimistic. One-shot solutions, few-shot solutions, rarely work. Unlike holding out your hand to save the drowning child, helping someone in need generally requires a major investment of time and resources.

This problem applies not only to the individual, face-to-face cases I have just been considering, but also to the cases of large-scale aid that are our primary focus here. We wonder what proportion of our charitable contributions lines the pockets of bureaucrats, or corrupt dictators. We hear many stories about how aid does not go to the people it is intended for.

If we believe these stories, that will certainly dampen our incentive to give aid. Of course, it is convenient for us to believe them. But it is also likely that many people would give more if they were convinced that their contributions would go where they ought to go, and for good purposes.

Such beliefs about the effectiveness of aid are beliefs about facts, about how things are rather than about how they ought to be. But such beliefs have important consequences for people's behavior.

OVERESTIMATING OUR GENEROSITY

There is a further way in which people's beliefs about facts can affect their attitudes and practices concerning giving to others. When asked whether the United States spends too much on foreign aid, about 75 percent of (American) respondents say yes.[20] But underlying these answers are gross misperceptions of the amount the United States actually spends:

PIPA's poll asked respondents to estimate how much of the federal budget goes to foreign aid. They were told that they could answer in fractions of a percent as well as whole percentage points, thus implying that the amount could be quite low. Nonetheless, the median estimate was 15 percent of the federal budget, fifteen times the actual amount of approximately 1 percent. The average estimate was even higher: 18 percent. Only 7 percent of respondents guessed an amount of less that 1 percent.[21]

When asked how much the United States ought to spend on foreign aid, the median respondent suggested 5 percent of the federal budget – more than five times higher than the actual amount. The mean response was 8 percent. "When respondents are asked to respond to correct information about the current level of foreign aid spending, an overwhelming majority finds it unobjectionable," confirming the suspicion that miserliness rests at least partly on misinformation.

It would not be surprising if a similar misconception infected people's beliefs about their own personal giving – if people overestimated the amount they gave to charity. Of course, interpreting such mistakes, if they existed, would not be a simple matter. For believing one gives more than one really does could be convenient and comforting. Nevertheless, being confronted with the realization that one gives less than one had previously believed could change one's behavior.

DISTANCE

If we're lucky, suffering typically takes place among people not present to us. Such people are ordinarily both abstract – we don't know their names or faces or indeed anything personal about them at all, except that they are suffering – and physically distant. Contemporary philosophers often treat distance as an important moral category. They speak of our moral obligations to distant strangers; this volume is concerned with morality and distance. The suggestion is that, with some notable exceptions, a linear relationship exists between moral connection, or the feeling of moral connection, and physical distance. The further away people are, the less tied to them you are or feel. The metaphor of concentric circles morality, which has become prevalent, reinforces this view.

But distance is a misleading metaphor. Clearly moral connection is not a matter of physical distance per se, but rather of relationships that are strongly although contingently connected to it: relationships of family, community, country, and the like. My parents or my children might live across the country or around the world, but that does not diminish my ties to them. And there are people living only a few blocks or a few miles away with whom I have no felt moral connection at all.

So, it appears, concentric circles morality treats physical distance as a contingently important but secondary factor. What matters more, on this view, is relationships. As many contemporary philosophers have argued – reinforcing a popular view in our and perhaps most other cultures – people feel more tied, and ought to feel more tied, to members of their own community than to outsiders, more tied to compatriots than to strangers. But although this view is practically the conventional wisdom – about how people actually feel if not about how they ought to feel – I think it is much overstated. It is by no means obvious that most Americans are seriously disturbed by the fate of their most disadvantaged fellow countrymen, or that they are more disturbed than they are by the sufferings of Indian earthquake victims or Somalian famine victims. And that is perhaps surprising, since some of those fellow countrymen may live right down the street, or not much farther.

Of course there are other factors at work here as well. We are more moved by acute crises than by chronic crises; the earthquake captures our attention more than the famine, which is more eye-catching than longterm malnutrition.[22] These differences in what captures our interest and attention are compounded by media coverage, which, capitalizing on what may be natural reactions, in turn widens the gap between popular and forgotten causes.

Still, the fact remains that most of us are quite unmoved by the plight of people who live down the street or across town. The explanation, I believe, is not that we are cosmopolitans or universalists, who believe that all human beings are equal and that it is wrong to favor our neighbors or compatriots over strangers. It is rather that although our less fortunate compatriots may not be physically distant, still they are typically nameless, faceless, and *absent*. They are, in short, abstract. Without an intimate relationship of the sort involved in family or close friendships or working relationships, and without the rare serendipitous connections in which people occasionally bump up significantly against strangers, those living down the street might just as well be living across the world.

It is probably impossible to make human suffering on a large scale very much less abstract to the ordinary person than it is now. Most people have only so much psychological room to feel others' pain. It's not at all clear that we would want to make people more sensitive in this way if we could. The suffering most people encounter among those in their inner circle – through death, disease, and innumerable varieties of evil, stupidity, and ill-fortune – is quite enough.

But there is another way we might expand personal giving. I shall advance a simple hypothesis: the most practically relevant reason people are not more generous toward those in need is that other people are not more generous. The implications of this claim are very important: if we want people to give more, we must raise the general level of giving in a society.

There are several reasons why individual giving depends on what others around us are doing. Here I shall discuss three broad sorts of reasons.

THE RELATIVITY OF WELL-BEING

To an extent that is rarely recognized, our well-being is relative to the well-being of those around us. I do not mean this in the sense that if those near and dear to us are unhappy, we too will be unhappy. That is no doubt true, but I wish to focus on other aspects of the relativity of well-being.

Most human beings need a certain number of calories, shelter and good health and a few other things to lead even moderately satisfying lives. These goods might be called absolute necessities. But the satisfaction received from material goods beyond the basic level rests in great part on the fact that others around us enjoy these goods.[23] This is so for several reasons.

One has to do with the particular infrastructure of one's society and with what economists call networking effects. You may need a car (or two) because there is no satisfactory system of public transportation. The more other people drive cars, the more you need a car; a good system of public transportation makes private cars less necessary. Similarly, you need a computer in an information society to do what you might have done without one in a different kind of society, or to do new things that you would not have had to do in a pre-computer society; without a computer in an information society you fall behind. So what other people around you have is directly, materially relevant to what you need in order to function at a reasonable level.

A second reason for the relativity of individual well-being depends on what we might call salience, to use a term from cognitive psychology, or what the economist James Duesenberry called the demonstration effect.[24] I never would have wanted a flibbertygibbet if I hadn't seen my neighbor's and those ads on TV. I could have lived just as happily without one, had I not been exposed to it. But having seen it, I want one. (How ya gonna keep 'em down on the farm after they've seen Paree?) We can leave open the question of whether I am better off having it, or not having it as long as I don't know it exists: the important point is that if a flibbertygibbet is available and known to me, I am better off having it than not having it (for a while, anyway). Here again, my needs and desires for things – and consequently my relative unwillingness to part with the means to those things – crucially depends on what those with whom I have economic, social, and personal relations have and do.

A third reason people's well-being depends on the possessions and practices of those around them has to do with the status functions of material – and some nonmaterial – goods.[25] Some people assimilate all the relativistic reasons for consumption to this function; they believe that to want what others have must be a matter of keeping up with the Joneses in the traditional sense. I hope to have shown why this is not the case – why we might want or need things because others have them but not want them simply for status reasons, rather because of infrastructure and networking effects or through salience and the demonstration effect.

Nevertheless, at least part of the reason we want things and are disinclined to part with the means to them (i.e. money) rests on the desire to be seen as at least as good as, or even better than, others around us. In every society, certain things – mostly material things but also some nonmaterial things – function as symbols or markers of respect and self-respect. To be a member of the society with dignity you must possess those things. No one has improved on Adam Smith's formulation of the point:

By necessaries I understand, not only the commodities which are indispensably necessary for the support of life, but whatever the custom of the country renders it indecent for creditable people, even the lowest order, to be without. A linen shirt, for example, is, strictly speaking, not a necessary of life. The Greeks and Romans lived, I suppose, very comfortably, though they had no linen. But in the present times, through the greater part of Europe, a creditable day-labourer would be ashamed to appear in public without a linen shirt, the want of which would be supposed to denote that disgraceful degree of poverty, which, it is presumed, no body can well fall into without extreme bad conduct. Custom, in the same manner, has rendered leather shoes a necessary of life in England. The poorest creditable person of either sex would be ashamed to appear in public without them.[26]

Which things serve this purpose varies from society to society. And, in addition to the "necessaries" that constitute the sine qua non of respectability, there is also a range of objects that serves to distinguish people of higher from those of lower status. Many would argue that these are at least as important, because people do not simply want to be viewed as equal to others, they want to be thought superior.[27]

But we do not need to settle this issue here. Even if it is superiority rather than equality people are after, the point holds: what it is important for a person to have depends crucially on what others have. Insofar as this is true – insofar as the reasons for consumption are relativistic in the ways I have described – it follows that people could get along just as well with fewer things, living at a lower level of consumption, as long as others in their society did likewise. Getting along on less would not involve a sacrifice of well-being.

THE POWER OF SHAME

Adam Smith alludes to shame in describing the feelings of a person without a linen shirt or leather shoes in a society in which these are considered "necessaries." Shame can also play a positive role if our goal is to motivate people to act in the interests of others. I suspect it may be more effective than guilt, because shame seems more tied to people's self-image than guilt and so is more subject to manipulation, particularly in an era like ours where narcissism is widespread.

How could shame be used to propel people to give more? As the habit of giving became more entrenched, those who did not live up to the standard would feel ashamed. An interesting question is whether feeling shamed depends on having one's failure be known. On the face of it the answer seems to be that it does depend, because shame is inherently tied to how one appears to others. Nevertheless, as we internalize the values that involve shame, we may feel ashamed even when no one actually knows what we do or fail to do.[28]

Experiments conducted by Elizabeth Hoffman and her colleagues shed some light on the phenomenon of shame generally and the extent to which it depends on others' knowledge.[29] In these experiments, a subject is asked to divide $10 between himself and an anonymous counterpart in another room. The subject can divide the money however he chooses and the counterpart must accept the decision (thus the name "dictator game"). The experiments vary in how much anonymity and social isolation they provide the subject – that is, whether or to what extent others will know what he decides – and these factors affect the subject's decision. Thus, for example, when no one, including the experimenter, knows how the subject has divided the money, he is likely to give less to the counterpart than if his decision is known. In general, the less anonymity and social isolation the subject has, the more she is likely to give the counterpart.

The experimenters conclude that when someone gives up money in a dictator game, he is "consuming" the good of reputation.[30] But this is something of a stretch, since typically the subject will never see the experimenter or anyone else in the experiment again. That fact suggests that once the mechanisms of shame are internalized, whether other people actually know what one does may be less important than the subject's awareness of prevailing social trends, which tell him what people *would* think if they *did* know.

Imagine that people's charitable contributions were listed publicly in the newspaper. Or that the contributions of employees of a university or company were listed on the bulletin board or the institution's website. A professor at a law school recently proposed that faculty members be required to report how much pro bono activity they do every year, and that this information be made public. The measure was strongly opposed by other faculty members.

In a society dominated by the ideals of freedom and individuality, such measures may seem draconian if not Orwellian, and I am not necessarily recommending that we adopt them. But their seeming harshness only confirms the view that most people's behavior is strongly influenced by both the behavior and the opinion of others around them. This is hardly a new and revolutionary idea; there is nothing more common than the view that people want approval from their peers and on the whole prefer to conform to what others around them are doing. If the thought of one's giving habits becoming known is so horrifying, we must care a great deal about what others think.

DROPS IN THE BUCKET

Let me suggest one further reason we might be less likely to give unless others give. We can call this reason the "drop in the bucket" effect. Suppose I am thinking about famine in a distant country, or even closer to home. My own contribution, even if generous, will make only a small dent in the problem. Rationally, this should not discourage me; after all, helping only one person or a few people stave off disaster, even if thousands need to be helped, is a fantastic contribution. And if I stop to think about the individual rather than the mass, I may feel motivated. But in these cases we do not know the individuals who would be affected, so it may be difficult to appreciate the value of our contribution. If 60,000 people a day die of starvation (a number often cited), and one's contributions could prevent five of those deaths, one is still left to believe that 59,995 people will die. Looked at in this way, we will not notice the difference. Here again the abstractness of the problem – our lack of acquaintance with any concrete individuals – is likely to dampen our motivation to act.

The "drop in the bucket" effect – and to some extent the other hypotheses discussed in this section – appear to be inconsistent with well-known experiments by social psychologists showing that people are *less* likely to intervene in "Good Samaritan" situations as the number of other bystanders increases. It is worth looking at these experiments to see if indeed they present counterexamples to the view I have presented.

John Darley and Bibb Latané conducted a series of experiments in the wake of the Kitty Genovese murder in 1964, where thirty-eight people watched from their Queens apartments as a young woman was killed outside. In one such experiment, subjects filled out applications while sitting in a waiting room, either alone, or with two other naïve subjects who also filled out applications. Smoke began pouring out of a hole in the wall. Three quarters of the Alone subjects (which included 24 people) reported the smoke before the experimental period came to an end after six minutes. In the three-person groups, of the 24 people in eight groups, "only one person reported the smoke within the first 4 minutes before the room got noticeably unpleasant"; "in only 38 percent of the eight groups in this condition did even one person report."[31] So people were twice as likely to report the smoke if they were alone than if they were in groups. Darley and Latané's other experiments produced similar results.

Darley and Latané offer several possible explanations for these results. One hypothesis is diffused responsibility: each person believes, or hopes, that others will intervene; when fewer are present the sense of responsibility, and the potential sense of guilt, falls harder on each individual. Another explanation is that subjects define and interpret the situation partly by noticing how others define it. When we come upon a person staggering in the street, we may not know whether he is drunk (with the implication that he ought to be ignored) or suffering a heart attack. If we look around and see others paying no attention, we are more likely to choose the former interpretation over the latter – and ignore the staggerer. A related but distinct idea Darley and Latané mention, almost in passing, is that people are concerned about how they appear to others around them, and don't want to make fools of themselves; when alone, people do not worry about their image and are therefore more likely to act.

Rather than disconfirming the view I have been advancing, these experimental results, and the preponderance of the hypotheses offered to explain them, serve to support it. They show that people are influenced enormously by the perceptions and behavior of those around them. If one reason an individual doesn't come to the aid of someone in need is that she thinks others who are not responding will think she looks silly, then the active involvement of others in helping would give her reason to help as well; she might fear being shamed if she didn't help. And if people interpret situations largely by looking around and seeing how others interpret them, the "helping behavior" of others will be a spur to their own action.

That leaves only the diffusion of responsibility hypothesis as a possible threat to the view I have been defending. According to this hypothesis, people are more likely to help others if they are alone than if they are in groups because when alone they cannot blame anyone else for the results of their inaction. But the experimental situations this hypothesis is meant to explain differ in important respects from the cases of large-scale aid in which we are ultimately interested, and I believe that these differences makes the diffusion of responsibility hypothesis less relevant, and perhaps altogether irrelevant, to the case of large-scale aid. One difference is that the potential harm in the experimental cases is immediate and palpable, not abstract and distant. When harm is abstract and distant, I would argue that the psychological mechanisms described earlier overwhelm any motivation to act rooted in the fear of guilt and self-criticism. Out of sight, out of mind. A second difference is that in the experimental cases the problem can be solved by a single action, while in the cases of large-scale aid – as well as in many of the real-life individual situations we confront – one-shot efforts are ineffective or insufficient.

Altogether, then, the evidence from these experiments does not pose a threat to the view I have been defending; indeed, it provides confirmation for it.

CONCLUSION

Philosophers have been preoccupied for more than a generation with trying to decide how extensive the obligations of the more fortunate of this world are to the less fortunate. I have argued that, partly for philosophical reasons, and partly for practical reasons, we ought to change the subject – that we should concern ourselves less with the question of obligation and more with the question of motivation.

The natural motivation to give aid to distant peoples is generally weak and unreliable. (By "distant" here I do not necessarily mean physically distant, for reasons I gave earlier; I mean people not present and not tied to us by close personal relationships.) If we want to equalize resources and improve the well-being of the disadvantaged, we cannot rely on individuals' altruistic impulses. Instead, we need to harness the powerful human impulse to conform: the dependence of people's behavior, and their desire for goods and status, on what others around them have and do.

But the impulse to conform presents us with an especially recalcitrant problem. Subjects in the Darley and Latané experiments did not act when others around them did not act, at least in part, it seems, because they took their cues about how to interpret the situation from others and did not want to appear strange or abnormal. How can we change the norm so that the ungiving person is the strange one? It is hard to get from where we are to where we want to go unless some individuals change their behavior, but if I am right individuals will not be strongly motivated to do so unless others do as well.

It seems to follow that we must either rely on some freethinking, free-acting individuals who set an example that others are inspired or otherwise moved to follow, or else think about new ways to design our institutions so that some of the problems I have described here can be overcome. Given the complexity and importance of the issue before us, it is almost certain that both approaches will be indispensable.

NOTES

I am grateful to audiences at the University of Florida, the University of Oslo, Brandeis University, and the US Naval Academy, as well as colleagues and graduate students at the University of Maryland, for helpful discussions of earlier drafts.

1 *Philosophy & Public Affairs,* 1 (1972), reprinted in Charles Beitz et al., *International Ethics* (Princeton: Princeton University Press, 1985).

2 Peter Singer, "The Singer Solution to World Poverty," *New York Times Magazine*, September 5 (1999).

3 Singer included, it seems. Singer gives 20 percent of his income to alleviate poverty. (Michael Specter, "The Dangerous Philosopher," *The New Yorker*, September 6 (1999), 53.) While this is far more than all but a tiny fraction of people give, it still falls short of the principle outlined in "Famine, Affluence, and Morality" and more recently in the *New York Times* article.

4 For a discussion of the reasons classical utilitarians did not focus on maximizing utility and therefore did not confront this issue, see Judith Lichtenberg, "The Right, the All Right, and the Good," *Yale Law Journal*, 92 (1983), 544–63.

5 "Famine, Affluence, and Morality," in Beitz et al., *International Ethics*, p. 249.

6 Karen W. Arenson, "Charitable Giving Surged Again in '99, by an Estimated 9 percent," *New York Times*, May 25 (2000), citing a report by the American Association of Fund-Raising Counsel. Personal giving has not been as high since 1973. These figures include giving to all kinds of charities. The largest proportion ($82 billion) went to religious charities, with educational organizations second ($27.5 billion). "The sharpest gain in percentage terms was to organizations focused on international affairs, like Doctors Without Borders and the United Nations Foundation, although the total still remained relatively small" ($2.7 billion). Of course some of the funds received by religious charities such as Catholic Charities no doubt goes to poverty and disaster relief.

7 Robert Putnam, *Bowling Alone: The Collapse and Revival of American Community* (New York: Simon and Schuster, 2000), p. 123.

8 Isaac Shapiro, "Trends in US Development Aid and the Current Budget Debate," revised May 9, 2000, Center on Budget and Policy Priorities, at www.cbpp.org/4-25-00bud.htm.

9 Quoted in Paul Krugman, "Delusions of Generosity," *New York Times*, July 19 (2000), A29. As Krugman points out, however, the paucity of our foreign aid budget may be due to misinformation rather than, or as much as, stinginess. See the section below on "Overestimating our generosity."

10 Many of the terms in use are loaded. Terms like "help," "aid," and "assistance" suggest that the person who aids is not causally responsible for the situation of those who need aid; they suggest charity and optionality rather than justice and obligation.

11 See, e.g., Robert Nozick, *Anarchy, State, and Utopia* (New York: Basic Books, 1974), and Judith Thomson, "A Defense of Abortion," *Philosophy & Public Affairs*, 1 (1971). Thomson's famous examples loom large: the person finding himself hooked up to the violinist, who needs his body for nine months, or the person whose life can only be saved by "the touch of Henry Fonda's cool hand on my fevered brow." You have no right to these things, according to Thomson, even though it would be "frightfully nice" of Henry Fonda to fly in from the West Coast. Nozick's view is similar: talk of rights and obligations is misplaced unless one person has harmed another or unless there exists a contractual arrangement between them.

12 See, e.g., Rabbi Joseph Telushkin, *Jewish Literacy* (New York: Morrow, 1991), pp. 511–12. Similarly, *mitzvah* is often translated as "good deed," but literally means "commandment."

13 See Singer's discussion of these issues in "Famine, Affluence, and Morality," in Beitz et al., *International Ethics*, p. 254. Kant provides an intermediate view with the idea of imperfect duties. We have duties to help other people, according to Kant, although we have discretion as to "time, place, and manner" about how to discharge these duties. It might be argued that the elbow room Kant allows is so great that in effect it lets people off the hook and makes charity supererogatory in spirit if not in letter.

14 "Modern Moral Philosophy," *Philosophy*, 33 (1958).

15 Ibid., p. 5.

16 For a good discussion see Elaine Scarry, "The Difficulty of Imagining Other People," in Martha Nussbaum et al., *For Love of Country: Debating the Limits of Patriotism* (Boston: Beacon Press, 1996), pp. 98–110.

17 See Melvin J. Lerner, *The Belief in a Just World: A Fundamental Delusion* (New York: Plenum Press, 1980).

18 See the references below in n. 32.

19 Of course this contingency is a feature of all aspects of human life: if I hadn't taken *this* job, which resulted from losing that one, I wouldn't have lived *here*, met *these* people, followed *this* path, met *this* partner; if we hadn't conceived on *this* night, rather than that, I wouldn't have had *this* child.

20 About the same percentage agreed in 1995 polls conducted by *Time*/CNN, the University of Maryland School of Public Affairs' Program on International Policy Attitudes (PIPA), and pollsters Hart and Teeter. When asked specifically about foreign aid to poor countries, the percentages dropped to 43–8 percent, depending on the poll. See Steven Kull and I. M. Destler, *Misreading the Public: The Myth of a New Isolationism* (Washington: Brookings Institution Press, 1999), p. 123.

21 Ibid. For the accurate figures about US aid, see above, text accompanying n. 9.

22 The thought processes at work here are no doubt related to those that affect people's attitudes toward risk: people fear cancer more than diabetes, air crashes more than car crashes.

23 For an extended discussion of these issues see Judith Lichtenberg, "Consuming Because Others Consume," *Social Theory and Practice*, 22 (1996), 273–97; reprinted in David Crocker and Toby Linden, eds., *Ethics of Consumption: The Good Life, Justice, and Global Stewardship* (Lanham, Md.: Rowman and Littlefield, 1998).

24 James Duesenberry, *Income, Saving and the Theory of Consumer Behavior* (Cambridge: Harvard University Press, 1949), pp. 26–7.

25 Obvious examples of non-material goods that perform such functions are schools, educational credentials, and jobs and occupations. In some societies, such as England, accents and speech patterns fall into this category as well.

26 Adam Smith, *An Inquiry into the Nature and Causes of the Wealth of Nations*, originally published 1776 (New York: Modern Library), b. v, ch. 2, pp. 821–2.

27 I have discussed this issue at greater length in "Consuming Because Others Consume" (see n. 23), pp. 284–90.

28 For a useful discussion, see Bernard Williams, *Shame and Necessity* (Berkeley: University of California Press, 1993), esp. endnote 1: Mechanisms of Shame and Guilt.

29 Elizabeth Hoffman, Kevin McCabe, and Vernon L. Smith, "Social Distance and Other-Regarding Behavior in Dictator Games," *American Economic Review*, 86 (1996), 653–60.

30 Ibid., p. 659. Reputation "is largely explained as self-regarding, that is, people act as if they are other regarding because they are better off with the resulting reputation. Only under conditions of social isolation are these reputational concerns of little force."

31 Bibb Latané and John M. Darley, "The Unresponsive Bystander: Why Doesn't He Help?," in Zick Rubin (ed.), *Doing Unto Others* (Englewood Cliffs: Prentice-Hall, 1974), p. 116; see also Latané and Darley, "Group Inhibition of Bystander Intervention," *Journal of Personality and Social Psychology*, 10 (1968); Darley and Latané, "Bystander Intervention in Emergencies: Diffusion of Responsibility," *Journal of Personality and Social Psychology*, 8 (1968); Latané and J. Rodin, "A Lady in Distress: Inhibiting Effects of Friends and Strangers on Bystander Intervention," *Journal of Experimental Social Psychology*, 8 (1969). The experiment I describe here is not obviously a "Good Samaritan" situation: the subject may act to save his own skin at least as much as someone else's. The other experiments conducted by Darley and Latane are pure Good Samaritan cases, but are more complex to describe. The differences do not matter for present purposes. Indeed, it's interesting that even where the subject's own safety and well-being are at stake, he is inhibited from acting by the presence of others.

PART II

Communities and obligations

Chapter 6

Moral closeness and world community

RICHARD W. MILLER

Ordinary moral thinking about aid to needy strangers discriminates in favor of the political closeness of compatriots and the literal closeness of people in peril who are close at hand. For example, in ordinary moral thinking, I have, as an American citizen, a much more demanding duty to support tax-financed aid to the poor of the United States than to support such aid to the foreign poor. I have a duty to save a drowning toddler I encounter at the cost of ruining my four-hundred-dollar suit, but not a duty to donate four hundred dollars to save children in a distant village from a yet more ghastly death from dysentery.

One of my goals is to defend these biases, showing that they express a deep commitment to moral equality. The other is to show that a proper understanding of their justification establishes substantial, if less demanding duties to help the foreign poor. In this way, a vindication of ordinary moral favoritism toward closeness grounds a case for extensive foreign aid that could be believable to the vast majority of non-philosophers, who find it unbelievable that a strong duty of impartial concern for neediness, whether near or far, determines what should be done to help needy strangers.

A MORALITY OF EQUAL RESPECT

My framework for defending this favoritism is a cluster of interconnected moral judgments that provide a partial interpretation of the principle that a choice is wrong just in case it could not express appreciation of the equal worth of all. The elements of this cluster are individually plausible and mutually supportive, providing a coherent perspective of moral equality from which the biases toward political and physical closeness can be assessed.

If appreciation of the equal worth of all required equal *concern* for all, there would be little hope of reconciling it with the ordinary biases. But this equation of equal valuing of persons with equal concern is much too strict. I do not have the same concern for the girl who lives next door as for my daughter, but I certainly do not regard my daughter as having greater worth. Rather (to offer a first interpretive precept) my equal appreciation of their worth is a matter of equal respect, not equal concern.

Equal respect is not just a matter of non-interference. In refusing to rescue the drowning toddler at the cost of ruining my suit, I would show a failure to respect him, a failure to ascribe the same worth to him and to myself, even if I did not push him into the water. If I appreciate everyone's equal worth, I must take anyone's neediness to be a reason to help. But I may decline to help, while expressing equal respect, because of a legitimate excuse, i.e. a special consideration in virtue of which my not helping is not wrong.[1]

One important source of such an excuse is a response to sharing a part of one's life with a person that constitutes the proper valuing of one's relationship.[2] This form of valuing primarily consists of responding to a certain type of shared history (one's child's dependence, for example, or mutual liking, activities enjoyed in common and mutual emotional openness) with certain forms of special concern (parental nurturance, for example, or the loyalties of friendship.) If I properly value parenting, then I respond to my young child's dependence on me by embracing a special responsibility for her wellbeing. In recognizing that this is the right response for me to have, I recognize that similar responsiveness is right for others and that it is desirable to help others respond to a similar history by doing well in pursuing similar goals of caring. But my appreciation of the special goodness of this nurturant response to parenthood is primarily expressed in my own special engagement in it, engagement which precludes impartial concern to promote the relationship regardless of whose it is. Although I appreciate the goodness of anyone's parental nurturing, I would not express a proper valuing of it by abandoning my child because this enables me to help two other people to become nurturant parents of two other children.

With their usual zest for vivid examples, philosophers have filled the landscape of partiality based on special relationships with water accidents and fires, in which the very life of the dear one is at stake. If I probably will have just one chance to rescue and a person is drowning on each side of the lagoon, my attempting the less likely, more distant rescue first is normally wrong, but not if the more distant one is my daughter. But special responsibilities based on special relationships extend much farther than saving from death. The most extensive such responsibilities, toward one's dependent children, involve a special commitment to help a particular person gain access to a life in which she pursues worthwhile goals, with which she identifies, enjoyably and well, goals exercising a broad range of important capacities. Thus, my proper valuing of my relationship to my daughter provides an adequate reason to spend money to send her to a good college that could, instead, be donated to an Oxfam project that will probably save several children in a village in Mali from early death.

Not only can reasons for special concern deriving from special relationships make the expression of impartial concern non-obligatory, if they are sufficiently important they can make impartial conduct wrong. To abandon my child as part of a project of adding to the net frequency of nurturant parenting or to abandon my friend to free up time needed to introduce friendship into the lives of two friendless people would constitute a failure to respect the person to whom I am tied. By the same token, I can rightly refuse to treat my child or my friend as just one locus of needs among others on the grounds that this is incompatible with my self-respect.

Three further observations will also be useful in the moral assessment of aid to needy strangers. First, if a special responsibility for someone else's well-being can justify neglect of more urgent needs of others when this threatens to make her life worse by jeopardizing the pursuit of worthwhile, important personal goals, then what threatens to worsen one's own life can also provide one with such an excuse. For surely one appropriately takes responsibility for one's own life. The doctor who would do the most good as a workoholic emergency room physician in an understaffed inner-city hospital, nearly but not quite "burnt out" by his job's demands, does no wrong if he continues his suburban dermatology practice instead, in order to avoid worsening his own life.

A further consideration, which also tends to increase the scope of excuses for neglect of the neediest, is a certain primacy of rules. Full appreciation of everyone's equal worth is a feature of someone's character, the general dispositions she expresses as circumstances arise. So someone's excuse for neglect of another's urgent need on a particular occasion may depend on the costs of a standing commitment that would dictate this assistance, rather than the burden of aid on the occasion in question. World poverty and effective charities such as Oxfam produce many occasions on which a relatively affluent person in the per-capita best-off countries could donate enough to save a desperate stranger from dire peril at small cost to herself and those to whom she has valuable and demanding relationships. But someone who appreciates the equal worth of all need not take such an opportunity to give on a particular occasion, if a standing commitment to respond in this way would jeopardize her special responsibilities and her capacity to pursue her worthwhile goals enjoyably and well.

Finally, the rules for living determining the difference between right and wrong are not just private rules that someone can embrace as an expression of legitimate personal goals. They have a distinctive potential social function: the terms of self-governance in virtue of which someone conducts herself in a morally responsible way are terms that she could want all to share while respecting all. This potential social role is the basis for further alternative formulations of the nature of moral duty. An act is wrong just in case its performance in its circumstances violates all moral codes that anyone who respects all could want all willingly to embrace as part of a shared moral code. Equivalently, an act is wrong just in case it violates every code that all could self-respectfully share. (One respects all in seeking to live by a moral code that all could self-respectfully share, and one disrespects another if one wants her to regulate her life in a way that is incompatible with her self-respect even if the regulation is shared.) These connections between moral duty and universally acceptable shared commitment are a final general resource that I will use to assess duties of aid to needy strangers in a morality of equal respect.

TAX-FINANCED AID

Even assuming (as I do) that such centrally important intimate relationships as that of being someone's parent, child, or friend provide reasons for neglect of strangers' needs, it is by no means clear to what extent forms of closeness which bind one to some, but not all, needy strangers justify special concern for them. I will begin inquiry into the moral status of these colder types of closeness with the case that is central to public policy, the standard political bias toward compatriots.

In ordinary moral thinking, one has a duty to put needy compatriots first in political choices concerning tax-financed aid, even if one lives in a per-capita rich country, one knows that the most desperately poor mostly live abroad, in countries lacking adequate resources to relieve their dire burdens, and one thinks that it is typically cheaper to relieve a burden on a poor foreigner through foreign aid than a burden on a needy compatriot through domestic aid. How can this bias be reconciled with an appreciation of the equal worth of all?

When I make political choices, a morally central difference between my relationship to poor compatriots and my relationship to poor foreigners is that I take part, and willingly so, in the creation of laws and policies that my compatriots are forced to obey. Proper valuing of the compatriot relationship provides a reason for the patriotic bias, partly because of the special requirements for justifiable participation in a project of coercion.

Suppose that someone taking part in political choice realizes that she lives under a regime of inequality of the following kind. The current system of laws gives rise to situations in which some people lack the same opportunity as others to live a good life. This system is, let us say, a capitalist regime in which, inevitably, some lose while others win, and children of losers (or of successive generations of losers) have special difficulty leading a good life. There is an alternative (I assume it is capitalist, as well) in which those who suffer the most from inferior social opportunities under the present system would have better opportunities to lead a good life, through measures whose burdens on an advantaged compatriot would not be as great as the consequent improvement in life-prospects of the disadvantaged. This is a powerful moral reason for a citizen to support a shift to the more equal alternative. In general, one can respect others while refusing to worsen one's own life to relieve worse burdens of theirs. But one does show disrespect if one helps to force others to accept rules of self-advancement generating life-worsening disadvantages for them and opposes a change that worsens one's life by reducing benefits of social advantage, when the change is necessary to relieve more serious burdens due to the social disadvantages one helps to impose.

The duty of special concern for disadvantages imposed by shared political arrangements limits the pursuit of globally impartial beneficence, not just the pursuit of self-interest. A participant in the process of collective self-rule ought to treat the relief of an important burden suffered by a compatriot due to the system of laws that she helps to impose as a stronger reason to change the laws than an unmet need of a foreigner, even one that can be satisfied more efficiently than her compatriot's need. To fail to accept this special responsibility for reducing burdens that one would otherwise help to impose coercively is to fail properly to disvalue political subordination. It is as disrespectful as an overlord's telling his exploited serfs that his exactions are justified by his using them to improve the well-being of the more miserable serfs of a fellow-baron.

Still, this argument from coercively sustained social disadvantage would not support the duty of patriotic bias in its whole extent. Even if politically enforced rules of self-advancement gave rise to no burdensome inferiorities, some compatriots' access to a good life would be drastically restricted by calamitous natural, as opposed to social, processes, for example, specially long-lasting, severe illnesses. There is, in ordinary thinking, a duty to provide these sufferers with some tax-financed aid, if this would supplement their own, inadequate resources in an effective and dignified way. Moreover, ordinary moral thinking shows patriotic bias in this matter: it would be quite wrong to neglect these afflicted people, "our" afflicted people, because foreign aid is a more effective means of relieving affliction worldwide.

The moral basis for this further bias is the proper valuing of joint loyalty on which a life-determining collective project depends. Suppose that we are willing, self-respecting participants in a joint project, that is, we have willingly joined in it or, in any case, we would not willingly do without it. Its success has an important impact on the success in life of each of us, and its success depends on potentially demanding loyalty on the part of participants. Proper valuing of participation in such a project is expressed in special loyalty to the other loyal participants, that is, a commitment to use one's influence on the project to show special concern for them in times of special need. As in other cases of loyalty, for example, friendship, this special concern, while responsive to beneficial sharing, is not simply a consequence of gratitude and is not always required for fair play. (I am grateful for the pleasure of hearing Maurizio Pollini, but I have no duty of loyalty to him. A compatriot who is unable to do much to express her loyalty to the common political project or who has actually been called upon to do very little still merits substantial concern.)

This duty of mutual loyalty arises in many shared cooperative activities. Consider the duty of the healthy members of a philosophy department to give a colleague a break if her voice has begun to weaken from Parkinson's Disease and she can no longer teach the sort of large service course, which no one wants to teach, that is part of everyone's expected mix of courses. It would be quite wrong for the healthy colleagues to say,

"We are glad that you have been loyal to the department. But our sharing this loyalty is enough, without our being loyal to you." More specifically, loyal co-participation should lead to loyalty to the co-participant which governs decision-making in the joint project: everyone in the department has a duty of loyalty to support a departmental decision in favor of special concern, but if the majority of one's colleagues were to vote for callous disloyalty in the crucial department meeting one would have no duty to use one's own salary to reduce the harm. (Without a restriction to aid via the joint project, a requirement of loyal aid to co-participants makes each, as a potential benefactor, too vulnerable to consequences of others' disloyalty.)

How much provision for needy participants a duty of mutual loyalty entails depends on the importance of the project to all concerned, on how potentially demanding the required institutional loyalties are, and on how effective the cooperative project is as a means of helping the needy. Such proportionality is needed to ration the demands of mutual loyalty in a cooperative project, which compete, in anyone's life, with the demands of mutual loyalty in other projects, with other special responsibilities and with legitimate self-concern. These considerations of proportionality make the political project of collective self-rule the source of a specially extensive duty of concern. For the institutional loyalty it requires is potentially extremely demanding, its effects on members' lives are pervasive and fundamental, and it is a particularly effective means of attending to members' needs.

Extensive as its political demands have turned out to be, the proper valuing of civic loyalty might seem incapable of explaining one further component of the duty of special concern for afflicted compatriots, as most people see it. This duty extends to those so afflicted since birth that they have never been in a position to be loyal participants. Suppose that we live in a country, among the most affluent per capita, in which some children are orphans who suffer from a painful, severely debilitating congenital disease which permanently prevents their political participation – say, a form of spina bifida. Whatever the legitimate excuses for withholding tax-financed aid might be, the following seems quite inadequate: "We will let these children among us with spina bifida suffer because the money that might go to their care is more effectively spent preventing afflictions just as grave by improving sanitation in poor foreign countries." How can special concern for our most pitiable compatriots be a duty, when all who suffer as much worldwide are equally deserving of our pity?

Obviously, any active compatriot's duty of concern for one of the orphans with spina bifida will not respond to any duty of this severely afflicted compatriot actually to engage in activities helping to sustain their shared institutions. Still, both the able and the severely afflicted compatriot can fall within the scope of an obligation to do what one can loyally to sustain the shared political institutions. If you are born in the territory of a government worthy of loyalty, then you have a duty loyally to participate in the shared political process if you can, unless you emigrate. If people did not generally recognize this duty, governments could not be stable and effective vehicles of justice.

In light of this principle, someone born with a severe disability, such as the paralysis of spina bifida, has the same duty as any compatriot loyally to participate if she can – but she cannot. She is like an utterly impoverished parent who has any parent's duty to do the best he can to guard his child's health, but who can do nothing to discharge this duty, since he cannot afford the only medicine that could help his child. So, if the concern that *active* participants in a worthwhile political project have a right to expect from each other is concern for each as someone doing what she can to discharge a duty to participate, it would be arbitrary of them not to show the same concern for congenitally severely disabled compatriots, who are also doing the best they can, viz., nothing, to discharge the same duty. And in fact, doing what one can to discharge the conditional duty of loyalty *is* the basis on which active participants properly expect concern.

The mutual loyalty that responsible active participants seek involves using their common project to express special concern *for one another*. So their well-wishing must not be contingent on the good fortune of being able to meet the ability-condition. Imposing this condition for aid, in this context, would show that one was not concerned for the other, but only for the pay-off of her participation. Even if I am never disabled until death suddenly strikes me down in vigorous old age, my compatriots have never been concerned for me if they would tell me, if I were disabled, "You are not useful to us and resources for insurance were equally distributed, so your distress is no concern of ours." Such well-wishing might constitute concern to avoid disproportion between what I contributed or would have if called on and what I receive, but not concern for me as a person.

It follows that if I withhold special concern from those who are bound to a common political project by the same duty of loyalty as me, withholding it because they are physically unable to follow through, I do not have an attitude of concern toward them that I ought to expect from others and show toward others, as part of a proper valuing of loyal joint citizenship. So, in withholding this special concern, I would be making an arbitrary distinction, discriminating in a way that violates moral integrity. But I make no arbitrary distinction in withholding the same concern from similarly needy foreigners who, similarly, do not and cannot participate in my political project. For the shared special concern that I ought to seek and offer among compatriots reflects the sharing of a duty of loyal participation which foreigners do not share.

FOREIGN AID

These ways of grounding bias toward compatriots in political choices on a morality of equal respect for all are very far from justifying utter nonprovision of humanitarian aid to poor foreigners by the governments of countries in which average material well-being is high on a world scale. On the contrary, each rationale implies a reason (albeit a less weighty reason) why aid should be provided – in response to current institutions, not just common humanity.

Political coercion that could be supported by someone who respects all does not solely affect people within the governed territory. It can be used, and is, in fact, used to keep needy foreigners out and to exclude them from exploitation of domestic natural resources. Those who suffer from closed borders or an inferior local share of the world's resources ought to receive what they would enjoy in an impartially justifiable scheme of access.

Similarly, the commitment to mutual loyalty has an international echo. One can imagine a world in which the governments of poor countries are disposed to expropriate the property of foreign investors, cancel foreign financial obligations, and invade richer countries whenever this would benefit their citizens on balance. Perhaps this is our world, and fear of the consequences *is* the only current constraint. Still, someone rationally committed to self-respectful unforced acceptability to all will not want to live in such a world. For the rationality of his willingness to forgo benefits that are not justifiable on the basis of self-respectful unforced acceptability involves a desire that the reliability of others not depend on their fear of retaliation. After all, the basing of reliability on self-respectful trust is what he would lose if he were Louis XIV, depending on the reliable oppression of peasants – and this luxurious situation repels him. So a morally responsible citizen of a rich country will want the reliability of international norms to depend on loyal self-respectful support in rich and poor countries. Extrapolating domestic reasoning, she will, then, want our norm-governed international system to become one in which concern for others throughout the world responds to such freely given loyalty. In part, foreign aid is a first step in the construction of such a system, a first step incumbent on the richest countries, since their citizens are less needy, their resources for aid are greater, and their economic dominance puts them in a position to abuse others' loyalty to international norms.

Despite their importance, these considerations dictate less aid than their domestic analogues. In all or virtually all countries, even those with average income that is high on a world scale, the duties deriving from the need to justify domestic coercion produce much larger claims on resources for aid than the corresponding international duties.[3] Suffering due to transnational political coercion that could be supported by someone who has equal respect for all is a relatively small part of world poverty. For example, sovereign control over natural resources is rarely a major determinant of national prosperity or poverty, which largely depends, instead, on commercial and technological capacities. Similarly, while immigration restrictions significantly affect the prospects of some, most of the world's poor would be in no position to take advantage of the removal of those obstacles; they might, indeed, be hurt by the flight of specially skilled and productive compatriots. In any case, in a country which is among the best-off per-capita, aid needed to compensate for burdens imposed by immigration restrictions is apt to be far less than aid needed to compensate for imposed domestic disadvantages. Since all per-capita well-off countries with substantial immigration restrictions jointly contribute to suffering due to the blocked opportunities, they share in the duty to alleviate it. In contrast, people in a per-capita well-off country have a unique duty to attend to the social disadvantages of their own compatriots, and this can be extremely expensive: consider how expensive it is to provide victims of the severest social disadvantages in such a country with access to secure, interesting, valued work.

As for the relevant duties of mutual loyalty: they are proportionate to the potential demands of the needed institutional loyalty and the impact of the shared institutions. Since international institutions are less important on both dimensions, duties of loyalty will dictate less concern for fellow-participants in international institutions than for compatriots.

Still, the rationales for patriotic bias do entail substantial reasons for foreign aid, grounded on special relationships that now bind humans one to another worldwide, not just on the ancient fact of common humanity. The existence of global relationships sharing the moral authority of compatriotism to some significant degree is a grain of truth in the idea of world community.

PRIVATE AID

Taxation in the per-capita richest countries, especially the United States, often leaves intact large personal surpluses over and above what is needed to discharge special responsibilities to intimates. (Certainly, tax-financed non-military aid to less developed countries is no threat to these surpluses in the United States. In 2000, its per-capita cost was $35.[4]) In this setting, discussions of the moral significance of closeness rightly give much prominence to the morality of voluntary giving: in what ways, if any, should relationships of closeness affect the allocation of voluntary aid to needy strangers? My case for patriotic bias in tax-financed aid concerned the avoidance of disrespectful political coercion and the use of shared political institutions to express a proper valuing of institutional loyalties. So no guidance concerning the question of voluntary giving results – and fortunately so. One wants to avoid the patriotic stupidity of condemning Americans who check the "Where the need is greatest" box, rather than the "United States only" box, when they tell the Save the Children Foundation whom they want to help through their private donations.

Questions about biases in aid are not, as such, questions about the total extent of duties to aid. However, a description of the extent of one's general duty to respond to neediness with aid will turn out to be a help in assessing both the importance of closeness and the claims of world community in nonpolitical choices. In the morality of equal respect that I sketched at the outset, this duty of beneficence is described in a precept that I will call "the Principle of Sympathy":

One's underlying disposition to respond to neediness ought to be sufficiently demanding that giving which would express greater underlying concern would impose a significant risk, on balance, of worsening one's life, if one fulfilled all further responsibilities; and it need not be any more demanding than this.

By "one's underlying disposition to respond to neediness," I mean the responsiveness to neediness with aid that would express the general importance one ascribes to relieving others' burdens, apart from special relationships and circumstances. Such ultimate concerns are not precise and determinate. So a change to a different, more demanding sensitivity in response to the same background of worldwide need would be expressed in a substantial increase in giving.

If the Principle of Sympathy is valid, such a substantial increase in giving may, at present, be an obligation of most affluent people. For a reduction in funds to spend on non-philanthropic pursuits need not worsen one's life just because the reduction makes it more difficult to satisfy desires expressing one's worthwhile goals. Given my goal of aesthetically interesting eating, I have desires that are more easily satisfied if I have more money to spend at nice restaurants. But being served a mediocre meal when I would have been in a position to have a better one if I had given less to charity does not, in itself, make my life worse. Even fairly frequent disappointment of this kind need not make for a worse life. On the other hand, one's life is worsened by the inability to pursue, enjoyably and well, the range of worthwhile goals with which one intelligently identifies, or could readily intelligently identify, as giving point and order to one's choices. If I could hardly ever afford to eat at a restaurant serving interesting and delicious meals (unless I sacrificed a worthwhile goal which is as important to me as my goal of gastronomic exploration), my life would be worse.[5]

Both the duty-generating aspect and the permissive aspect of the Principle of Sympathy can be derived from the morality of equal respect. If I could be more responsive to neediness without imposing a significant risk of worsening my own life or neglecting further responsibilities, then the costs to me of greater responsiveness are not an adequate excuse for my neglect of people's needs, not a basis for reconciling unequal concern with equal respect. Lesser underlying concern for serious deprivation in others motivated by fear of trivial expected costs to oneself expresses the attribution of lesser importance to others' lives. Yet such personal costs of greater responsiveness are the only excuse that is left if further responsibilities have been taken into account, as they are in the Principle of Sympathy. On the other hand, as I argued before, I have an adequate excuse not to ascribe greater importance than I do to others' neediness as such if the consequent increased disposition to give would impose a significant risk of making my life worse. The responsibility to a dependent that justifies a refusal to display concern for neediness as such that imposes a significant risk of worsening his life corresponds to a similar prerogative in the case of one's ultimate dependent, oneself.

Perhaps my life would have been better, happier and healthier, if I had never developed my gastronomic interest, or my sartorial interest in displaying my aesthetic sensibility and engaging in the fun of mutual aesthetic recognition, and had formed a deeper commitment than my own to serve the world's poor. But the activities with which one can intelligently readily identify as the basis for a life that is rewarding to oneself are not the same as those with which one once could have identified. After all, poverty worsens the lives of those who would not be worsened if a different upbringing had given them the outlook of monks and nuns in ascetic orders.

MERE CLOSENESS

Returning from the question of how concerned an individual must be to relieve neediness in general to the question of favoritism toward needy strangers who are in some sense close, one encounters a stark contrast in ordinary moral thinking between those with urgent needs who are literally close to a potential benefactor and those who are not: we ordinarily take ourselves to have a strong (i.e., potentially quite demanding) duty to rescue someone in peril close at hand, but no strong duty, in general, to rescue someone in peril, regardless of distance. In light of further reflection, this ordinary bias in aid has sometimes seemed perverse. In the essay at the origins of current discussions of closeness and aid, Singer notes this aspect of ordinary moral thinking and protests, "If we accept any principle of impartiality, universality, morality or whatever, we cannot discriminate against anyone merely because he is far away from us."[6] An adequate defense of the discrimination in duties must show that the ordinary special connection between closeness and the duty to rescue is justifiable in a perspective of equal respect for all.

Obviously, ordinary morality does acknowledge plenty of demanding duties to help imperiled distant strangers, based on special responsibilities (e.g., the forest ranger's, as she surveys the vast forest from the observation tower) and special histories (e.g., the negligent toxic-waste-disposer's obligation to help the now dispersed victims of his negligence.) So the live issue concerning literal closeness and aid to needy strangers is not whether strong duties to help strangers stop at the boundary of the near. Obviously, they do not. Also, ordinary insistence on a strong duty to rescue those in peril close at hand presupposes normal background circumstances of human interaction. In a ghastly circumstance of frequent encounter, every day, with innocents in imminent dire peril, it might even be morally permissible for someone to neglect a drowning toddler close at hand, because he must ration individually easy aid to nearby victims to take adequate care of his loved ones and his life. In a science fiction in which humans have become so adapted to contact via the internet that attention and control are much easier at a distance than closeby, there seems to be no strong duty of nearby rescue.

The live issue in the assessment of the ordinary connection between closeness and obligatory aid is the justification of the presence in an otherwise acceptable moral code of (something like) the following principle, asserting a special linkage between potentially demanding rescues and closeness, taken to govern rescues in the normal background circumstances of human interaction:

(The Principle of Nearby Rescue.) One has a duty to rescue someone encountered closeby who is currently in danger of severe harm and whom one can help to rescue with means at hand, if the sacrifice of rescue does not itself involve a grave risk of harm of similar seriousness or of serious physical harm, and does not involve wrongdoing.

I will offer reasons why the morality of equal respect precludes a revision of ordinary morality giving rise to a moral code lacking the Principle of Nearby Rescue or any similar special connection between closeness and rescue. What reasons come into play in the course of this vindication depends on what alternatives are to be precluded.

If the question is whether the reference to closeness should be deleted in the Principle of Nearby Rescue, then the crucial consideration is one that helped to sustain the Principle of Sympathy, namely, the avoidance of excessive demands. In what are now the normal circumstances of human interaction, which include the prevalence of severe peril and inadequate local resources in some parts of the world and farreaching means of aid elsewhere, many of the world's better-off can reject the distance-deleted alternative to Nearby Rescue, without showing unequal respect: such a standing commitment to help those in peril near or far would involve their imposing on themselves a serious risk of a worse life, for lack of resources needed to pursue, enjoyably and well, worthwhile goals to which they are attached. In contrast, commitment to a moral code including the Principle of Nearby Rescue imposes no risks that someone who ascribes equal value to everyone's life can reject. Because of our shared human vulnerability, our shared need to monitor goings-on close at hand and our typically greater capacity to intervene nearby with means close at hand than to intervene in distant processes or with distant means, the expected net cost of a shared commitment to Nearby Rescue is trivial at most, in the course of a morally responsible person's life. One may gain, as beneficiary, from the shared commitment, on account of vulnerability. One may lose, as benefactor, but the *ex ante* probability of substantial net loss in the course of a life in normal circumstances is nil or minute. Because the expected loss from shared commitment to the rule of nearby rescue is trivial, at most, rejecting this commitment to save people in dire peril because it demands too much would show a failure to appreciate the equal worth of every person's life.

Of course, commitment to the Principle of Nearby Rescue could come due in costly ways in unusual circumstances. But this is true of quite uncontroversial moral principles, which clearly are requirements of equal respect, for example, principles requiring the keeping of a promise that has become surprisingly costly when the stakes to the promisee are substantial and the possibility of adequate compensation is uncertain.

However, considerations of demandingness will not justify the inclusion of the Principle of Nearby Rescue *in addition to* the Principle of Sympathy in a shared system of principles that must be acceptable to anyone who equally respects all. Here, the vindication of Nearby Rescue must rebut the objection that the singling out of nearby victims is arbitrary, not the objection that it requires too little giving. Although commitment to rescue from nearby peril is one relevantly nonburdensome way for someone to respond to neediness, the same could be said of other rules enjoining specific kinds of aid that are not mandatory, for example, "Give at least a small amount to the prevention or treatment of cancer every year." In general, people have a broad prerogative to pick and choose among possible ingredients in the total personal practice of giving that expresses their ultimate concern for others' neediness. Singling out a worthy cause as mandatory almost always justifies a complaint of arbitrariness on the part of those who specially care about other causes, as potential beneficiaries or benefactors. Why isn't it arbitrary to insist that the Principle of Nearby Rescue be in everyone's package of beneficent rules?

The answer to this question must appeal to special values of closeness that provide everyone who respects all with a reason for including Nearby Rescue among her rules of aid. There are at least three such reasons.

(a) *The relationship of encounter.* Personal encounter is our minimal special relationship, the pervasive (if usually fleeting) basis for mutual recognition. Quite apart from the value of assurance of aid in case of disaster, life goes better if people encountering each other are in a position to assume that the other would benevolently attend to a peril that strikes in the course of the encounter. Even if I know that I will never collapse on a sidewalk, my encounters with passersby are better if I know that they would not simply step over me if I did collapse. So a proper valuing of special relationships is expressed in special attentiveness to the needs of those closeby.

(b) *Coordination.* A special inclination to help those in peril close at hand is pervasive among us humans. It functions reasonably well as a way of assigning responsibility to those able to help, avoiding buckpassing and inefficiency without making relevantly excessive demands. No rival, relevantly undemanding basis for coordination of personal efforts to aid is feasible. So this is a disposition that one would want to continue to be prevalent, if one values everyone's life. One would, then, be a parasite not to share the disposition.[7]

(c) *Trusteeship.* A self-respecting person expects others to be inclined to respect her space, giving her free passage and letting her continue to leave her imprint on her environment. Of course, the spatial prerogative that we rightly claim is hardly absolute. Still, others' obligation not to interfere with my movement and not to keep me from going about my business where I happen to be is more demanding than their general obligation to take my interests into account. Stopping someone in his tracks is, in general, much more serious than creating a reason for someone, now distant, to take a different path. On the other hand, it shows a failure of equal respect to insist that others be specially concerned to leave one in control of one's immediate environment without accepting a responsibility to pay special attention to events within this space that provide a serious reason for concern. A moral code that all could self-respectfully share will include both the spatial prerogative and the correlative responsibility of trusteeship.[8]

The appeal to specific values of closeness is essential in explaining why the special connection between closeness and the duty of aid is nonarbitrary. But this appeal does not provide a convincing explanation of why reference to closeness should not be deleted in the Principle of Nearby Rescue, a move to a morality which would require aid to nearby victims and much more, besides. So, when morally relevant values of closeness are described in a defense of the ordinary connection between closeness and obligatory aid, there is legitimate cause for concern that these considerations lack the power to justify neglect of dire need. On the other hand, when the ordinary connection between closeness and obligatory aid is defended on the ground that the restriction to those closeby avoids excessive demands, there is cause for concern that strong demands have been avoided at the cost of an arbitrary distinction. These worries are overcome by taking account of the distinctive role of each kind of consideration at a different stage in the vindication of the ordinary connection between literal closeness and obligatory aid.

FROM CLOSENESS TO DISTANCE

Like the case for special concern for compatriots in tax-financed aid, the case for Nearby Rescue rests on an appreciation of closeness that also suggests considerations supporting duties of concern for distant strangers. To some extent, the support is direct: considerations that I have labelled "values of closeness" lend special value to caring interactions between a potential beneficiary and a distant imperilled stranger, sustaining a duty of special concern. For example, considerations of encounter and coordination create a special duty to help when emergencies arise in the course of communication, however remote. If the distant salesperson taking down my order over the telephone shows unmistakable signs of having a heart attack, I have a duty to help him in addition to any background duty to help victims of heart attacks in general. I believe that the values of closeness sustain other such duties of aid to particular distant people in circumstances that are sufficiently similar to closeness. But these duties would not connect many people in the richest countries with many people in poor countries, in the relatively moderate morality that I am exploring. In general, the monitoring and fulfillment of a farflung network of obligations to particular people engendered in ways beyond the agent's control would constitute an excessive distraction from the pursuit of worthwhile personal goals.

The most important contribution of the case for Nearby Rescue to the case for aid to distant strangers is less direct. The justification of Nearby Rescue depended on the moral relevance of certain values, singling out nearby victims, to anyone's choices of whom to aid. Analogously, a different universal value, which also commands the attention of any morally responsible benefactor, could provide a reason to implement the general demands of sympathy in ways that benefit needy people in poor foreign countries. Specifically, in current world circumstances, the proper valuing of willing cooperation has a crucial moral role to play in channeling aid from affluent people in rich countries to the foreign poor. Those benefactors must be sensitive to the exploitive relationship between their affluence and desperate foreign needs; without this sensitivity, they would be free to regulate their beneficence by considerations that are apt to crowd out aid to the foreign poor.

Suppose that a citizen of one of the per-capita richest countries is at least fairly affluent, and has worthwhile personal goals, valuable relationships and special responsibilities that are not unusually demanding. The Principle of Sympathy will require substantial aid to help others avoid deprivations. However, even if giving to the desperately needy in poor countries is the most efficient way of relieving the most desperate needs, one must not conclude, in the absence of further considerations, that such a person has a duty to send substantial aid abroad. People with serious needs that are not the most severe or with burdens that are hard to lift could rightly complain of a general requirement that private aid to needy strangers always be channeled in ways that do the most to relieve the most serious needs. So could benefactors who seek to give in ways that express special values and acknowledge special relationships that enrich their lives. Benefactors express their love of opera and ballet through giving that avoids cultural deprivations. Preferential attention to needy compatriots or needy people in one's city or neighborhood is justifiable, even if it is not dictated, by a variety of considerations. It can be an expression of civic friendship, that is, a way of expressing appreciation of good will and courage in the face of adversity on the part of the disadvantaged who take part in one's own social milieu, through which they contribute to mutual respect and trust. Often, such local aid involves a commitment to continue an inherently valuable tradition and expectation of sharing. If the suffering of the domestic disadvantaged reflects a shortfall in meeting the special demands of domestic justice, a special interest in helping them is one way, even if it is not an obligatory way, of affirming the importance of the underlying values of political respect and loyalty.

If good causes that would crowd out aid to the foreign poor are close to the benefactor's heart, what compelling moral reason could there be for such a person to allocate a substantial portion of his aid to needy people in poor countries? This question has great practical importance. In the actual charitable donations of typical affluent

people in the per-capita best-off countries, the allocation to needy people in poor countries is not substantial. In the United States in 2001, only
2 percent of donations to tax-exempt non-profit organizations went to
those whose primary interest was international, including those concerned with international security, foreign affairs and cultural exchange
as well as those concerned with development assistance and humanitarian relief.[9] Only about 7 percent of households made any contribution to
any of these international agencies.[10] Development assistance by private
voluntary agencies based in the United States amounted to $16 per US
resident.[11]

In implementing the demands of sympathy, someone who regards
the lives of all as equally valuable must count efficiency in relieving the
burdens of the neediest as a significant reason to donate to a cause. Still, it
does not seem that this consideration – which I take to favor poor people
in poor countries – must play an important role, in the final analysis,
in the benefactions of affluent people in per-capita rich countries, given
the pressure of competing good causes which are close to their hearts.
What does require a substantial allocation of aid to desperately needy
people in poor countries is a more specific obligatory concern, the proper
valuing of willing cooperation, entailing a concomitant disvaluing of
exploitation.

Someone who respects all, equally valuing their lives, must value
cooperative relationships in which no party benefits from severe bargaining disadvantages of others that deprive them of access to a good
life. One could hardly rationally commit oneself to observing a moral
code whose terms of self-governance everyone could willingly, self-
respectfully share if one did not care whether one benefited from the
extraction of burdensome concessions from others that they are forced
to yield on account of dire need. If I benefit from others' agreeing to
work on terms incompatible with a good life because their bargaining-
position is weak, then a proper valuing of willing cooperation requires
a special disposition on my part to use my gains to help relieve their
disadvantages, at least if this does not impose a significant risk of worsening my life or interfering with my special responsibilities. My use of
these gains from the severe disadvantages of some in charitable relief
of the deprivations of others would be an expression of contempt, unless, perhaps, this use much more effectively relieves needs at least as
serious or effectively relieves much more urgent needs. My using benefits from the weak bargaining power of people fleeing grinding rural
poverty for the sweatshops of Southeast Asia to help the needy of my

hometown would be wrongful channeling of beneficence, like rushing past a toddler sinking into quicksand in order to visit a lonely sick friend before the end of hospital visiting hours.

These days, affluent people in the per-capita richest countries are apt to derive considerable material benefits from such bargaining disadvantages of poor foreigners. They gain from the consequent cheapness of labor and raw materials while their own special skills or financial assets shield them from costs that globalization can impose on their less affluent compatriots. Moreover, this transnational benefit does not just derive from desperate neediness of foreigners actually engaged in the advantageous transactions. Well-positioned buyers are advantaged by actual sellers' fears of concessions that might be made by even more desperately needy potential sellers, elsewhere. So, in their charitable activities (which might have to be extensive, given the Principle of Sympathy), affluent people in per-capita rich countries ought to give substantial and distinctive consideration to the neediest foreigners, in general. These are people whose desperation contributes to their prosperity.

Once the duty to channel substantial aid to the foreign poor is established, it contributes to the political duty to support tax-financed aid, as well. For everyone adequately responsive to foreign needs has reasons to favor significant reliance on taxation as a means of discharging such responsibilities, reasons which include the importance of scale and coordination in the development of infrastructure in a poor economy, the absence of adequate voluntary responsiveness to foreign needs, and the danger that those who voluntarily do as much as they should in their charitable endeavors will, by giving up financial resources, place themselves at a competitive disadvantage to those who give much less than they should. In principle, increases in tax-financed foreign aid could end the moral pressure on the affluent to show substantial concern for poor foreigners in their private contributions. But typical affluent people in per-capita well-off countries have not reached this point, and people in the United States are especially far from it.

CONCLUSION

The conflict between reasons expressing the moral importance of neediness as such and reasons expressing the independent importance of relationships of closeness is a recurrent, troubling feature of moral experience. At present, the outcome of this conflict among most people in the per-capita best-off countries (and, especially, in the United States) is a low level of effective concern for neediness in poor countries. If (as I believe) this level is too low, the underlying moral error might seem to be a failure to appreciate the ultimately greater authority of the perspective of impartial concern. But the arguments of this essay suggest that this is a false diagnosis, diverting attention from the arguments most apt to help the world's poor.

The authoritative moral perspective is one of equal respect, not equal concern. In seeking to specify the demands of equal respect, the friends of the world's poor have no need to debunk ordinary biases toward closeness. For a sympathetic understanding of these biases uncovers powerful rationales for concern for needy strangers who are not close. The avoidance of disrespectful coercion and valuing of loyalty that justify the political bias toward needy compatriots also provide important reasons for tax-financed aid to needy foreigners. An understanding of the rationales for a specific, potentially demanding duty to aid those in peril close at hand helps to explain why typical affluent people in rich countries have a duty to allocate substantial donations to aid needy people in poor countries.

The strength of these moral reasons to aid distant strangers reflects the nature of current transnational interactions, for example, the importance of global institutions that ought to be sustained by global loyalties, the significance of immigration restrictions as a barrier to opportunities, the existence of farreaching transnational facilities for aid, public and private, and the extent of transnational benefits from neediness abroad. Because these interactions give rise to such important transnational duties, public and private, the world is now a moral community. The moral importance of this farflung community is illuminated, rather than obscured, by a proper appreciation of the moral importance of closeness.

NOTES

1 There is another usage in which excuses reduce the blameworthiness of a person for doing what is wrong, typically on account of some diminished capacity. My topic, in using the term, will always be the wrongness of what is done.

2 To adopt a phrase of Scanlon's; see T. M. Scanlon, *What We Owe to Each Other* (Cambridge: Harvard University Press, 1998), p. 89 and elsewhere. Samuel Scheffler, "Relationships and Responsibilities," *Philosophy & Public Affairs*, 26 (1997), 189–209 is another recent examination of special relationships that is generally supportive of my view of their role in moral obligation.

3 The exceptions would be per-capita well-off countries within which it is easy to remove all serious burdens due to inferior social opportunities and to do what can be done to alleviate specially severe natural misfortunes. I am not sure such countries exist.

4 This includes concessionary loans less repayment of principal, as well as grants, and contributions to multilateral programs, as well as bilateral aid. See *World Development Indicators: 2002* (Washington: World Bank, 2002), pp. 358f. In 1995, 72.7 percent of this aid was subject to restrictions on procurement sources, presumably favorable to US manufacturing and agricultural interests (ibid., p. 357, where no more recent figure is provided for the United States)

5 Some might disagree with my assessment of the impact of the disappointing meal, claiming that it makes my life worse but only insignificantly so. I do not think that this disagreement matters for present purposes. At the cost of some awkwardness, those who have this alternative assessment can take "worse" to abbreviate "significantly worse," wherever the disagreement would otherwise lead them to resist my arguments about aid.

6 Peter Singer, "Famine, Affluence, and Morality," *Philosophy & Public Affairs*, 1 (1972), 232.

7 In "The Possibility of Special Duties," *Canadian Journal of Philosophy*, 16 (1986), 651–76, Philip Pettit and Robert Goodin emphasize the benefits of widely shared norms allocating special responsibilities. They are not concerned, however, with the moral status of closeness and deploy a rule-consequentialist framework which has very different consequences, especially for foreign aid, from the morality of equal respect that I am exploring.

8 Here, I have benefited from Kamm's intriguing tentative suggestion that the duty "to take care of what is associated with oneself: for example, the area near one" is "the flip side" of the "prerogative to give greater weight to one's own interests rather than giving equal weight to oneself and to others." (See Frances Kamm, "Faminine Ethics," in Dale Jamieson, ed., *Singer and His Critics* (Oxford: Blackwell, 1999), p. 200.) However, an alleged duty to take care of what is associated with oneself seems much too broad in scope. After all, the former owner has no responsibility to continue to take care of his distinctive, monogrammed cast-off clothes. One needs to find a prerogative specifically concerned with what is closeby that directly generates a responsibility for what happens there without further appeal to mere "association."

9 Center on Philanthropy at Indiana University, *Giving USA 2002* (Indianapolis: AAFRC Trust for Philanthropy, 2002), pp. 19, 125. This amount included corporate and foundation as well as individual giving.

10 Ibid., p. 147.

11 See Table 13, OECD, *2002 Development Cooperation Report*, www.oecd.org/xls/M00037000/M00037866.xls.

Chapter 7

National responsibility and international justice

DAVID MILLER

When we think about what justice requires us to do for other people, we often find ourselves pulled in opposite directions. On the one hand, human beings are needy and vulnerable creatures who cannot live decent, let alone flourishing, lives unless they are given at least a minimum bundle of freedoms, opportunities, and resources. They must have freedom to think and act, the opportunity to learn and to work, the resources to feed and clothe themselves. Where people lack these conditions, it seems that those who are better endowed have obligations of justice to help provide them. On the other hand, human beings are choosing agents who must take responsibility for their own lives. This means that they should be allowed to enjoy the benefits of success, but it also means that they must bear the costs of failure. If people have poor or otherwise inadequate lives because of decisions or actions for which they are responsible, then outsiders have no obligation of justice to intervene. It might still be a worthy humanitarian objective to provide aid to those who are responsible for their own impoverishment, but it is not a matter of justice, and it would be wrong to compel people to pursue it.

This dialectic between respecting people as beings with essential needs and respecting people as responsible agents is played out in many contexts, for instance in debates about the form that the institutions of a welfare state should take within a political community. In this essay I want to explore how it should shape our thinking about international justice, and especially our obligations to poor people in distant countries. The idea that millions of malnourished, unhealthy, desperate people might in some sense be responsible for their own plight may strike readers as so barbarous a thought that they are disinclined to pursue this line of enquiry any further. But given the central role played by ideas of choice and responsibility within liberal philosophy especially, that conclusion would be premature. We must follow the dialectic where it leads and, as I shall try to show in the course of the essay, it need not lead to the conclusion that we have no obligations to the distant poor. On the contrary, our obligations may be quite substantial. But we need to be clear about their basis and their limits.

Liberal thinking about problems of international justice is often distorted by an individualism that refuses to attach ethical significance to membership of communities and groups, and especially politically organized communities such as nation-states. Liberals recognize, of course, that these collective bodies may play a crucial role in *delivering* justice – in providing freedoms, opportunities, and resources to those who need them – but they tend to ignore their existence when spelling out what justice requires in the first place. Thus a claim frequently made is that such memberships are morally arbitrary: it is unjust if one person enjoys a greater share of advantages than another merely because the first belongs to one community while the second belongs to another. This has the corollary that the principles of justice that apply internationally should be exactly the same as those that apply within nation-states or indeed within communities of other kinds. It may be more feasible, on this view, to implement justice domestically than it is to implement it globally, but this is just a matter of practicalities. The principles themselves are invariant.

I describe this view as a distorted one because I believe that it misconstrues the significance of community membership, even from a liberal perspective. The fact that our world is not made up simply of individuals with differing capacities, tastes, needs and so forth, but also contains distinct communities, often with their own political structures, matters for two reasons at least. First it means that people are immersed in distinct cultures that shape both their general conceptions of value and more specifically their understandings of justice itself. Moreover they identify with those cultures, in the sense that they do not regard their cultural attachments as burdensome but as defining positively the kind of people that they are. In saying this I don't mean to deny that people often have different levels of cultural identification – for instance that alongside national identities they may have ethnic, religious, political and other such identities. Nor do I mean to suggest that there is no overlap in the content of what people belonging to different communities believe. If we look, for instance, at how social justice is understood in different parts of the world, we find much common ground as well as some divergence (the extent of the divergence also varies: Swedes and Norwegians have conceptions of justice that are much more alike than those of Americans and Japanese).[1] Nonetheless cultural difference matters, for reasons that I will give in a moment.

Second, where communities are politically organized, as in the case of nation-states, people are empowered, within limits, to take decisions that will later affect the freedoms, opportunities, and resources available to the members of each community. The extent of this political autonomy is controversial. It is often claimed that global economic forces have reduced the scope of national decision-making, in economic policy especially, virtually to nothing. I do not share this view, but I would add that in any case there is still much scope for decisions that affect people's life-chances in a fundamental way outside of the economic sphere (think of decisions that concern the security and freedom of women, for example). Where someone's share of opportunities and so forth can be traced back to a decision taken or a policy followed by her political community, and where she was involved in taking that decision, there seems prima facie to be a case for saying that her having that share is just, according to principles of responsibility such as those referred to in the opening paragraph. Of course there is a significant gap between *individual* responsibility for outcomes and *collective* responsibility, and this is an issue that will concern us later in the essay. For the moment, I want only to underline the fact that we live in a world in which there is not just one centre of political decision, but many centres, and this fact, I claim, must shape our understanding of international justice.

What can justice mean in a world made up of culturally distinct communities each enjoying some degree of political autonomy? It cannot require that everyone everywhere must enjoy the same bundle of freedoms, opportunities, and resources – a view that I shall refer to as global equality of opportunity.[2] It cannot require this because people in different communities will want to have these advantages distributed in different ways. In particular, they will attach different relative weights to different components of the bundle. In some places, people may attach very great importance to personal freedom – the freedom to execute one's own individual plan of life with as little outside interference as possible – and so they may wish to limit the scope of government control and economic redistribution as far as they can. Elsewhere people may place more value on democratic participation and the opportunity to exercise collective control over their social environment. In other places still, economic security – having a guaranteed job and/or a guaranteed income – may be rated above either personal freedom or democratic control. (These examples are not, I hope, purely hypothetical.) In that case, why should justice require that an identical package of benefits be provided for the members of each community? Why shouldn't the priority rules and the trade-offs between different elements in the bundle that a particular society adopts correspond to the judgments made by its own members rather than outsiders?

Consider next the impact of cultural factors and political decisions over time. Suppose each community were to begin with a roughly equal share of natural resources per capita , so that we could say that in one important sense their starting positions were equal.[3] How those resources are used, however, will depend upon a host of factors, such as the system of property rights that is established by law, the form of work organisation that is adopted, the level of enterprise and industry displayed by the members, and so forth. We have no reason to expect that a few decades later per capita resources will still be equal across communities. Nor does there seem to be any injustice about this, since the differences that emerge can be traced to the cultural values and political choices of the members of each community, and these in turn are features for which the members in question are properly held responsible.[4] Justice in a world of nations cannot mean global equality of opportunity for individuals.

The picture I have just painted is of course an idealized version of the actual world that we inhabit. In the actual world, many states are culturally divided, their members have little control over the direction in which their society develops, and communities impact on one another in such a way that the options open to some may be quite limited. These are important factors that we must take into account as we proceed. But equally we should not lose sight of the considerations presented above. These are powerful enough for us to reject the claim that membership in a political community is morally arbitrary, and that the principles of global justice are simply the principles of social justice writ large. We need to begin our thinking in a different place. We need in fact to go back to the two potentially conflicting requirements of justice with which we began.

These ideas, to recall, were first that justice requires us to provide human beings generally with the means to lead a minimally decent life; but second that people should be treated as responsible agents and asked to bear the consequences of their own actions and decisions. If we want to apply these ideas in the international arena, we have to address three basic issues. First, we have to be able to specify a minimum bundle of freedoms, opportunities and resources that are considered universally necessary for a decent life, and that justice therefore requires us to secure for everyone in the first instance. Second, we have to decide when it is reasonable to hold people responsible for their own condition, even if this should mean their having less than the minimum bundle, and to decide this in settings where responsibility is collective rather than individual. Third, in cases where people have less than the minimum bundle, and are *not* responsible for having less, we have to allocate what I shall call remedial responsibility – we have to decide who else to hold responsible for bringing them up to that threshold. Once all three issues have been addressed, we will be able to spell out at least some of the core requirements of international justice – in particular to determine what obligations fall on the citizens of rich nations to transfer resources and other forms of aid to those in poor countries.[5]

SETTING INTERNATIONAL STANDARDS OF DECENCY

What drives the thought that justice may require us to provide aid to distant strangers? It is surely our sense that people in many places are forced to live lives that we regard as intolerable. We cannot see how anyone could lead a worthwhile life without physical security, adequate food, the opportunity to work, and so forth. Presented with concrete cases, we have no doubt about what justice demands. But it is harder to set down the principles that guide such judgments, particularly in the light of what has been said already about cultural difference. How can we be sure that our notions of decency do not simply reflect our own culturally specific conceptions of the good life?

We might turn for guidance here to the various manifestos of human rights that were issued in the second half of the twentieth century, especially perhaps to the seminal document in this area, the *Universal Declaration of Human Rights*, adopted by the UN in 1948. After all the aim of these manifestos was to lay down for the international community a set of standards that every state should be expected to meet, and so in intention at least the list of human rights they contained was to be cross-culturally valid. Yet it should come as no surprise that the documents in question proved to be controversial in practice, for on closer inspection they ranged between rights that do indeed correspond to the basic conditions of human decency (such as the right not to be tortured and the right to freedom of movement) and rights that are closer to being aspirations, in the sense that they form part of the manifesto-writers' conception of the good polity. Take for instance the right to take part in the government of one's country (Article 21 of the *Universal Declaration*). Liberals will certainly regard this is an essential requirement of any just society, and, provided the form that the right takes is not specified too closely, their view may be echoed elsewhere. But ought we to say that human beings cannot lead decent lives unless they are able to participate in the government of their community? To say this would imply that, since democracy barely existed before the twentieth century, few human beings could have led minimally worthwhile lives before that period. But this is a highly implausible view. When we contemplate the lives of the great artists, scholars, scientists, and explorers of the Renaissance, for example, it hardly crosses our mind to ask whether they enjoyed rights of political participation. No doubt some did as a result of their success in their chosen field. But this is tangential to the question of how adequate their lives were.

One reason that official lists of human rights overshoot the mark, as far as our question is concerned, is that they make no distinction between rights that correspond directly to basic human needs, and rights whose importance is primarily instrumental. The right to political participation surely falls into the latter category. Although many people do indeed find value in engaging in political activities, the chief reason for regarding political participation as a right is that it serves to safeguard other rights that are more basic. Regimes that are subject to democratic control are far less likely to starve their subjects, torture them, deny freedom of expression, and so forth. This well-supported generalization fully justifies including the right in manifestos whose aim is the broader one of laying down conditions for the just state. But our interest is narrower. We want to know how to set standards of decency that may ground international duties of justice.

A more promising starting point is Amartya Sen's idea of basic capabilities.[6] Sen argues that rather than look for psychological indicators of human well-being such as happiness, or material indicators that are at best imperfectly correlated with well-being such as income and wealth, we should begin with the idea of a functioning – an activity or a condition that a person is able to perform or achieve. Being in good health, being adequately nourished, being able to move around, being able to speak freely, are examples of functionings in Sen's sense. A person who is able to achieve a functioning is said to have the equivalent capability, whether or not she actually chooses to realize that functioning. Thus a person who chooses voluntarily to fast but otherwise has access to suitable food has the capability to be adequately nourished. For any given person we can construct a capability set, in other words a list of all the capabilities that the person possesses. Sen suggests that we can use the capability set to measure that person's substantive freedom.

The advantage of Sen's approach, for our purposes, is that it focuses directly on what people can and cannot do, and this seems the right focus if we want to set a decency threshold (people who are starving fall below that threshold because they cannot be adequately nourished, whereas people who are fasting voluntarily do not). But it also contains some problems. First, the idea of a capability does not by itself distinguish between capabilities without which people cannot lead decent lives – like the capability to be adequately nourished – and capabilities which are valuable, but not in that way essential – like the capability to read and understand books of philosophy. Sen implicitly draws a distinction between basic capabilities and the rest, for he defines poverty as "the deprivation of basic capabilities" and gives as examples of such deprivation premature mortality, undernourishment, and illiteracy.[7] These examples are intuitively convincing, but Sen does not explain the principle that underlies his distinction.

A second problem is that cultures may vary in the weights they attach to realizing capabilities of different sorts. One culture may place a high premium on achieving material success, another on reaching a state of spiritual grace. If that is so, it may prove impossible to evaluate capability sets in a way that is genuinely neutral across cultures. Sen acknowledges that there is a real evaluative issue here, and eventually appeals to "public discussion" as a way of assessing the relative value of different capabilities. But this may mean that there is significant variation in the way that capability indices are constructed in different political communities. That does not matter if the indices are being used to guide domestic policy-making, but it does cause problems if our aim is to establish principles of international justice. For suppose that many people in society S fall below some decency standard according to the capability index that members of that society themselves endorse, but that according to the index that *we* favor they are above the line (suppose that the capacity to practice religion weighs heavily in their index but not in ours). We might legitimately wonder whether we have obligations of justice towards the members of S, given that they are deprived only in relation to cultural values that we do not share.

It might then seem that we should proceed as follows. First, we should look at each political community in turn and see how its members define the set of capabilities that are required for someone to have a minimally decent life (let's assume that there is rough agreement on where to set the threshold within each community). Then we should look at the intersection of all these sets – at the capabilities that *every* community agrees are essential. This would give us a genuinely international standard of decency. If someone fell below it, it would be universally agreed that his or her life was less than decent.

The trouble with this approach is that it makes the international standard hostage to what in some cases may be ill-informed beliefs about the conditions for a decent life. This is especially so when what is at stake are the needs of women. Members of some communities, including female members, may believe that women can have a decent life without capability C – access to contraception, or the opportunity to take paid work, for instance – whereas it can be shown, empirically, that women who lack C do not in general have adequate lives, even within the societies where the beliefs prevail.[8] The intersection approach might not rule out even such barbaric practices as foot-binding or female circumcision if there turn out to be communities whose members believe that these practices do not compromise decency.

So we need to take a more objective approach, one that tries to determine what is *actually* necessary for people to lead decent lives in different cultural contexts, as opposed to what people in those cultures may believe is necessary. And here we must appeal to the fact that there are activities that humans engage in that are reiterated across contexts – activities such as working, playing, building dwellings, raising families, and so forth – so that although the form the activity takes may vary from community to community, the activity itself can be described as universal.[9] Let us refer to these as *core* human activities. Then we can say that a person has a decent life when she has a capability set that enables her to engage in each of the core activities, given the conditions prevailing in the society she belongs to. She is able to work, play, and so on, without having to bear unreasonable costs, and also without having to forgo some other core activity – so that a life would not count as decent if, say, the person in question had an opportunity to work, but only if she gave up the opportunity to raise a family.

The reference to prevailing conditions here is meant to capture the elementary point that whether or not one has capability C may depend on both physical and social features of one's surroundings – to decide whether a person is adequately sheltered from the elements one has to know about the local climate, but equally to decide whether a person has the capability to work one has to know enough about local norms to say what penalties would be applied if the person in question began to work. We need to draw a line between obstacles that result from the social environment, and barriers that result from a person's own beliefs and preferences. Consider a person living in a country where the eating of pork is regarded as abhorrent, and imagine the unlikely situation in which the only available source of protein in that place is indeed pork. On the view I am defending, that person does not have the capacity to be adequately nourished. In contrast, someone who as a result of personal conviction is a vegetarian in a society where meat-eating is routinely accepted does have the capability in question, even if, because of the limited availability of vegetables, he would need to eat meat to realize it. This would be a case in which the person can achieve a functioning but chooses not to do so. Of course, in the former case, what prevents people from leading a decent life is a shared belief, enforced by social sanctions, that eating pork is sinful, and this opens up the question of where responsibility lies for the failure of decency – a question to be pursued shortly. At this point I am simply sketching an account of how an international decency standard should be set, and my claim is that to decide whether A does or does not have capability C we have to take as given the social conditions in which she finds herself.

So, to sum up, questions of international justice come into play whenever we encounter people whose lives are less than decent, which means that they cannot engage in the range of core human activities that we find recurring across culturally varied societies and that we may therefore take as central to human life. The question we should ask is not whether a given person does or does not engage in one of these activities – she may choose not to – but whether she has the relevant capability. Nor should we ask whether people in S themselves regard one of the activities in question as falling within the core – they may have culturally specific reasons for excluding a particular activity, or at least for denying its relevance to a particular sub-section of S. Our judgment must in this respect be more objective, which explains why we may be obliged by justice to provide the members of S with a certain resource, even though they themselves might prefer to have some other benefit that is irrelevant to decency – we might have an obligation to supply medical aid, but not consumer goods, even though the members of S, who don't attach much importance to bodily health, would prefer the latter. However to say that failures of decency bring questions of international justice into play is not yet to answer them. We must also ask about how to assign responsibility for such failures. I take up that problem in the section that follows.

NATIONAL RESPONSIBILITY

I remarked earlier that many people find repugnant the idea that nations might be held responsible for their own condition, when this idea is put forward in debates about global poverty. Yet in other contexts the idea of national responsibility is widely accepted. In particular, where nations have acted through their representatives in ways that cause harm to other peoples – taking aggressive military action, expropriating resources by unfair means, dumping polluting substances, and so forth – it is acknowledged almost without question that the nations in question owe debts of compensation, and that their members can rightly be made to bear the cost of paying those debts. This even extends to cases in which the harmful acts were perpetrated by previous generations. That we rely on ideas of national responsibility in making these judgments is not sufficient by itself to show that such ideas are coherent, but it does underline the point that abandoning the notion altogether would radically change the way we make political judgments – just as abandoning the idea of individual responsibility (if we could do it) would revolutionize large areas of our ethical thinking. So what can be said to support the claim that we may be justified in holding nations responsible for the results of their actions and policies?

National responsibility is clearly a species of collective responsibility, and this wider notion seems to make sense, at least in some relatively clear-cut cases. Let me sketch in a couple of these, as a way of introducing two models of collective responsibility that will be important later.[10] A gang of teenage boys, out on the town for the night, come across an old truck and decide to go joy-riding. They urge each other on, hand round bottles of beer, take turns at driving the truck with greater and greater displays of bravado, until finally the inevitable happens and one member of the gang is seriously hurt as the truck swerves off the road. Here it seems natural to hold the gang collectively responsible for the injury. Although in a narrow sense we could say that the person whose hand was on the wheel at the time of the accident was responsible, in a broader and morally more relevant sense we can attribute the accident to the behaviour and frame of mind of the whole group, to which each member contributed. Inside the gang, a collective ethos is generated: this is never spelt out explicitly, but the gang members nevertheless share ideas about how to behave, how to dress, and so on. Moreover they identify with their group and its common ethos. These facts are sufficient for us to hold members collectively responsible for the results of that ethos, without having to trace the exact causal relationship between the actions of any one particular member and those consequences.

For our second example, consider a small firm owned and managed by its employees, whose economic activities impose certain costs on the surrounding environment – for instance they involve dumping pollutants into a river. The employees know about these costs, and from time to time they discuss whether to change to a cleaner technology, but the majority are unwilling to make the capital investment that this would require. Here, too, we can hold the group collectively responsible for the results of their behaviour, and this may justify us in making them clean up the river, for instance. What generates collective responsibility here is not a common ethos, but a practice from which all the participants benefit (we can assume that decisions were taken democratically and that each employee shared in the net profit of the firm).

These cases were chosen because they were relatively clear-cut, and it may seem that we are taking a large step if we try to extend the idea of collective responsibility to nations. There appear to be two major points of divergence. First, it may be asked whether it makes sense to treat nations as collective actors in the same way as we treated the gang and the firm. Although we often speak loosely of Spain doing such and such or the people of Canada reaching this or that decision, it may be said that these expressions are indeed loose, and what we really mean is, for instance, that the Spanish *government* did something, or that a certain percentage of Canadians voted for policy P rather than Q. Second, it may be argued that we cannot treat nations either as embodiments of a genuinely shared ethos or as practices from which every member benefits; they are too culturally diverse, and contain too many sub-groups with conflicting interests, for either of our models of collective responsibility to apply. I shall consider each of these issues in turn.

National responsibility as it is commonly understood extends not only to the effects of formal political decisions and public policies, but also to the consequences of social practices (such as religious traditions, forms of family life, and so forth). When we attribute responsibility to nations in this way, we assume that these phenomena reflect widely shared beliefs and values. Suppose, for example, that a certain religious practice in society S has economic effects, reducing overall productivity. If we are to hold the members of S responsible for those effects, then we must show that the practice embodies their own beliefs, and had not been imposed on them by a priestly caste, for instance. Similarly if a political decision is at stake, we need evidence that the decision reflects the values of the wider community. This will be easiest to provide in societies that are democratically governed, where we can point to electoral competition, attitude surveys, and so forth to demonstrate popular support for the policies pursued by the ruling party. However it would be too restrictive to say that national responsibility can only obtain in democratic societies. Even in autocratic regimes, the authority of the ruling elite may depend on the fact that they hold values and pursue policies that correspond more or less closely to those favoured by the population at large. Suppose that the rulers of a theocracy issue a decree that results in the death of some person deemed to be an apostate. If the issuing of the decree stems from religious norms that are generally accepted throughout the population, then we can properly say that responsibility for the death lies in some degree with the people as a whole.

An objection to this line of argument is that we cannot treat people as wholly responsible for their beliefs and values in the first place. We know about the effects of social conditioning, and we also know about the power of established regimes, especially autocratic ones, to brainwash their subjects into holding beliefs that may prove extremely damaging to their interests in the longer term. So why talk about national responsibility in these cases rather than the responsibility of those who hold the levers of power? This is a difficult issue that cannot be addressed properly here, but my brief response is that we need to make judgments about how far people can be expected to retain the capacity for independent thought and decision in the face of sustained propaganda efforts and the like. In the face of brainwashing of a certain intensity, we may conclude that it would take a heroic effort of will to resist, and that ordinary people must therefore be relieved of responsibility for the effects of the policies they are induced to support. But this is very different from normal processes of socialization whereby people are brought up to accept certain values and assumptions, come to regard those values and assumptions as part of their identity, and proceed to act on them politically. To deny collective responsibility in this more normal case is tantamount to denying responsibility altogether.[11]

This objection does however reinforce the point that national responsibility is most easily attributed to political communities that are free and democratic, so that policies and decisions can be openly debated, alternatives presented and people encouraged to reflect on their beliefs and values. Under these circumstances many traditional practices will doubtless still be followed, but because they are always open to challenge in principle, we can say with some confidence that they reflect sincerely held beliefs. Conversely, the more autocratic the community, the more hesitant we should be about attributing responsibility, and the less ready we should be to hold back from helping people whose lives are less than decent on the grounds that they are responsible for their condition.

Such an appeal to democratic processes does, however, lead us directly to the second of the two problems with the idea of national responsibility identified above, the problem of dissident minorities. How can we hold minorities responsible for the consequences of decisions or policies that they have opposed, or practices that they have refused to engage with? The argument about responsibility might work if every member of a national community had essentially the same values and interests, but as we know that is very far from being the case. It seems as though the effect of introducing notions of national responsibility into debates about international justice will either be to penalize or to unfairly advantage minority groups for decisions taken and practices upheld by majorities.[12]

In answer to this problem I want to make two points. First, insofar as we are talking about *national* responsibility, and not merely the responsibility of the citizens of a particular state, we may assume that members of the nation share a set of overarching values that are articulated in the public culture, notwithstanding the fact that they may disagree quite radically over many more specific cultural questions. This is simply part of what it means to constitute a nation.[13] Of course this definitional point would have no interest unless it were true that in the real world we could find nations that fit the definition. But it is indeed true, nor is it hard to understand how the processes that have shaped national identity historically have created populations with overarching values of this kind. The implication is that minority groups within nations do not adhere to beliefs and values that are completely at odds with those of the majority; instead we find areas of overlap, and insofar as the decisions, policies and practices we are discussing reflect those overlapping beliefs and values, it is not wrong to attribute responsibility to members of the minority too.

Second, people may become responsible for the consequences of decisions and so forth as a result of engaging in democratic politics, even if they find themselves in a minority. Democratic politics works on the basis that individuals or groups win on some issues but lose on others, and in either case are bound to accept the results of the democratic process. They have, for instance, an obligation to abide by laws that they voted against (an obligation that can, however, be overridden if the law is seriously unjust). By the same token, they must share in the responsibility for the decisions that are reached, in the sense of bearing their share of the costs when these decisions turn out to have negative consequences.[14] This is a requirement of fairness: when a group finds itself on the winning side, it benefits from the compliance of the minority who opposed the decision, and so by the same token it can be asked to comply in turn when it is on the losing side. All of this assumes, however, that minorities are not permanent – that the same people do not routinely find themselves on the losing side when decisions are reached. If this happens, the argument that they should be asked to bear the cost of those decisions becomes much less plausible.

My argument, in short, is that nations, and especially *democratic* nations, conform to varying degrees to the two models of collective responsibility I outlined earlier. Their members subscribe to a common public culture, despite individual differences in belief and value, and they participate in mutually beneficial practices whose shape they have a chance to influence. The more strongly these conditions obtain, the more appropriate it is to hold nations responsible for their political actions and decisions, and the consequences that flow from these.

THE LIMITS OF RESPONSIBILITY

Does acceptance of national responsibility mean that global poverty should not be our concern, because it is the people whose lives are poor who are themselves responsible for their own condition? By no means, for reasons we shall come to shortly. What *does* follow, however, is that international inequality may not itself be unjust, when the inequality can be traced back to actions and decisions for which the people in question can properly be held responsible. And indeed this is something that we accept, when our attention is turned away from societies that fall below the decency threshold towards inequalities between comparatively rich nations. It is rarely argued that differences in living standards between, say, the Germans and the Greeks are unjust, because these differences are in part explicable by cultural and political differences between the two nations in question. Such cases are not morally problematic. But how should we view societies that appear unable to provide their members with the resources to lead decent lives? Should we acknowledge obligations of justice to help them?

There are several reasons why we should. First, it may well be that the conditions for national responsibility do not apply in such cases. I made it clear in the last section that there is a strong link between national responsibility and democratic government. Conversely, people cannot be held responsible for the effects of decisions taken by autocratic rulers that they would have opposed if they had had the opportunity to do so. It would be too neat a solution to say that failures of decency can always be traced back to autocratic government, and therefore that questions of responsibility never arise in practice. Nevertheless, it is not hard to see how democratic mechanisms – political accountability, freedom of the press, and so forth – will encourage governments to act to prevent significant shortfalls of this kind. Sen points out in particular that "no substantial famine has ever occurred in a democratic country – no matter how poor," and gives plausible reasons why this is so.[15] So it is at least a reasonable presumption that when we encounter gross breaches of the decency standard, we are looking at people who cannot be held responsible for the policies that have brought them to this point.

Second, we need to think carefully about the effects of interaction and interdependence between nations, especially economic interaction. If we take any nation at random and ask the question why its members have the living standards that they do, then the answer is likely to refer not only to the cultural values they espouse and the political decisions they have taken in the past, but also to the impact on them of *other* nations' actions and decisions. This is an obvious enough point when the external impact takes unjust forms such as economic exploitation. But it is less obvious when the impact takes the form of policies that are damaging to the nation in question, but not in themselves unjust. Consider, for example, the economic position of Cuba, whose poorer citizens were unable, in the 1990s, to buy sufficient food to maintain a nutritionally adequate diet. Our first thought might be that this was the result of Communist economic policy over the previous thirty years, and that since the people had consistently given their support to Castro's regime, they can legitimately be held responsible for the outcome. But we must surely also consider the impact of the ongoing United States trade embargo, given that before Castro's revolution more than two-thirds of Cuba's foreign trade had been with that country, and equally the withdrawal after 1989 of very substantial trade subsidies from the Soviet Union.[16] We might regard these politically motivated policies as legitimate expressions of national self-determination by the two countries in question; yet given their effects on the Cuban economy, we might also want to attribute some share of responsibility for the deprivation suffered by ordinary Cubans to these two superpowers.

The problem this raises is that attributions of responsibility have to be made against the background of a "normal" state of affairs that is taken for granted. Suppose that I cannot support myself because, although I have been offered several perfectly acceptable jobs, I insist on having a job that is not now available. We would say that I am responsible for my own condition, because we build into the background the assumption that no one else has a responsibility to give me the job that I most prefer. My situation is different from that of someone who has no chance to get a job of any kind. But it may not be so clear how the "normal" state of affairs should be defined. In the case we are considering, is free trade between countries to be taken as the norm, or should we say that each nation is entitled to decide who it does and doesn't wish to trade with, so that if the US decides to embargo Cuba, that is simply a background fact in the light of which Cubans' responsibility for their own economic condition is to be assessed? This question is difficult to answer categorically. What we can perhaps say is that in cases where the actions and policies of powerful state S1 have a severely negative impact on the capabilities of members of relatively powerless state S2, then some share of responsibility must attach to S1, even if the policies themselves were justifiable as a legitimate expression of national self-determination.

So far we have examined two reasons why we may be obliged by justice to support people whose lives are less than decent: one is that they are not themselves responsible for their condition, but the victims of autocratic rule; the other is that the responsibility is only *partly* theirs, since their condition has been significantly affected by the actions of other nations. But what if neither of these reasons applies, and we can attribute poor and barren lives to cultural beliefs and political choices for which the people in question are indeed wholly responsible (unlikely as this scenario might seem)? I believe that even here we remain under an obligation to intervene, though it is an obligation that can be overridden by more stringent obligations to people who are *not* responsible for their condition. This is tantamount to saying that if we have to decide between respecting people as beings with essential needs and respecting them as responsible agents (to revert to the dilemma that I introduced at the start of the essay), we should choose the former. But note that by parity of reasoning we need not respect the cultural values that led them into this predicament. If we commit resources to bring people who are collectively responsible for their condition to the threshold of decency, we may at the same time mount an assault on the beliefs and the practices that led to them falling beneath it.[17] If we say that in the last resort the sustaining of basic capabilities is more important than the principle of responsibility, we cannot treat as sacrosanct cultures that condemn their followers to lives that fall below that threshold.

In all these cases there remains the problem of how to distribute the responsibility for getting people over the decency threshold. Although currently millions of people worldwide live lives that are less than decent, the wealth of the developed nations is such that there are many possible ways in which the costs of putting this right could be distributed. In these circumstances, it is understandable that potential donor nations should hold back in the hope that the burden can be shifted elsewhere, and the result is that overseas aid budgets are typically only a small fraction of what would be needed to bring people everywhere across the threshold. Clearly, we must look for principles that determine where remedial responsibility should fall.[18] More specifically, we need principles that will connect the members of rich nation A to the members of poor nation B so as to justify our saying that it is A that bears a special responsibility towards B. Such principles exist, but they are plural, and there is no obviously correct way of rank-ordering them. For instance, we might ask how far A is causally responsible for B's present plight as a result of policies pursued by A in the past. Alternatively, we might ask the connected, but different, question how far A can be held *morally* responsible for the condition of B. A third possibility is to ask whether A has particular capacities that other nations do not have to remedy shortfalls in B – capacities due to resource endowment, geographical location and so on. Finally we might ask whether any kind of special relationship exists between A and B – an affinity of language or culture, for example – such that members of A feel a sense of community with those in B. Each of these principles identifies a form of connection between A and B that can ground special remedial responsibilities on A's part, and avoid the situation where, because there are many nations that *could* help B, but none has a particular reason to act, each holds back in the hope that others will step in first.

Unfortunately, however, the principles cited in the last paragraph may pull in different directions in a particular case. The nation that has played the biggest causal part in bringing B to its present condition may not be well positioned to provide the resources that would now permit members of B to lead decent lives. There is an urgent need to develop international conventions to deal with such conflicts of principle, as well as an institutional structure that is able to apply such conventions, ensuring that impoverished nations do not fall though the net just because no rich nation recognizes a special responsibility towards them. I shall not try to describe such an institutional structure, since my concern is with the underlying principles of responsibility rather than with their implementation. But the underlying aim should be clear. Nations already acknowledge, through their relief and development programmes, that they have some responsibility to remedy global poverty. Institutional cooperation would allow them to coordinate their efforts by allocating specific tasks to specific countries where appropriate, or pooling resources in cases where no nation bears a special responsibility for the condition of the B in question.

My aim in this essay has been to show that we can take the idea of national responsibility seriously and still recognize substantial obligations towards the world's poor. On the one hand, I have rejected visions of global justice that require some form of global equality of opportunity. On the other hand, I have dismissed the claim that national responsibility entails looking after one's own and nothing more. We can establish international standards of decency that entail an obligation to provide support for people whose lives are currently less than adequate by those standards. It is not wrong to ask how far the people in question are responsible for their own condition – the idea of collective responsibility makes sense, I have argued – but we should not jump too quickly to the conclusion that they must be. And even if, after investigation, it turns out that they *are* responsible, that may affect the way the obligation is discharged, but it does not nullify it. A just world, on this view, would be one in which the principle of national responsibility was given full play, and which would therefore exhibit considerable diversity (including diversity of living standards), but in which remedial responsibilities were also fully acknowledged, so that no one was condemned to live a life that fell below the threshold of decency.

NOTES

This chapter draws in part on collaborative work done with Cécile Fabre, and I am grateful to her for allowing me to make use of it here. I also thank her, along with Deen Chatterjee, Matthew Festenstein, and Sue Mendus, for written comments on earlier drafts of this chapter, and audiences at the Universities of Oxford, Sheffield, and York for many helpful criticisms and suggestions.

1 I have looked at some of the evidence relevant to this question in D. Miller, "Popular Beliefs about Social Justice: a Comparative Approach," in S. Svallfors, ed., *In the Eye of the Beholder* (Umea: Bank of Sweden, 1995).

2 For defences of this view, see B. Barry, "Humanity and Justice in Global Perspective" and "Justice as Reciprocity," in B. Barry, *Liberty and Justice* (Oxford: Clarendon Press, 1991); T. Pogge, "An Egalitarian Law of Peoples," *Philosophy & Public Affairs*, 23 (1994), 195–224; S. Caney, "Global Equality of Opportunity and the Sovereignty of States," in A. Coates, ed., *International Justice* (Aldershot: Ashgate, 2000).

3 In fact there are difficulties with this supposition, arising from the fact that in a culturally plural world there may be no metric in terms of which we could determine whether an international distribution of resources is equal or not, as I have argued in "Justice and Global Inequality," in A. Hurrell and N. Woods, eds., *Inequality, Globalization, and World Politics* (Oxford: Oxford University Press, 1999). But I set those difficulties aside in order to make the point that follows.

4 Compare here John Rawls, *The Law of Peoples* (Cambridge, Mass.: Harvard University Press, 1999), section 16, and my own earlier discussion in "Justice and Global Inequality." It might seem that the observations made here pose no challenge to global equality of opportunity, since the latter idea permits inequalities that can be traced back to values and choices. However the values and choices that equality of opportunity accommodates are always *individual* values and choices, whereas I am pointing in the text to resource differences that stem from the *collective* decisions and practices of different peoples.

5 I say "some of the core requirements" because I do not aim here to give a complete account. A full theory of international justice would have to deal with several other questions, including the issue of the terms on which members of different political communities should interact economically with one another, the issue of territorial rights, the issue of compensation for acts of historical injustice and so forth. My focus here is on what is owed as a matter of justice to people who are inadequately endowed with freedoms, opportunities and resources.

6 This idea has been spelt out by Sen in a number of works, including *The Standard of Living* (Cambridge: Cambridge University Press, 1987); *Inequality Reexamined* (Oxford: Clarendon Press, 1992), ch. 3; "Capability and Well-Being," in M. Nussbaum and A. Sen, eds., *The Quality of Life* (Oxford: Clarendon Press,

1993); *Development as Freedom* (Oxford: Oxford University Press, 1999), esp. chs. 3–4. It has been used in the construction of the Human Development Index and the Human Poverty Index featured in the *Human Development Reports* issued annually by the United Nations Development Programme.

7 Sen, *Development as Freedom*, pp. 99–103.

8 One should not, however, conclude too quickly that women go along with dominant male views about their not needing certain capabilities. See the powerful argument advanced by Martha Nussbaum in *Women and Human Development* (Cambridge: Cambridge University Press, 2000) that poor women in India have learned to value the capabilities that Nussbaum takes as central to an adequate human life.

9 In saying this I do not mean to imply that every human being engages in all the activities. Some choose not to raise families, for instance.

10 I consider these two models at greater length in "Holding Nations Responsible," *Ethics*, forthcoming.

11 Distinguishing between what I here call "normal processes of socialisation" and the coercive inducing of beliefs and values is admittedly difficult. There is a spectrum of cases, at one end of which we find liberal societies in which people are encouraged through the education system to think for themselves, there are a range of religious and other cultural options to choose from, and so forth; at the other end there are societies with an officially promoted ideology, religious or secular, where stiff penalties applied to anyone who expresses dissent in thought or deed. In between we find a range of traditional societies. In these intermediate cases, we need to make judgments about how far people "could have thought otherwise" and therefore how far they can reasonably be held responsible for their beliefs and values.

12 Minority groups will be penalised in case the decision or policy they favour would have brought them a larger share of resources, and unfairly advantaged in case it would have brought them a smaller share.

13 See my discussion of nations and national identity in D. Miller, *On Nationality* (Oxford: Clarendon Press, 1995), ch. 2.

14 It is important to keep in mind here that the form of collective responsibility we are discussing is responsibility for the costs that follow from a group's or a nation's following a certain course of action, not moral responsibility in the narrower sense that is connected to praise and blame. It would clearly be wrong to hold a group morally responsible, in the sense of blameable, for a policy that they had opposed in a public forum. But it may not be wrong, according to my argument, to hold them responsible, along with other groups on the majority side, meaning that they may be held liable for their fair share of the costs associated with the policy. For a fuller analysis of these different senses of responsibility, and of the importance of keeping them disentangled, see my "Distributing Responsibilities," *Journal of Political Philosophy*, 9 (2001), 453–71.

15 Sen, *Development as Freedom*, p. 51. See also J. Dreze and A. Sen, *Hunger and Public Action* (Oxford: Clarendon Press, 1989).

16 The impact of these policies is well described in S. E. Eckstein, *Back to the Future: Cuba under Castro* (Princeton, NJ: Princeton University Press, 1994).

17 "Mount an assault" metaphorically rather than physically – I mean that we are justified in using whatever carrots and sticks will lead the people in question to adapt their culture so that it allows them to lead decent lives, so long as the methods we use do not themselves violate their basic rights.

18 I draw here on my much fuller discussion in "Distributing Responsibilities."

PART III

The law of peoples

Chapter 8

Women and theories of global justice: our need for new paradigms

MARTHA NUSSBAUM

The life of a Christian wife who is compelled to live against her will, though in name only, as the wife of a man who hates her, has cruelly treated her and deserts her, putting an end to the matrimonial relation irreversibly, will be a sub-human life – without dignity and personal liberty. It will be a humiliating and oppressive existence, without the freedom to remarry and enjoy life in the normal course. It will be a life without the freedom to uphold the dignity of the individual in all respects as ensured by the Constitution of India in the Preamble and Article 21. The impugned provisions . . . are highly harsh and oppressive and as such arbitrary and violative of Article 14 . . .

> High Court of Kerala (India)[1]

> We had tongues but could not speak.
> We had feet but could not walk.
> Now that we have the land
> We have the strength to speak and walk!
>
> > Peasant women in Bodhgaya, Bihar
> > (East India), on first receiving rights
> > to land in their own names in 1982[2]

We discuss how we can increase our income and how we can develop ourselves . . . If anybody's mind is depressed, after participating in the meeting, her mind will be refreshed. After coming to the meeting everybody states their plans. Somebody says that she thought about this and someone else says that she thought about that. Their plans are discussed and reviewed during the meeting.

> Women in a women's collective sponsored by the
> Bangladesh Rural Advancement Committee[3]

147

AN INCOMPLETE RESPONSE TO ENTRENCHED
INEQUALITIES

As John Rawls memorably wrote, "Each person possesses an inviolability founded upon justice that even the welfare of society as a whole cannot override" (*TJ* 3).[4] But of course that is a normative statement, which
does not correspond to current reality in many parts of the world. To take
the salient example that will be my theme, women in most nations of the
world (in some respects, in all nations) do not have sufficient protection
for that inviolability. They are often unequal under the law: for example, they often lack the property rights, the employment opportunities,
the assembly and travel rights, and the rights of civil capacity that are
granted to males. They often lack equal access to the political process,
and they almost always lack equal representation within it. Within the
family, they suffer from sexual abuse, marital rape, and domestic violence, often without realistic legal recourse. They are much less likely
than men to be literate, and still less likely to have pre-professional or
technical education. Should they attempt to enter the workplace, they
face greater obstacles, including intimidation from family or spouse,
sex discrimination in hiring, and sexual harassment in the workplace –
all frequently, again, without effective legal recourse. Burdened, often,
with the "double day" of taxing employment and full responsibility for
housework and child care (work that is arduous but unpaid and often
not respected), they lack opportunities for valuable forms of friendship
and self-cultivation. All these factors take their toll on emotional well-
being: women have fewer opportunities than men to live free from fear
and to enjoy rewarding types of love – especially when, as often, they
are married without choice in childhood and have no recourse from a
bad marriage.

In the very basic area of health and nutrition, the female-male gap
is significant, and in some nations is getting worse. In India, for example, the sex ratio in the 1990 census was 92 women to 100 men,
the lowest since the census began to be taken early in the twentieth century. The current census results are not yet final, but it seems
likely that the ratio will dip to 85 to 100. (It is estimated that when
equal nutrition and health care are present, women live, on average,
slightly longer than men; thus one should expect a sex ratio of 103
women to 100 men.) And those are government statistics. House-to-
house counts in some regions by reliable nongovernmental organizations have produced far more alarming figures: in a region of rural

Bihar, 75 women to 100 men; in a region of Karnataka, 65 women to 100 men.[5]

In short: however we conceptualize the "primary goods" that a just society ought to distribute justly, the liberties, opportunities, powers, income and wealth that figure in Rawls' approach, and in other related approaches, whether we conceive of them as resources or rather as capabilities,[6] women have grossly unequal access to them, in a way that seems to raise urgent questions of justice.

John Rawls is very sensitive to these inequalities. In fact, in some respects he singles women out in *The Law of Peoples* for special treatment. And yet, as I shall argue, there are features of his overall approach to international issues that make his theory of international justice inadequate and half-hearted in the remedies it offers for such wrongs. Thinking about why the approach does not do justice to women's situation in the world is a way of thinking, more generally, about what might be inadequate about it. Thus, although this paper focuses on women and on the developing nations, it is not at its conceptual core a paper about women as much as it is a more general diagnosis of some shortcomings in Rawls' theory, shortcomings that affect its dealings with all marginalized or subordinated groups. And yet it is still useful to focus on the problems of women, both because it seems good to keep the reader's mind fixed on these issues of urgent importance and also because these issues provide a powerful lens through which to study some more general problems that might otherwise escape us.

Why should a paper concerned with sex equality in the international arena focus on Rawls' theory of global justice? Most obviously, this focus is appropriate because Rawls is one of the most distinguished political thinkers of our era, and his approach to issues of global justice is both important and highly influential. But Rawls' theory is not only his own, in a sense: it represents a very long tradition of thinking about justice among nations that goes back at least to Kant, and in many respects to Cicero, in which the nation state is seen as the primary unit within which justice is to be secured, and issues of justice between nations are to be handled afterwards, and between the nations, so to speak, rather than in a way that makes the rights of the individual the primary focus of a theory of global justice.[7] Rawls' theory is subtle, as we shall see; this description does not fully capture the way human rights figure in his account. Nonetheless, there are reasons to question whether any such theory can be fully adequate to the complex and multifaceted international society in which we live, in which connections among persons are mediated not only by nation states but also by a wide range of international agencies, treaties, and other documents, as well as by the global market. Thinking in detail about what is promising and what defective in Rawls' theory of justice among the nations is thus, I believe, a very good way to start thinking about global justice as we try to write theories that are adequate to this complex and changing world.

Two problems in Rawls' theory of international justice that pertain to his dealings with sex inequality will not concern me here. One of these is the failure of the theory to support redistribution of wealth and income from richer to poorer nations.[8] It is pretty obvious that sex inequality is to some extent independent of general poverty. Women are not fully equal even in the world's most prosperous nations, and nations with similar levels of general prosperity can vary greatly in their level of sex equality.[9] Furthermore, some of the worst sex-specific abuses do not seem to be at all ameliorated by a high living standard. Although reliable figures for rape and domestic violence are very hard to come by, the United States surely ranks high up among the nations of the world on these crimes. But in some areas there is at least a modest correlation between general prosperity (in the sense of GNP per capita) and high human development (in the sense of the wider set of issues that are pursued in the *Human Development Reports*) for women: thus in no prosperous nation do we find the staggering disparities in sex ratio that we find in South Asia, North Africa, and some parts of Latin America. We do not find them in some extremely poor nations either: Sub-Saharan Africa, where women are major agricultural producers, does surprisingly well, or at least did before the scourge of AIDS, reliable recent figures being hard to obtain. A high living standard, while not a necessary condition for roughly equal nutrition and health care, would appear to be a sufficient condition for that. Equal education of boys and girls, once again, is usually found, up to a certain point (primary and secondary education), in nations with a high living standard. Again, poor nations or states within nations may attain this equality (the Indian state of Kerala is an impressive example); but again, prosperity seems to be at least a sufficient condition for a roughly equal distribution of primary education.[10]

Thus we might expect that one concern of a theory of international justice that attempts to undo the ways in which individuals are violated, deprived of basic life chances, through morally irrelevant features of their environment would have to be the redistribution of wealth and income across national borders. Rawls' rapid dismissal of this whole issue seems to me one of the grave weaknesses of his theory. That weakness, however, is an issue for another time.

Another issue that I shall also bracket is the issue of the family. A serious defect of Rawls' theory, both in its domestic and in its transnational form (and I think it is not just accidental that "The Idea of Public Reason Revisited," with its essay on the family, is published in *The Law of Peoples*) is his refusal to countenance much state intervention into the family, which he tends to treat as a pre-political entity that exists by nature. I have discussed this question at some length elsewhere, and made my own proposals, so I do not repeat those arguments here.[11]

Instead, I shall focus on an issue that goes to the heart of Rawls' argument in *LP*: his insistence that the liberal principle of toleration requires us to tolerate hierarchical societies, provided that they meet certain minimum conditions of reasonableness and respect for human rights. Thus the stringent requirements of justice that obtain within the domestic sphere, curtailing the privileges of religious and other groups within each liberal society, are relaxed when it comes to other parts of the world. I shall argue that Rawls' argument for giving this much deference to the so-called decent hierarchical societies is unsuccessful, resting on a misleading analogy between peoples and persons. In the transnational realm as elsewhere, there are no good arguments for making groups, rather than individuals, the basic subjects of a theory of justice,[12] and some very strong arguments why we should insist that the individual is the basic subject. More generally, there are no obstacles to justifying the same norms, in the area of basic entitlements, for all the world's people.

There is, however, an issue that ought to give us pause: the issue of implementation. I shall argue that although we may successfully justify certain norms as applicable to persons in all nations of the world, and thus rightly recommend (through international instruments, and so forth) that all nations incorporate these norms into their domestic political structure, there are good reasons why it would be wrong to seek to implement them from without, reasons having to do with the special role of the basic structure of the state in the lives of its citizens and the special character of its accountability. Worries about colonialism and paternalism rightly surface here, in the domain of action and implementation, although I believe they have little bite in the area of justification. But to make this point successfully, I shall be forced to call into question another aspect of Rawls' argument: his strong distinction between states and peoples, and his claim that issues of international justice primarily pertain to relations among peoples, not to relations among states. I shall argue that the basic structure of the state, and its special role, is what ought to prevent us from most types of intervention. I shall then conclude by saying what I think a decently respectful type of persuasion, in the transnational sphere, would look like, and what means it might employ.

HISTORY: WEST AND NON-WEST

An initial problem we have, when we approach Rawls' theory, is that some of his arguments rest on a very shaky historical understanding – or at least on a very incomplete portrayal of the relevant history. Rawls typically presents liberalism, and political liberalism in particular, as a response to a peculiarly Western historical experience. In *PL*, for example, he writes: "[T]he historical origin of political liberalism (and of liberalism more generally) is the Reformation and its aftermath, with the long controversies over religious toleration in the sixteenth and seventeenth centuries" (xxvi). This understanding is important to him: he suggests that for this reason the justification of the principles of political liberalism holds only within a society whose shared political culture derives from this specifically Western history.

In "LP", liberalism continues to be characterized as "Western", even as based on "Western individualism" (69), even though Rawls is also at pains to insist that the reasonable law of peoples he proposes, because of its treatment of decent hierarchical societies, is not peculiarly Western (48, 29). In the book version, however, references to the Western tradition are dropped, in favor of a schematic distinction between liberal and non-liberal societies. It seems, however – although the abstract character of Rawls' formulations makes this somewhat unclear – that by "liberal" Rawls is still thinking above all of the Western democratic nations, and not, for example, of India or Bangladesh or South Africa, all of which have adopted liberal constitutions out of a history that is quite distinct from the European history that is Rawls' focus in *PL*. Insofar as Rawls appears to believe that liberal societies have different traditions from nonliberal societies, and that these traditions help to justify their continued nonliberal status, it seems most likely that he does so with the ideas of *PL* in view.

Are the core ideas of Rawls' books peculiarly Western, then, as *PL* suggests? We should begin by objecting to the shopworn conceptual division of the world into "Western" and "non-Western," which is surely an obstacle to correct historical perception, suggesting singleness where in real life there is a complex multiplicity. The classification, bad enough when we are talking about the Euro-American traditions, is particularly unhelpful for the "non-Western," since the very concept "non-Western" is obviously a Western artifact which draws together civilizations of Africa, East Asia, South Asia, and Africa,[13] and others, which would not understand themselves as parts of a single "non-West." But let me follow Rawls' usage, in order to question other aspects of his account.

So: even if these ideas had their origin only in the "West," that would hardly entail that they can be applied only there. All human beings are ingenious borrowers of ideas. The West got all of its (usable[14]) mathematics from the Arab world, and the Enlightenment could not have taken place without that borrowing; nonetheless, we do not consider that we have no right to claim those ideas. Similarly, even were it true that the ideas of political equality, democracy, human dignity, and toleration were basically Western Enlightenment notions, this would not prevent and has not prevented many other nations and peoples of the world from putting them into their constitutions, from fighting and dying for them, and so forth; such a deliberate staking of one's future on the ideas would seem to make the ideas theirs even more firmly than they are ours, who got them by habit. If, moreover, we were to adopt the principle that the ideas of a people are only the oldest ideas in their tradition, we ourselves would have to go back to Homeric Greece, perhaps, where none of the Rawlsian ideas can be found in anything like its modern form, as he himself notes in *PL* (xxiv). (Not to mention the fact that many of "us" would trace our origins back to Africa, China, India, the shtetls of Eastern Europe, etc., all with their different ideas.) Why should we allow ourselves and not others the ability to change and to borrow?

Moreover, the historical record of any culture is the record, largely, of its most powerful voices; we have little record of what poor illiterate people have thought about the world they live in, or what women of any social class have thought of their lives. So even if non-Western cultures, as we best know them, did insist on corporatist and hierarchical principles such as we might find in the Western Middle Ages, this would not tell us that the society as a whole, or the "people" as a whole, endorses those ideas. Those at the bottom of the hierarchy might well endorse very different, more egalitarian, ideas. Even if they cannot be known to have done so, we might conjecture that they would quickly endorse them, were the ideas presented to them in a context free from threat. Thus, to the extent that we agree to be guided by the written record of a people in asking what we should expect of it, we are agreeing not to take very seriously the possibly quite different voices of those who suffer from the inequalities imposed by that tradition. For example, when we say that a given tradition holds such and such ideas about the role of women, we are just failing to take women seriously, for if we think for a little while we can easily see that the tradition that denigrates them was neither written nor freely endorsed by them. It's always convenient for those in power to brand women's demands as "Western" and anti-traditional: but in response we should inquire, whose tradition was this anyhow? Was it ever theirs? For many women, the ideas of feminism are more intimately theirs, more their tradition, than whatever it was that oppressed them.

But we do not need to reach this point. For it is actually mistaken of Rawls to suggest that his core ideas are parochially Western, even in the sense of their historical origin. Indeed, what would be parochially Western, it seems to me, would be the confident assertion that these ideas are especially Western. It's not impossible for other people to come up with the idea of human dignity and respect for persons. Even some of the more specific ideas in Rawls' conception have deep roots in other cultures. For example, ideas of religious toleration and reasonable pluralism were worked out in India from at least the edicts of Ashoka in the fourth century BC, and a highly sophisticated set of doctrines of political respect for religious difference was elaborated during the Moghul Empire in the fifteenth to sixteenth centuries – well before "our" "invention" of such ideas.[15] More or less every component part of the Enlightenment idea of human rights and basic liberties has its counterpart in the cultures of India and China, although the Enlightenment configured those ideas in a particular way. In fact, if one regularly reads Indian legal writings, one will see that ideas of equality and autonomy are cited again and again by justices as core ideas of Indian culture.[16]

At the same time, it is obvious that corporatist and hierarchical ideas are right at home in the Western European tradition, especially in some of its major religions. My first epigraph records the fact that Christianity, which was brought to India from Europe, is seen by Indian courts as holding more organic and communitarian ideas of the family than are common elsewhere in Indian culture, with its emphasis on the dignity of the individual. Even if the dignity of the individual is not always honored in the observance in other major religions either, it is at least a shared ideal toward which the society is seen as striving, and with regard to which Christians are seen as lagging behind.[17]

I conclude, then, that to the extent that Rawls might have wished to argue that liberal ideas are more easily justified for Western than for non-Western societies, on account of pervasive differences of history and tradition – a line of argument he strongly suggests in *PL* – that argument has not been and could not plausibly be made good.

THE TOLERATION ARGUMENT

The argument on which I want to focus is given very briefly in "LP," so let me begin with that formulation:

> Surely tyrannical and dictatorial regimes cannot be accepted as members in good standing of a reasonable society of peoples. But equally not all regimes can reasonably be required to be liberal, otherwise the law of peoples itself would not express liberalism's own principle of toleration for other reasonable ways of ordering society nor further its attempt to find a shared basis of agreement among reasonable peoples. Just as a citizen in a liberal society must respect other persons' comprehensive religious, philosophical, and moral doctrines provided they are pursued in accordance with a reasonable political conception of justice, so a liberal society must respect other societies organized by comprehensive doctrines, provided their political and social institutions meet certain conditions that lead the society to adhere to a reasonable law of peoples.   ("LP" 42–3)

In other words: Just as Americans are required to respect the comprehensive doctrines of believing Roman Catholics, and Buddhists, and Muslims, and Jews, and atheists, provided that they pursue their doctrines in accordance with the reasonable political conception of justice defended in *PL*, so too a liberal society (let us suppose that America is one) is required to show respect both for other liberal societies and for decent hierarchical societies, provided that these societies adhere to the constraints and standards spelled out in the law of peoples.

In *LP*, the argument remains the same, but several features are spelled out in more detail. Toleration is said to require not only refraining from exercising military, economic, or diplomatic sanctions against a people, but also recognizing the non-liberal societies

> as equal participating members in good standing of the Society of Peoples, with certain rights and obligations, including the duty of civility requiring that they offer other peoples public reasons appropriate to the Society of Peoples for their actions.

Liberal societies are to cooperate with and assist all peoples in good standing. If all societies were required to be liberal, then the idea of political liberalism would fail to express due toleration for other acceptable ways (if such there are, as I assume) or ordering society. (*LP* 59)

And then the analogy is spelled out in exactly the same way as in "LP". Rawls explicitly rejects the argument that all societies should be judged by the liberal standard of treating all citizens "who possess all the powers of reason, intellect, and moral feeling as truly free and equal" (60).

Let us now examine this analogy. The problem on which I want to focus is that there is both analogy and disanalogy here. Inside a liberal society, there are many hierarchical conceptions of the good. These conceptions will be tolerated, in the sense of being respected as reasonable, provided that their adherents accept, as a module or constituent part within their comprehensive doctrine, the principles of justice that shape the basic structure of their society.[18] In other words, the religious conceptions must include the principles of justice inside themselves, even if originally they did not do so. Religions that at one time in their history taught that it is right to treat women as unequal in society must affirm, as a part of the comprehensive doctrine itself, the political doctrine that women are fully equal as citizens, and that it is just that the basic structure of society be organized so as to accord to women all the major liberties, opportunities, and powers on a footing of full equality. This may not be incompatible with retaining some teachings about sex difference or even sex hierarchy, where this pertains to the spiritual sphere, but note that the family is part of the basic structure, so it would appear that the religions may not even maintain that men and women are unequal within the family.[19] And Rawls is clear that retaining any sort of hierarchy, even in the spiritual sphere, will impose some strain, if the religion really does affirm the full justice of the principles underlying the basic structure.

Comprehensive doctrines that promulgate teachings conflicting with the requirements of political justice will not find their speech suppressed, except in the very exceptional conditions Rawls specifies in his highly protective doctrine of free political speech. Nonetheless, they will not be respected, in the sense of being regarded as members of society's overlapping consensus; nor will their proposals be allowed to come forward for straightforward majority vote.

In the transnational case, things are very different. The religious or traditional source of value is tolerated, in the sense of being recognized as belonging to the community of peoples, whenever certain far weaker conditions obtain. There must still be respect for a small list of fundamental human rights, an issue to which I shall return. But it is clear that a people may win respect in the community of peoples even if property rights, voting rights, and religious freedom are unequally assigned to different actors within the society.[20] The stringent requirements of political democracy, the equal worth of liberty, and universal suffrage[21] are replaced by the far weaker requirement of a "reasonable consultation hierarchy." Even free speech need not be accorded to all persons, so long as certain "associations and corporate bodies" ("LP" 62) allow them to express dissent in some way, and take their views seriously.

Let us consider this difference as it structures the lives of women. And let us take as our example the case of the Catholic Christians in Kerala, South India, which I have already discussed. In India, which is a pluralistic liberal democracy and must be counted by Rawls as one of the liberal nations, the Roman Catholic Church, according to Rawls, can be counted among the reasonable comprehensive doctrines only insofar as it accepts not only the doctrine of toleration and mutual respect for other religions that Rawls rightly associates with the work of John Courtney Murray, but also some further very stringent limitations on what its views can be. Agreeing with the High Court of Kerala, Rawls will insist that the Catholic Church must uphold stringent standards of respect for human dignity and equality. Roman Catholics, that is, must hold as a module within their comprehensive doctrine the view that women are fully equal as citizens, entitled to equal religious liberty, equal political rights, and equal economic opportunities. With regard to all the primary goods, there should be no differentiation between women and men, and in general life chances should not be deformed in these very basic areas of life on grounds of sex. The Catholic Church may teach that metaphysically women are different from men, but not in a way that contravenes this deep and extensive political equality. Such a teaching probably can be used to legitimize the denial of certain key religious functions to women; but the minute the Church practices discrimination in employment, or, as in the case at issue, discrimination in the very basic issue of exit options from abusive marriages, it would appear to run afoul of Rawlsian principles. Similarly, if we consider an issue that arose earlier concerning the Christian Church in Kerala, the Church will not be permitted to grant women unequal inheritance rights.[22] Here again, Rawls agrees with actual decisions of Indian courts.

Let us now imagine that at the time of Independence in 1947 Kerala was not made part of the nation of India. Instead, it became a separate nation.[23] Because Catholic Christians predominate in the state,[24] the decision is made that Kerala will be a Roman Catholic nation. They justify their decision to refuse membership in India by saying that they are a distinct people and that they want to govern themselves by laws deriving from their own tradition, which is very different from that of other Indian regions. (It is useful to focus on this Christian example, rather than the fictional Islamic state of Rawls' text, to bring home the fact that this so-called Western religion[25] has just the same problems as does an Islamic republic, let us say Bangladesh, and that both liberal ideas and the resistance to them are typically found in every nation. Demonizing Islam is a popular industry to which one should avoid contributing.) In the new nation of Kerala, following centuries of Catholic teaching, the Founders set things up in such a way that women have rights and liberties very unequal to those of men. They have unequal property rights.[26] They don't vote, although men are asked to consult them, and it is a part of the country's "common good conception of justice" that their views are to be taken seriously. They are not encouraged to work outside the home, and there are no non-discrimination laws to protect them when they are in the workplace.[27] Women have no right to petition for divorce, except where they can prove both adultery and either desertion or cruelty: in other words, cruelty alone is not a ground of divorce. Men may divorce on grounds of adultery only.[28] Although men cannot divorce for cruelty alone either, the law creates deep asymmetries between women and men, chaining women to abusive marriages, given that domestic abuse is overwhelmingly committed by men against women. Because rape within marriage is not a crime in Kerala,[29] and because the nation has borrowed from British ecclesiastical law the remedy of "restitution of conjugal rights,"[30] women may be and often are forced to have intercourse they don't want, and to bear children they don't want.[31] It is difficult for women to change these things, given their unequal access to property, thence credit, and given their unequal access to the political process. All of this is defended with reference to a common-good conception of justice: for example, unequal property rights are defended by an argument that failed in Indian courts, namely, that giving equal property rights to women would "destroy the traditional harmony and goodwill that exists in Christian families."[32]

So far as I can see, it is Rawls' view that the nation of Kerala will be regarded as a member in good standing of the community of peoples.[33]

Why, according to Rawls, are the women of the nation of Kerala so much worse off than Catholic women in the state of Kerala in India? In both the domestic case and the transnational case, there is a group that holds a comprehensive conception of the good, and this group maintains that their tradition requires certain inequalities between women and men. In the domestic case, Catholic men will have to choose between their commitment to these inequalities and membership in the overlapping consensus. If they want their doctrine to be respected as among the reasonable ones, they will have to drop or modify those features that clash most directly with the political doctrine. If they somehow manage, in some region of the world, to get into a sufficient majority that they can make laws for themselves, enacting the norms of their tradition, they get off the hook.

Put in other terms, it looks as if in the domestic-pluralism case women get to count as fully equal persons. The dignity of the person, and the full equality of persons, are key features of the Rawlsian basic structure, as indeed they are of the Indian Constitution. The reason why the Catholic doctrine does not get to propound or enact certain key inequalities between the sexes is that each person is an equal subject of the theory of justice. In the case of the nation of Kerala, which of course (as I've designed it) is, so far as history and tradition go, the very same case,[34] suddenly women don't get to be full persons. They are absorbed into the corporate body of the Church, and they get only such rights as the Church permits. In both cases, a tradition said that women should be treated as parts of this organic whole, but only in the case of the independent nation of Kerala did that tradition get to determine how things would be for women. Why this sudden difference? Why, in the transnational case as well as the domestic case, don't we have exactly the same principle of toleration, namely: we will respect the Roman Catholics of the state of Kerala, or the Roman Catholics of the independent nation of Kerala, provided that they respect certain stringent norms of political justice and graft them into their comprehensive doctrine? It is the same doctrine with the same history, the same tendencies, the same difficulties: so why should the contingency of setting up as a separate nation make such a huge difference to the way both people and groups are treated?

In the domestic case, it appears that Rawls' principle of toleration is actually a person-centered principle: it is a principle about the importance of respecting persons and their comprehensive conceptions of the good. In the transnational case, although Rawls depicts himself as applying the same principle, it appears that the principle is fundamentally different: it is a principle that respects groups rather than persons, and that actually shows deficient respect for persons, insofar as it allows their course to be dictated by that of the dominant group in their vicinity, whether they happen to like or belong to that group or not. Rawls still retains awareness of the person as subject to the extent that he does insist on a list of human rights. But he clearly allows tradition and group desire to have a power in the national case that they do not have in the internal case.

This asymmetry is especially peculiar in light of the fact that Rawls' central objection to Utilitarianism, in *TJ*, was that it is not sufficiently person-centered: By treating the community as a super-person and treating all satisfactions as fungible within this single structure, it neglects the fundamental distinctness of persons and their lives, treating them as "so many different lines along which rights and duties are to be assigned" (27).[35] Rawls' theory of international justice does what his domestic theory of justice persuasively argues against; it neglects the inviolability of each person that was a key to Rawls' domestic theory. But persons are persons, and violation is violation, wherever it occurs.

Furthermore, in the domestic case, any concessions that are made to the group are made against the background of exit options: persons are always free to depart from one religion and to join another, or to have no religion at all. Rawls knows well that the basic structure offers no exit options; this is a key reason why he thinks it is so important that the institutions that form part of the basic structure should be arranged in accordance with principles of justice. The basic structure shapes people's life chances pervasively and from the start. And yet in the transnational case, Rawls appears to have lost sight of this insight, allowing a religion to shape people's life chances pervasively and from the start, in ways that depart from principles of justice, even though there are no exit options for those who do not endorse that doctrine. For of course the women of Kerala the nation are actually worse off than they would be were they in a state of Kerala within India that was allowed to go on behaving badly to women in the ways described: for then, they could move to another state that did things better.[36] In the nation case, they probably cannot.

Let us recapitulate. Rawls' analogy seems to be defective for the following reasons:

(1) *Same groups, different circumstances.* Rawls suggests that there are these "peoples" in the world that have a mysterious sort of unity,

different from the bonds that hold together members of religions and other groups that exist within nations. But in reality, in the world, so far as I can see, we do not find these "peoples." We find just the same groups we have on our hands already – religions, ethnic groups, with all their comprehensive doctrines. Roman Catholicism in independent Kerala is just the same doctrine as Roman Catholicism in India; it is simply in different circumstances, where it has become the numerical majority rather than a subgroup. Rawls has given no reason why the same group should be treated differently when it manages to form a state, why this fact should give it license to dominate over minorities when it would not be permitted to do so otherwise. Groups, however close and intimate, are always internally plural: they contain hierarchies and inequalities.[37] Why do those inequalities get political recognition in one case and not in the other?

(2) *Hierarchy and subordination are still unfair to persons.* In the case of liberal India, Rawls' doctrine holds that certain sorts of hierarchy that exist within groups are unacceptable. The basic structure ought to protect the dignity of the person. In the case of independent Kerala, persons and their dignity suddenly get less protection – apparently, only because some powerful male leaders have managed to win a particular sort of political settlement. The women don't like being unequal in the independent nation any more than they do in the liberal pluralist nation, and there is no reason to think that they endorse the way of life that keeps them subordinated. So, once again: the accident of some arrangements made or not made in 1947 are permitted to make the difference between being equal and not being equal. Because Rawls acknowledges, in his defense of human rights, that the person remains the ultimate subject of justice, this concession to groups seems especially odd.

(3) *The fact that it's the basic structure makes things worse.* As a Catholic woman in the state of Kerala, Mrs. Mary Roy, denied equal property rights, had options. She could, and did, seek to exit from the system that oppressed her.[38] In the independent nation of Kerala there would be no courts independent of the Christian hierarchy to which she could appeal. In India, again, there was a just basic structure in place, and a Constitution that defined her as a subject of justice with a definite set of fundamental rights and a dignity equal to that of men. So the indignity she suffered at the hands of the Church was not only remediable, it was localized. In the independent Nation of

Kerala, the unjust basic structure would determine her life chances pervasively and from the start. In short, we have reason to be more, not less, vigilant about inequalities when they are dominant in an independent nation and determine the shape of its constitution.

(4) *And what about the group of women?* Rawls' argument permits certain groups to have great power over the lives of individuals, wherever those groups have geographical concentration and power such that they are able to form an independent state. But of course there are many groups that are very important to people's comprehensive doctrines and sense of self that will never have this power, because they are dispersed around the world.[39] As one feminist activist in India put it, after Parliament had passed a law that deprived Muslim women of certain rights enjoyed by other Indian women, "If by making separate laws for Muslim women, you are trying to say that we are not citizens of this country, then why don't you tell us clearly and unequivocally that we should establish another country – not Hindustan or Pakistan but Auratstan (women's land)."[40] Auratstan, however, will not exist at any foreseeable time, because women do not have sufficient geographical concentration or power to set up as an independent nation. For this reason, a woman's choice to identify her life course with the group of women will never get the same respect in Rawls' system as the choice to identify one's life course with an ethnic or religious group that might possibly form a nation. I am not very sure what a "people" is, but it seems plain that the dispersed group of women is not one, at least in the sense that Rawls seems to have in mind, since he does not even mention the possibility that there might be a "people" that is dispersed among many nations.[41] But why not? Why is the group of women less worthy of respect, and, more to the point, why do the people who choose to identify with this group rather than with one of the more geographically concentrated groups get less respect?

I conclude that Rawls' analogy is deeply flawed, in ways that are explained, but not justified, by the lack of concreteness and realism in his discussion as a whole.

Rawls would probably make three replies to this argument. First, he would insist that in fact women's interests play a very important role in the constraints on so-called decent hierarchical societies. In "LP" he refers to "the subjection of women abetted by unreasonable religion" as among the greatest evils of poorer societies (77), and suggests that his emphasis on human rights will "moderate, albeit slowly," this subjection (77). In LP he adds to the account of a reasonable consultation hierarchy the proviso that "any group representing women's fundamental interests must include a majority of women" (110). This is indeed an important step: but who can tell what its result will be, in a nation whose constitution gives women unequal property rights and few exit options from bad marriages? The presence of women in a group, in short, does not guarantee that their voices will not be deformed by fear and material inequality. As for the claim that his weaker constraints would modify women's lot over time, well, perhaps: but note that the Catholic property and divorce laws of Kerala lasted from the seventeenth century until 1986, in the case of property, and 2000, in the case of divorce, and both ultimately yielded to pressures from women, and the liberal Indian state. Sexism is tenacious, and, as Mill observed, men who typically adopt a presumption in favor of liberty in other contexts adopt the opposite presumption when women's equal liberties are under consideration.[42]

Rawls will argue, second, that his view still offers protection for a central group of fundamental human rights, and that this feature is sufficient to make the remaining inequalities for women tolerable. I dispute this claim. If there are good arguments from respect for persons that lead to the more stringent constraints of the Rawlsian liberal state, then these arguments seem to me pertinent to the independent state of Kerala as well. To the extent that the list of human rights in *LP* omits features that are guaranteed for all persons in the Rawlsian state, it omits features that there are good reasons to include. And in fact the list omits some features that are of particular importance for women. Equal property rights are surely among the most important determinants of women's life chances, as are equal grounds for divorce.[43]

Third, Rawls might suggest that my argument presupposes a peculiarly Western concern with the individual. In "LP", for example, he writes, "Many societies have political traditions that are different from Western individualism in its many forms" (69).[44] Now I have already argued that there is nothing particularly Western about the idea that each and every person has certain basic rights, just as there is nothing particularly Western about corporatist or associationist views of rights – a point that Rawls seems to grant in *LP* by citing Hegel as an example of the latter view. In the state of Kerala, a Western corporatist tradition was inhibited by ideas of human dignity that derive from a long Indian tradition of thought about persons and their dignity. In independent Kerala, those same Western traditions got to rule the roost. What we are really seeing, then, is that the very same traditions, whether Western or non-Western, are treated differently because of the accident of setting up as a separate state, not because of any deeper phenomenon of organic unity or universal consent.

But we can go further than this: it seems extremely likely that there is no tradition anywhere, nor ever has been, in which women simply endorse the lower lot in life they are offered. Women are often cowed, isolated, unable to resist effectively. But their "everyday resistance" has been amply documented all over the world.[45] And my third epigraph records a fact that can easily be observed all over the world: that as soon as women are able to get together in groups, and talk to one another about their situation, they begin to resist more effectively, taking charge of their own lives. So the very idea that women do *not* see themselves as persons who have lives to plan, separate from those of the males with whom they live, is an idea that would be extremely difficult to establish, and one that probably could not be established. Even women whose preferences are in many ways deformed by hierarchy and fear still recognize themselves as separate from other persons, and they do not confuse their own hunger with the hunger of a child or a husband.[46]

JUSTIFICATION AND IMPLEMENTATION

Rawls has not presented a good argument against the application of liberal norms to all the world's societies. So far as his argument goes, at least, there seems to be no moral obstacle to justifying a single set of human rights, or human capabilities, as fundamental norms for all persons.

But there is another issue that troubles Rawls, and that ought to trouble us. Rawls clearly thinks that if we conclude that another nation has defective norms we will intervene in some way, whether through military intervention or through economic and political sanctions. Usually he treats the question, "Is this nation worthy of respect as a member of the society of peoples?" as if it is equivalent to the question, "Should we refrain from intervening in that nation to seek the implementation of our own moral standards?" Indeed, it is in large part because, for

Kantian reasons, he believes that intervention into the sovereign affairs of another republic is morally deeply problematic that he is eager to conclude that we may respect hierarchical nations as members of the society of peoples.

But of course the two questions need not be linked in this way. We may, that is, think that the standards of the nation of Kerala are defective, and that we can justify as applicable to independent Kerala the more extensive menu of basic rights and liberties recognized, for example, in the Indian constitution, without thinking that we have the right to intervene in the affairs of Kerala, either militarily or economically and politically. We may take this line if we believe that there are independent grounds for refraining from interference with other nations, grounds that do not depend on our believing that we ought to express respect for the hierarchies around which this society has organized itself.

What might those independent grounds be? I believe that they are the very grounds suggested by Kant in *Perpetual Peace*: a moral loathing of colonial domination and a related moral belief that one should respect the sovereignty of any nation that is organized in a sufficiently accountable and republican fashion, whether or not one believes that its institutions are fully just. Recognition of the moral importance of the state as an expression of human autonomy is already a prominent feature of Grotius' discussion of humanitarian intervention in *De Iure Belli Atque Pacis*: by forming sovereign states and giving themselves laws, human beings assert their moral autonomy.[47] Because one respects the citizens of a nation, and because one believes that the nation is, if in many respects imperfect, still above a certain threshold of democracy and accountability, therefore one will refrain from military intervention into the affairs of that nation, and one will negotiate with its duly elected government as a legitimate government. Unlike Kant, and extending Grotius' doctrine of humanitarian intervention,[48] I would make an exception for some classic cases where humanitarian intervention has typically been taken to be called for: genocide, mass rape and torture, etc. In many such cases (e.g. Rwanda), one will have reason to think that the government doesn't have democratic legitimacy. But sometimes tyrants really get elected, as Hitler was elected, and it would still be right to intervene to impede his heinous policies. It would not, however, be right to intervene, either militarily or through economic and political sanctions, simply in order to implement better human rights protections in the areas of sex equality that I have touched on (unequal property rights, unequal access to divorce). In such cases – as, for example, with the United States on capital punishment, which seems to me rightly abhorred by a reasonable society of peoples, diplomatic pressures and persuasion seem more fitting than any sort of coercion.

Thus, in the case of independent Kerala, much though one might deplore the inequalities of women under the Keralan constitution, it would not be right to intervene in coercive ways, so long as one judged that the state was above a certain threshold in terms of democratic accountability. These threshold conditions would be much weaker than those required for fully being respected as a just society in the society of peoples. Most nations in the world today are unjust in one or more respects, and it is right to argue that they are unjust and to hold up to them standards of full equality and dignity that one can recommend as applicable to them. But it would not be right to impose sanctions on them, so long as they pass a much weaker test of accountability, a test that today's United States and today's India will both easily pass, even though both fall well below the standards of full human rights protection that we can justify and rightly recommend.

To put it in terms of the idea of the basic structure: in a domestic case where rights and liberties are being violated, it is always right for the state to intervene, because the state has been legitimated by the people who are its citizens. Indeed, whatever account of legitimation we accept, whether Rawls' or another, we should grant that one major task of the basic structure is precisely to provide a basis for intervention (through laws and their enforcement) when rights and liberties are being violated. In the transnational case, there is no analogous process of legitimation, and no basic structure. We therefore lack a moral basis for intervention – although I would argue that traditional accounts of humanitarian intervention supply one for the narrow range of cases I have identified.

Someone might ask whether we do really show respect for a state and its people, if we criticize it and suggest that it violated important moral norms that can be justified for all? It is important to approach this question from the starting point that no existing state is fully just. All contain violations of important moral principles. It is not fully respectful of another nation when state actors criticize only other nations and fail to criticize their own. On the other hand, it is perfectly possible to express criticism in the context of an acknowledgement of one's own failure fully to live up to principles of justice.

Where there is a gap between what we can justify morally for all and what we are morally entitled to implement, what should we do? One obvious thing we may and should do is to work out international treaties protecting the human rights in our scheme and work to get the nations of the world to adopt and implement them. Beyond this, it seems to me that nations are often entitled to offer aid in ways that reinforce causes they believe important: thus it would be legitimate for the United States, in giving aid to India, to target education, health care, and, as Clinton did, the empowerment of poor women, and to try to make sure that the aid gets used on these things rather than on building more nuclear bombs. It would also be legitimate to use diplomatic exchange as a way of drawing attention to those issues, as when Clinton used the occasion of his visit to India to draw attention to the situation of poor rural women struggling for credit and property rights. The legitimacy of this way of proceeding is unassailable, given that the cause of female empowerment and equality is a deep part of the Indian constitutional tradition itself. To the extent that a nation, for example independent Kerala, fails to endorse such goals, we would be right to proceed in a more cautious and respectful way, but we would probably still be entitled to focus aid on projects that seem to us morally good. And of course individuals are always free to focus their aid on projects they favor.[49]

At this point Rawls might say that I have conceded his basic point: that we should treat nations as decent members in good standing of the society of peoples on a much weaker showing of liberal freedom and equality than we would demand within a liberal society. And indeed Rawls and I have converged in some respects on a set of practical principles. Am I not in effect conceding that we refrain from these impositions out of respect for a people and its traditions?

No, I am not. My argument has had no use for the concept of a people. I am arguing that we ought to respect the *state*, that is, the *institutions of the basic structure of society* that a given group of people have accepted, and that are accountable to them. The state is seen as morally important because it is an expression of human choice and autonomy: and of course it is the state that expresses the desire of human beings to live under laws they give to themselves, not the people. It makes no difference to my argument whether the inhabitants of the state can be said to constitute a people in Rawls' sense, that is, sharing traditions and a relatively extensive[50] conception of the good, or not. In independent Kerala there are quite a few human beings, anyway, who do share a comprehensive conception (though I think it is actually rare to find women fully sharing a common conception of the good with men, in a situation of entrenched sex inequality). In today's India, it would be utterly implausible to think that there is anything like a Rawlsian people in that nation as a whole. But my argument about implementation applies in a similar way to both.

Nor does my argument require us to relax in any way the moral judgments we make about the wrongness of actions in another nation, as Rawls' argument clearly does. It does not rely on any recognition of group rights, and it continues to maintain that the person is the basic subject of the theory of justice. It simply recognizes the fundamental bond between citizens and the basic structure of the state that is theirs, and it shows respect for that bond, as a way of respecting persons. Otherwise put, it is an argument about implementation, not justification, and it insists that there is a basic distinction between those two issues.

One possible drawback of my approach is that it suggests that any agreement reached between liberal and non-liberal societies is a mere *modus vivendi*, whereas the Rawlsian doctrine suggests, instead, that there is a society of peoples that is linked by a moral overlapping consensus.[51] But once again: let us distinguish justification from implementation. In the sense of justification, all societies, liberal and non-liberal, are linked by a moral law that applies to them, whether they recognize it or not. But it seems reasonable enough, when we are thinking of practical matters, to make a sharp distinction between societies that show respect for women (to pursue that example) as fully equal persons and societies that do not. An agreement with the former is surely a different and deeper sort of agreement from an agreement with the latter, in which women are inadequately represented.

Reflecting in this way about respect for states as a reason against intervention, we will be led, I believe, to reject another feature of Rawls' argument: his odd distinction between peoples and states, and his equally odd contention that the principles of international relations apply in the first instance among peoples and not among states. I have already said that I don't think the concept of "people" is a particularly useful concept. If it just means a group of people who share a comprehensive doctrine, or at least a set of traditions that come close to that, then it is a recognizable concept, but we should not kid ourselves that we will often find any coincidence between a people and national boundaries. Even in independent Kerala, where ex hypothesi the Roman Catholic doctrine prevails, we have seen that women may not share all aspects of the comprehensive doctrine; moreover, like any state, it contains religious and other minorities: Jews, Hindus, Muslims. In other words, if we count women as roughly 50 percent of the population, it is likely that fewer than 40 percent of Keralans will share the comprehensive doctrine of its male leaders, even if Roman Catholics are in a large majority.

Similarly, in the Bangladesh of my third epigraph, the women's group described by the speaker does not share very much with the *mullahs* who oppress women and forbid them to go out of the house – even though their influence is tremendous in the state as a whole. If we now turn away from small and *relatively* homogeneous states to larger nations such as India, Peru, and so on, we typically find very pronounced divisions of comprehensive doctrine within the nation, just as we do in the society envisaged by Rawls in *PL*. That is no accident, since Rawls has agreed with Larmore that reasonable disagreement about comprehensive doctrines is a characteristic feature of modernity.

Rawls suggests that the requirements for being a people are weaker: not full-fledged sharing in a comprehensive doctrine, but only "common sympathies" are required; and "common sympathies," in turn, does not require a common culture with common language and history, though these are certainly helpful in constituting a people (*LP* 24). I don't really know what he means. The concept is too vague to offer any guidance. It seems to me likely that women around the world have "common sympathies" with women in other nations to a greater degree than women do with men in nations characterized by sex hierarchy. Indeed when people live close together in conditions of inequality, resentment and lack of mutual sympathy are especially likely to be found, more likely than when people live at a distance and don't see each other much. To the extent that we're inclined to say that the people in a nation have "common sympathies" it is usually because we manage to overlook such facts of subordination and to take the dominant group's word for how things are. So I see no reason to think that there is anything like a Rawlsian people anywhere in the world. There may be small homogeneous groups within nations; though even here we should be skeptical, recognizing that even members of a small and traditional religion often differ profoundly over core elements of the religion's comprehensive doctrine (as Fred Kniss showed for the Mennonites in his wonderful book *Disquiet in the Land: Cultural Conflict in American Mennonite Communities*).[52] Certainly inside the borders of any modern nation there will be a reasonable plurality of comprehensive doctrines, including the doctrines of women, and those doctrines will give rise to many tensions.

If we leave "common sympathies" to one side, we are left with Rawls' other necessary condition for being a people, the willingness to live together under the same set of democratic institutions. But this brings us back to the state, and alludes to what I have called the fundamental bond between citizens and the state in which they live. We don't need any extra concept, like the concept of a people, to talk well about this, and there are good reasons, I've suggested, why we should not use this vague and unhelpful concept. Why, then, does Rawls show such skepticism about the concept of the state, and hold that international relations must be seen primarily as relations between peoples and not relations between states? At this stage, his argument takes a strange turn: for he speaks not of the state simpliciter, but of "states as traditionally conceived" (*LP* 25), and characterizes the state in a way that builds into it certain powers that states are traditionally believed to have, such as warmaking powers. Because he wants to deny that states rightly have such powers, in a well-functioning community of peoples, he concludes that the state cannot be the subject of a theory of international justice. Why not conclude, instead, that the traditional conception of the state is, in part, mistaken, and has ascribed to it certain powers that states, rightly understood, do not really have? I think that line of argument would serve Rawls' overall purpose far better.

Again, Rawls argues that states are rational actors pursuing self-interest alone (28); here he refers to traditional realist conceptions of foreign policy. But again: why not simply say that these conceptions, like narrow economic conceptions of the person, are mistaken: states are both moral and self-interested. Again, such a line of argument would have served Rawls' purpose better.

If Rawls had criticized the traditional conception of the state and advanced a more moralized conception, he would then have had no need for the idea of respect for putatively homogeneous peoples, which causes so much trouble in his argument. He could have acknowledged that in certain ways the presence of a democratic state imposes constraints on the actions of other states, while insisting that we can justify a single set of basic norms of human rights and entitlements as applicable to all modern states, and a desirable goal for their further human development.

This detailed confrontation with the ideas of John Rawls is also a confrontation with an entire tradition. Philosophers in the Western tradition have traditionally thought of justice as a matter that pertains primarily to the nation state, and only derivatively to the world of international relations. This paradigm has some obvious strengths, and has produced deep insight. I have argued, furthermore, that national sovereignty has moral importance, as an expression of human choice; it ought to be respected by any decent set of international institutions we advocate. Nonetheless, the nation-state paradigm is not fully adequate to the modern world, where a host of complex relationships link people across national borders, and the accident of birth in a given nation now looks in some ways as morally arbitrary as the accidents of race, class, and sex. We need to devote ourselves to working out new theories that will prove more fully adequate to this world. Rawls' theory, and the critique of it, are important guides as we get to work on that task.

NOTES

An earlier version of this chapter appeared in *Politics, Philosophy and Economics* 1 (2002), 283–306. I am grateful to the editors of the journal, Jerry Gaus and Jonathan Riley, for their challenging comments. I would also like to thank Michael Green and Vic Peterson for their very helpful comments on an earlier draft, and Michael Blake for his extremely incisive comments at the APA session at which this chapter was first presented.

1 *Ammini EJ* v *UOI*, AIR (1995) Ker 252, a case that has proved pivotal in pushing the Christian community to rethink its personal law of divorce, which was more oppressive than the laws prevailing in other religious communities, thus leading to the Christian Marriage Bill, passed in 2000. (Christian personal law must be passed by the national parliament, a body in which Christians, of course, form only a tiny minority; so even though by now the Christian hierarchy has approved the changes, that is hardly the end of the matter!)

2 Quoted in Bina Agarwal, *A Field of One's Own: Gender and Land Rights in South Asia* (Cambridge: Cambridge University Press, 1994), p. xvi.

3 Quoted in Martha Chen, *A Quiet Revolution: Women in Transition in Rural Bangladesh* (Cambridge, Mass.: Schenkman, 1983), pp. 154–5.

4 In what follows, I shall refer to works of Rawls as follows: *TJ* = *A Theory of Justice*; *PL* = *Political Liberalism*; *LP* = *The Law of Peoples* (book); "LP" = "The Law of Peoples" (Amnesty Lecture).

5 The figure for Bihar is from Viji Srinivasan, of Adithi; the figure for Karnataka is from Barbara Harriss-White, an economic historian who is studying demographic change in that region. Some of the downward shift is imputable to access to information about the sex of the fetus: although sex-determining procedures are illegal for most purposes, they are widely available.

6 See my *Women and Human Development* (Cambridge: Cambridge University Press, 2000), hereafter *WHD*.

7 I discuss these historical issues in *The Cosmopolitan Tradition*, in progress; the section on Cicero has appeared in *Journal of Political Philosophy*, 8 (2000), 176–206. Other chapters concern Grotius, Adam Smith, and Kant; I argue that Grotius offers a very interesting balance between respect for international sovereignty and attention to rights of individuals.

8 This is the primary theme of *The Cosmopolitan Tradition*; I trace this failure to Cicero's distinction between duties of justice and duties of beneficence. I also discuss these issues in my 2002 Tanner Lectures in Human Values, *Beyond the Social Contract: Toward Global Justice*, forthcoming in the Tanner Lecture volumes.

9 This is shown graphically in the Gender Development Index in the *Human Development Reports* of the UNDP, which adjusts overall national rankings for sex equality. For example, Japan goes dramatically down, and Sweden, Norway and Finland go dramatically up.

10 See my "Women and Education: A Global Challenge," forthcoming in *Signs*, for more data pertaining to the unequal distribution of primary education in developing countries.

11 See "The Future of Feminist Liberalism," 2000 Presidential Address to the APA Central Division, in *Proceedings and Addresses of the American Philosophical Association*, 74 (2000), 47–79, and also ch. 4 of *Women and Human Development*.

12 Of course in another sense the basic structure of society is the subject of the theory, in the sense that it is about that structure that the theory primarily speaks; but it is the individual who is the subject in the sense of being the goal of the theory, and the test of its adequacy.

13 Of course even these labels are constructs, and controversial in their application to complex collections of linguistic and political traditions. On Africa, see Kwame Anthony Appiah, *In My Father's House: Africa in the Philosophy of Cultures* (New York and Oxford: Oxford University Press, 1992).

14 In the sense that Greek mathematics, which geometrized all numerical issues, was a dead end for many problems that needed to be addressed.

15 See Amartya Sen, "Human Rights and Asian Values," *The New Republic*, July 10/17 (1997), and my *WHD*, ch.1.

16 Indeed, in one very interesting case concerning solitary confinement, the Indian Supreme Court stresses that values of solitude and individualism are particularly at home in the Indian tradition, and they argue that, *even so*, imposing solitary confinement on death row prisoners is a cruel punishment: *Sunil Batra* v. *Delhi Administration*, AIR (1978) SC 1675.

17 Rawls does not deny that liberal ideas contend with other more hierarchical ideas in the Western tradition. But to the extent that he grants this, he would appear to obscure a distinction he plainly wants to draw between "West" and "non-West", in the area of justification, and to raise the question whether a Western culture, organized along lines of what Rawls calls a "decent

hierarchical society," might not equally count as deserving of respect under a reasonable law of peoples. (I am grateful for this point to Jonathan Riley.)

18 For this language, see *PL* 144–5: "the political conception is a module, an essential constituent part, that in different ways fits into and can be supported by various reasonable comprehensive doctrines that endure in the society regulated by it."

19 See my "The Future of Feminist Liberalism" for the twistings and turnings of Rawls' position on these matters; see also my "Rawls and Feminism," in *Cambridge Companion to Rawls*, ed. Samuel Freeman (Cambridge and New York: Cambridge University Press, 2002).

20 See *LP* 65 n. 2: "this liberty of conscience may not be as extensive nor as equal for all members of society: for instance, one religion may legally predominate in the state government, while other religions, though tolerated, may be denied the right to hold certain positions."

21 See *LP* 71: "all persons in a decent hierarchical society are not regarded as free and equal citizens, nor as separate individuals deserving equal representation (according to the maxim: one citizen, one vote)."

22 See *Mrs. Mary Roy* v. *State of Kerala and Others*, AIR (1986) SC 1011, discussed in *WHD* ch. 4 and in Agarwal, *A Field*.

23 This is not implausible, because Kerala is simply the union of two former independent princely states of Cochin and Travancore, which were not very strongly linked with the rest of the subcontinent, and, because of their coastal location, had particularly strong connections, through trade, with Europe. Roman Catholicism was brought to the region primarily by Jesuit missionaries from Europe, particularly Portugal, in the seventeenth century.

24 There is actually quite a diversity of religions in Kerala, including Muslims, Hindus, and a substantial Jewish community (though much less numerous now than formerly); Christians are not more than half of the population, so this part of the example is to that extent fictional.

25 Though why Christianity should be thought especially "Western," given its place of origin, is anyone's guess. When I go to a University that lists the Bible on a list of "Great Books of the Western Tradition," as many do, I marvel at the propensity of arrogant Westerners to appropriate anything they revere.

26 *LP* 65 stipulates that the right to property is part of the basic list of human rights, but Rawls is careful to avoid insisting on equal property rights.

27 The requirement on *LP* 65 of "formal equality . . . (that is, that similar cases be treated similarly)" notoriously does not suffice for non-discrimination, since some allegedly relevant difference between women and men can always be produced. See generally Catharine MacKinnon, "Difference and Dominance," in *Feminism Unmodified* (Cambridge, Mass.: Harvard University Press, 1987), 32–45. In describing Kazanistan, Rawls states that "religious

and other minorities . . . are not subjected to arbitrary discrimination" (76), but (a) women are not included in this list, and there are many reasons in the text to think that Rawls will not consider all denial of equality to women discriminatory; and (b) the accent should fall on the all-important word "arbitrary": for, obviously enough, the very concept of a decent hierarchical society suggests that Rawls is not defining discrimination as many feminists would, in terms of an end to all systematic hierarchy and discrimination. He suggests, instead, that some types of discrimination are merely arbitrary and others are justified by some difference. That is the model of discrimination under which women have traditionally been denied many benefits available to men: see MacKinnon, cited above.

28 This is true, and was the central issue in the case cited in my epigraph.

29 Nor in fact anywhere in India, but that is another story. (In the United States, about half of the states have some form of marital rape exemption, either treating it as not a crime at all or treating it as a lesser offense than rape.)

30 Although this remedy was actually incorporated into Hindu, not Christian, law in India, it is Christian in origin, as Indian courts have pointed out, and thus this fiction seems plausible enough.

31 I see nothing in Rawls' list of human rights to rule this out, for surely the Keralans would contend, as Christians traditionally have, that marriage gives a presumption of consent to intercourse, and that the situation of a wife is thus very unlike "slavery, serfdom, and forced occupation."

32 P. J. Kurien, author of a Private Member's Bill seeking to block the legal effect of the Supreme Court decision in the Mary Roy case.

33 And this is not even to raise the question of Kerala's unequal treatment of members of other religions: around the time of Independence, the Jews of Cochin and Travancore (as I said, the two states out of which Kerala was formed) emigrated in large numbers to Israel, not for no reason! Some of the anti-Semitism of this region can be observed in Salman Rushdie's novel *The Moor's Last Sigh*; whether the anti-Semitism is that of the author has been a matter of controversy.

34 We could have told a similar story about Bangladesh, whose women would apparently have a different lot, under Rawls' view, had they stayed within India from the lot they now have in an independent Islamic republic. Bangladesh, however, has a liberal constitution and is in matters of sex equality quite progressive, in some ways more progressive than India. So I stick with the retrogressive Christian case.

35 Cf. *TJ* 27, 29, 185–9.

36 Freedom of travel, understood to include movement among the states, is guaranteed by Article 19 of the Indian Constitution. Article 19 also protects some instances of international travel (as in a famous case in which the removal of the passport of a political unpopular person was declared unconstitutional), but obviously enough, no nation's constitution can guarantee its

citizens the right to emigrate to another nation: they have to have somewhere to go.

37 See my "The Complexity of Groups," in *Philosophy and Social Research*, 29: 1 (2003).

38 In fact, as I've argued in *WHD* ch. 3, exit options are imperfectly guaranteed in the Indian system of personal law, because people are slotted into a given religious system at birth and hereditary property, and laws governing it are all bound up within that system, so that an individual cannot extricate her property should she wish to change religion. (This difficulty is compounded by the fact that under Hindu property law individuals own shares in a family consortium and cannot – or could not prior to some reforms that are unevenly enacted in different states – extricate their own shares.)

39 See here "The Complexity of Groups."

40 Quoted by Amrita Chhachhi in "Identity Politics, Secularism and Women: a South Asian Perspective," in *Forging Identities*, ed. Zoya Hasan (Boulder, CO: Westview, 1994), p. 74. See also Hasan, "Minority Identity, State Policy and the Political Process," in *Forging Identities*, 59–73, at 69–70: "Inevitably, through the Muslim women's Bill, the multiple identities which men and women possess were ignored, as was the distinction between minority and gender identity. Though the issue was one of women's rights, the State only acknowledged an ungendered identity for Muslim women."

41 Other "dispersed groups" include groups based upon occupation, sexual orientation, or a passion for a cause.

42 Mill, *The Subjection of Women* (1869), ed. S. M. Okin (Indianapolis: Hackett, 1988), p. 2.

43 See Agarwal, *A Field*.

44 Isn't it time to declare a moratorium on the use of the word "individualism," with its multiple ambiguities? If it means "egoism" (psychological or ethical) or even a belief that self-sufficiency is best, few Western thinkers have held such views. If it means that each person should be treated as an end, many Western thinkers have held this view (as have many "non-Western" thinkers), but it seems to be a good view to hold; and we would be unlikely to see "the notion that each person is an end" used as a term of abuse, as if just to bring it up made argument unnecessary. See my "The Feminist Critique of Liberalism," in *Sex and Social Justice* (New York: Oxford University Press, 1999).

45 See again Agarwal, *A Field*.

46 See my "The Feminist Critique of Liberalism," in *Sex and Social Justice*, and *WHD* ch. 1.

47 See my treatment of Grotius in *The Cosmopolitan Tradition*, forthcoming (under contract to Yale University Press).

48 *De Iure Belli Atque Pacis* II.20.40. His own list of examples is exceedingly peculiar, and a sign of the grave difficulty, even for a great thinker about this

very issue, in making the distinction he says must above all be made, that is, between mere custom and what belongs to universal moral law. (Although there are some reasonable items on his list, such as cannibalism and systematic murder of the elderly, there are also some items that can serve as a counsel of humility in such matters: for example, he recommends military intervention to stop same-sex intercourse.)

49 On these matters, see further my "India: Implementing Sex Equality through Law," *Chicago Journal of International Law* 2 (2001), 35–58.

50 In order not to say "comprehensive" – see below.

51 I am grateful to Jonathan Riley for raising this point.

52 New Brunswick, NJ: Rutgers University Press, 1997.

Chapter 9

Human rights as foreign policy imperatives

ERIN KELLY

INTERNATIONAL RESPONSIBILITY FOR HUMAN RIGHTS

In this chapter I will argue for a broad conception of moral responsibility with respect to human rights. This conception concerns requirements of justice that extend across borders. I will defend a principle of International Responsibility for Human Rights, according to which widespread human rights abuses require an international response.[1]

Under this principle, the particular obligations that individual states incur will vary as follows: all states are morally prohibited from profiting in their dealings with regimes that violate human rights.[2] Further, a state that is directly implicated causally in human rights violations in another state has a special obligation to support international efforts to halt those violations and to make reparations. This may include shouldering the costs of intervention across borders. And finally, as benefiting members of an international community, wealthier states are obligated to offer aid to poor states, when doing so will further the cause of human rights. I will not explore in any detail strategies states ought to take in order to satisfy the positive obligations the principle imposes. I focus instead on arguments that aim to show that societies in crisis must be brought up to a decent minimum. A reasonable consensus on human rights defines that minimum.

The argument I develop thus addresses the content of human rights as well as their function within international relations. Human rights must be conceived of narrowly if they are to play the role spelled out for them by the principle of International Responsibility for Human Rights. A narrow conception of human rights will not include many rights specified in the Universal Declaration of Human Rights. It will

177

not include, for example, the right to holidays with pay (article 24), the right to education directed at "the full development of the human personality" (article 26), or the right "to enjoy the arts and to share in scientific advancement" (article 27). Nor, more controversially, will it include the full liberal right to freedom of expression (article 19), the right to democratic political participation (article 21), or the right to equal pay for equal work (article 23).

Human rights advocates are likely to endorse the role that I claim human rights ought to play in international relations. They may be unhappy, however, with my narrow construal of the content of human rights.[3] By contrast, political realists who might endorse the narrow content as a matter of political accommodation or in the service of national interest would reject the strongly normative role for human rights that I argue is required by international justice.[4] My argument does not represent a compromise between these two positions. It grows out of a broader moral philosophy of the nature and limits of our obligations to other persons.

I begin with a sketch of the fundamentals of a moral philosophy that leads toward a principle of International Responsibility for Human Rights. A fundamental requirement of morality is this: we should reasonably be able to think that the principles that guide our social interactions are compatible with the basic interests of all persons involved.[5] These social interactions encompass behavior that either directly or substantially affects other persons. The requirement that our behavior be compatible with the interests of those affected by it conveys the idea that all persons have equal moral status. We should be concerned that persons who share the aim of meeting this requirement do not have reasonable objections to our conduct.

We should understand this "impartialist" moral requirement to hold across national borders. People who are committed to standing in morally acceptable relations with other people would affirm the equal moral status and claims of persons generally, regardless of national identity and physical location. Associative obligations to our fellow citizens cannot override the more fundamental moral requirement that the impact of our conduct on other people be compatible with their most basic interests. Distance between persons often gives some indication of when morally relevant interactions or interpersonal effects are present. But there is no reason to think that distance itself matters morally.[6] Our political and economic conduct is often closely connected with the life conditions of persons who live outside our borders. The goods we consume are produced in an international economy and the governments we elect are engaged in political interactions that affect the stability and prosperity of other societies around the world.[7] The rapid and growing exchange of information and the development of new technologies have global implications, including serious consequences for the natural environment. These and other indicators of increasing interdependence and mutual influence between societies only strengthen the moral intuition that the basic interests of other people matter no less when we do not share their culture, ethnicity, religion, national identity or geographical region.[8]

HUMAN RIGHTS AS URGENT NEEDS

Let us refer to societies that are minimally just as "decent" societies.[9] As I shall understand it, the goal of protecting human rights should be shared globally: this goal is at the core of a conception of global justice whose principles would secure joint acceptance by decent societies. That is, concern for human rights is fundamental to a cross-culturally shared (or shareable) conception of international justice. I have supposed that some concern for the basic needs of persons generally, regardless of national affiliation, is a requirement of morality for persons who are engaged socially or politically with one another. It should not be surprising, then, that states supported by morally concerned individuals would endorse some version of International Responsibility for Human Rights.

This principle will meet the normative requirement of joint acceptability, however, only when the role it articulates for human rights in international relations is restricted by a narrow understanding of the content of human rights. The content of human rights must be consistent with a range of not unreasonable understandings of justice that societies may adopt for regulating their internal affairs. We should not assume that all decent societies must be liberal. A society would be intolerant to assume that other societies with different histories and cultures should share the conception of rights particular to its own understanding of domestic justice. The prospects for effective joint deliberation and action in accordance with principles of international justice would thereby be remote.[10] A narrow conception of human rights is designed to avoid this problem.

The requirement of joint acceptability by decent societies of a conception of human rights aims to ensure that each party demonstrates respect and concern for the interests of the others, despite real disagreement over the nature of domestic justice.[11] This requirement is basic to a morality of states as distinguished from a mere *modus vivendi*. The idea that some substantial mutual concern is part of the concept of decency means that adherence to principles of global justice would not be the result of self-interested bargaining between states. There are, of course, self-interested reasons why states would care about the international protection of human rights; no society can guarantee its security against natural disaster, political corruption, internal conflict, or foreign aggression. But acknowledging the mutual concern that is basic to any plausible conception of morality and justice is needed to explain how a shared commitment to the protection of human rights globally could remain sufficiently strong and stable over time.

I submit that in view of their shared moral framework of mutual concern, decent societies would agree that human rights generate moral imperatives. An obvious and primary imperative of human rights is domestic respect and implementation. I take that for granted. My focus is on the idea that when domestic respect and implementation is lacking in a society, human rights generate foreign policy imperatives for other societies. They constitute imperatives for an international response. I now consider several relevant kinds of foreign policy imperatives.[12]

The first sort of foreign policy imperative concerns *prohibitions on engagement*, for example, in trade. All decent states have a moral obligation not to profit from dealings with regimes that systematically violate human rights. It is objectionable as well for countries to allow international corporations that contribute to the violation of human rights elsewhere to operate within their borders. Just as corporations are required to engage in a lawful business, they should be held to human rights standards. Generally speaking, profiting from injustice is wrong, and in the human rights cases with which we are concerned, the matter of injustice is severe. Due consideration to the severity of the injustice supports prohibitions on engagement. Economic disengagement with regimes that are involved with human rights abuses also places valuable pressure on those regimes to change their conduct.

A second sort of imperative involves *duties of aid*. Aid may come in many forms: cash payments, loans, food, clothing and equipment, medical care, education, training, and advice. Decent societies would agree that wealthier societies are under a moral obligation to aid those in need, when providing aid would further the cause of human rights. The inequalities between societies are tremendous and there is much that wealthy states could do to bring poor states up to a minimumly decent level of well-being, without incurring unreasonable costs.[13] A narrow conception of human rights helps to make the point that parties with more resources can help at minor cost to themselves, relative to the stakes involved. This may involve adjusting the terms of international trade, engaging in debt relief and establishing minimum wage regulations for international corporations. In other words, wealthier nations may be under pressure to reform international institutions as well as, in some cases, to provide more direct forms of aid to governments. As rescue examples help to show, it is commonly recognized that those who are in an advantageous position to further important moral aims have stronger obligations to act. This intuition is only strengthened by the fact that the standard of living in poorer countries has often been negatively affected by the conduct of wealthier countries in the international arena. These effects lend further weight to the argument that wealthier states ought to take steps to rectify the most egregious inequalities and to aid those in need up to a decent minimum.[14] It is hard to see how the denial of these duties of aid could be consistent with sincere affirmations of concern for the basic welfare of persons generally.

There is a third sort of imperative generated by the moral urgency of human rights: *requirements of intervention*. Sometimes clear and direct causal connections can be drawn between the conduct of one state and the human rights situation in another. If a state supports a regime that is responsible for widespread human rights violations or if it fosters economic activity that results in human rights violations or deprivations, that state bears a special moral responsibility for rectifying the damage. Its conduct has detrimental effects that are both substantial and direct. This constitutes a blatant violation of the moral compatibility requirement. When the international community reasonably deems it necessary to intervene across borders in order to halt abuses, those states that have been causally involved with the injustice are obligated to support that effort (with soldiers, supplies and money), when they have the resources to do so. Intervention may call for aggressive forms of diplomacy, as well as embargoes and other military operations. I stress the importance of diplomatic intervention, which can be neglected. Of course, given a state's history of questionable foreign policy, its reparative actions ought to be monitored and enforced by international institutions.

One might object that such causal connections are insufficient to support the special responsibilities I have described, since a state's economic or political support for another state's unjust regime might fall short of establishing the supporting state's moral blameworthiness for the abuses of the unjust regime. The supporting state is not the agent of those abuses and may even be ignorant of them. Still, the supporting state's role is, generally speaking, reason enough to establish that the state has an obligation within a collective scheme to attempt to rectify the abuses, even at significant cost and risk, such as incurring deprivations through sanctions or suffering military casualties. Placing special moral pressure on societies that are directly causally responsible for human rights violations is a practical way to end those violations and to organize an international response, and it does not seem unjust.[15]

Thus we have arrived at a certain understanding of how International Responsibility for Human Rights should be distributed. This principle is compelling because the injustices with which the principle is concerned are very serious. Bringing the worst off up to a very basic standard of living is a moral priority. The role played by this threshold represents an important restriction on the scope of the principle. International Responsibility for human rights is concerned with needs that are especially urgent. Moreover, such needs could be recognized by all concerned parties (provided each has some concern for the welfare of persons as such); that is, the urgency of these needs could be collectively endorsed.

Urgent needs, as I understand them, pick out a class of needs that affect the basic welfare of persons, but they do not include all the needs whose fulfillment or deprivation significantly affect how well a person's life goes.[16] Security and subsistence needs, for example, count as urgent. By contrast, winning an Olympic medal may be an important goal for someone, but this does not mean that she has an urgent claim on us to help her achieve it. This may be true even when winning the medal substantially affects her welfare; for instance, achieving her ambition may make a real difference to whether she judges her life as a whole to have been worthwhile.[17] Persons may disagree about the fundamental importance of many commitments and ambitions, including commitments to religion, education, or technological development. A standard of moral urgency, however, must be able to generate consensus among parties who aim for agreement and have some moral concern for one another. On the understanding of urgent needs I am proposing, human rights comprise a suitably thin moral standard of urgency within international relations.

The plausibility of the principle of International Responsibility for Human Rights depends on the possibility that decent societies would agree that human rights violations comprise harms serious enough to warrant an international response and, in particular, a response that would suffice to rectify the injustice. As I have suggested, the urgency of human rights entails that all states have an obligation to refrain from economic engagement with a regime that violates human rights. It also provides the basis for establishing duties for certain states to provide aid or to act more aggressively to change such a regime. In these ways human rights would assume priority in foreign policy. Recognizing the moral urgency of human rights can be viewed as the cost of membership in the international community.

THE COSMOPOLITAN ROOTS OF INTERNATIONAL JUSTICE

The view I have articulated so far fits within the broad framework for thinking about international justice put forth by Rawls in *The Law of Peoples*. In particular, I follow him in holding that a conception of international justice should be jointly acceptable to decent societies. Rawls develops this idea by supposing that principles of international justice are principles that would be chosen by representatives of decent societies behind a veil of ignorance. These representatives, we are to imagine, do not know the size of their territory or population, their relative strength, the extent of their natural resources or economic development, or whether they are liberal or non-liberal.[18] They do assume, however, that the societies they represent are decent. The principles that would be chosen include those that assert the equal status of peoples, the bindingness of treaties, limitations on the right to war and on its conduct, duties of assistance under unfavorable conditions, and the importance of human rights.[19]

The fact that societies rather than individual persons are represented in the hypothetical choice situation when the task is to formulate principles of international justice has led some critics to object that Rawls' law of peoples is insufficiently cosmopolitan.[20] A cosmopolitan view holds that the fundamental unit of moral concern is the person, and that all persons matter morally. Cosmopolitanism is thus individualistic and universalistic; states or societies can have moral claims only derivatively.

Charles Beitz contrasts cosmopolitanism with what he calls "social liberalism." According to the social liberal, the fundamental units of moral concern within a theory of international justice are societies, not individual persons. On this view, we are to understand the international community as a society of domestic societies characterized by a division of labor: "domestic societies are responsible for the well-being of their people, while the international community is responsible for maintaining background conditions in which decent domestic societies can flourish."[21] It is the corporate interests of peoples, rather than the fundamental interests of their members considered as individuals, that are to determine the choice of principles of international conduct.[22]

What is wrong with social liberalism, according to Beitz, is that insofar as it is compatible with concern for human rights, it leaves us without the right sort of justification for them. It is because all persons matter morally that human rights are a pressing concern, not because respect for human rights enables a society to function smoothly and to enjoy peaceful and productive relations with other societies. Our strategic interest in international stability is not what underwrites the moral status of human rights.[23] "For example, the reason why people have human rights not to be tortured," he writes, "does not seem to be that regimes that torture are dangerous to other regimes: although the latter fact (if it is a fact) might justify intervention, it does not imply anything about the moral situation of the tortured."[24]

Beitz is wrong, however, to classify Rawls as a social liberal. The criterion of decency for societies that Rawls puts forth is designed to be responsive to the basic interests of persons; the moral status of peoples or societies can and should be understood to be derivative. Rawls defines decency largely in terms of respect for human rights. I have suggested some further analysis. The content of human rights can be understood to be the subject of negotiation between societies that are supported by morally concerned individuals who affirm that the fundamental interests of all persons matter morally. Recall the moral intuition with which we started: the basic interests of other people matter no less when we do not share their culture, ethnicity, religion, national identity or geographical region. This intuition is central to a cosmopolitan moral philosophy.[25] Using this intuition to guide us helps to show how a conception of international justice that takes seriously the moral claims of peoples or societies can be situated within a cosmopolitan moral conception – one in which shared ethical concern for human rights generates international pressure to ensure that all societies are decent.

The reason we are led to imagine negotiation of the content of human rights taking place between societies or peoples rather than between individual persons is that this acknowledges that persons may have a basic interest in culture: an interest in group membership, in a sense of community, and in realizing shared values, including a collective sense of religious devotion, commitment to a particular language, or an understanding of political authority as, say, gendered or hereditary.[26] I group these sorts of considerations loosely together as cultural claims. Cosmopolitanism must leave room for the importance of cultural claims, since many persons care deeply about them and, properly constrained, cultural claims can be understood to be compatible with the basic human rights of persons as such.[27] It is natural and morally unobjectionable, generally speaking, to form special ties with particular individuals and groups with whom one shares interests and values that define a sense of one's identity. Common values may be expressed, for instance, in educational requirements, the declaration of a state religion, or restrictions on eligibility for political office.

The limitation that human rights places on collective autonomy, however, is serious and important in view of the fact that most societies are multi-ethnic and multi-religious. A narrow approach to human rights can acknowledge the importance to some members of their shared ends and attachments at the same time that it ensures protection for the human rights of members of minority groups. It achieves this by checking to see that its content is compatible with the interests of both liberal and non-liberal societies, provided that all such societies in turn represent the basic interests of all of their members. In other words, a narrow approach makes room for cultural claims while maintaining that all societies must be decent.

THE CONTENT OF HUMAN RIGHTS

I have argued that only a suitably constrained conception of human rights could be endorsed by all decent societies. A narrow conception contrasts with a conception that gives expression to a full-blown understanding of the elements of a good life,[28] or to what is demanded by a conception of justice fully adequate to order the affairs of some domestic society. A narrow conception of human rights must respect variance in local conceptions of justice at the same time that it provides the right sort of guidance within international relations – expressing what we might think of as the limits of toleration. It would be likely to include the following[29]:

(1) *Security rights*: the right to life and to bodily integrity.
(2) *Subsistence rights*: the right to a minimally adequate standard of living (food, clothing, housing, and rudimentary medical treatment, such as low-cost, life-saving vaccinations).[30]

(3) *Individual liberties*: freedom from forced labor, freedom of conscience, freedom of private expression and association, freedom publicly to protest the violation of human rights, free movement, the right to emigrate.[31]

(4) *Political rights*: the right to have reasonable and accountable political representation.[32]

(5) *Due process rights*: the right to public disclosure of criminal charges, a hearing or trial to assess the truth of the charges and public disclosure of the verdict and sentence; the right not to be subject to torture.

A regime that uses terror to "ethnically cleanse" some portion of its territory, for example, clearly violates the security rights of the targeted population. All states have a duty to refrain from economic engagement with such a regime. The case for intervention of some sort is strong when less invasive methods of addressing the problem are unlikely to be effective. Any states that have substantially supported the offending regime are obligated to assist in intervening when it is necessary in order to address the human rights crises.

The CIA helped to destabilize the popularly elected Allende regime in Chile in 1973 and was instrumental in empowering the Pinochet regime. (Let us accept these as the facts.) The Pinochet regime was subsequently responsible for widespread human rights violations – of security, individual liberties, political rights and due process. There is a good case to be made that the United States thus incurred a duty of reparations. A similar case can be made with respect to the human rights crisis in East Timor, given the history of United States support – economic, political and military – for the Indonesian government.

Left off the narrow list of human rights are:

(6) *Rights associated with liberal democracy*: the right to vote, the right to organize political parties, to conduct political campaigns and to run for public office, free public speech, freedom of the press.

(7) *Rights associated with a secular state*: the public teaching and practice of religion, sexual and lifestyle liberties that extend beyond private expression and association.

(8) *Rights associated with the value of equality*: the right to work and to receive equal pay for equal work, the right to education, the right to equal citizenship and to full equality before the law, the right to non-discrimination on the basis of sex, race, religion, and so on.

I certainly do not deny the importance of rights in these latter categories and, in particular, their common connection in practice with the narrow rights I have identified as basic.[33] These connections are important to understand, especially since I am arguing for a conception of human rights that includes subsistence rights. Security and subsistence may depend on non-discrimination. Subsistence may also depend on education and employment. Democracy and many due process rights may be necessary to ensure adequate political representation, and so on.[34] In such cases, human rights can be said to require protective and enabling rights, and the international community is required to support them. Nevertheless, there are good reasons not to count these enabling and protective rights as themselves basic human rights. The problem with classifying them as human rights is the potential conflict this may generate with what I have referred to as cultural claims.[35] Substantial majorities in some societies may reject the value of equality or rights associated with a secular state, majorities that could include groups that are denied these rights.[36] Even so, perhaps it is possible for a hierarchical and religious state, for instance, to secure basic human rights.[37] If it can do this while retaining the support of its population, why should it not retain good standing within the international community? We should take seriously the possibility that what would suffice to secure basic human rights may vary contextually. The narrow list of human rights, by contrast, would appear to concern non-negotiable aspects of basic welfare as well as to constitute preconditions of meaningful consent and the possibility of even limited personal and cultural expression.

Of course, any account of legitimate political authority must address the challenge posed by dissenting minorities. On the account I defend, the human rights, narrowly construed, of all groups within a decent society must be protected; denial or deprivation of these rights is intolerable. Provided that this healthy minimum is ensured, disputes some groups may have with their larger society about further rights (e.g., against discrimination) are not sufficient to undermine their society's decent international standing or to generate imperatives for other societies to respond. Some societies or some of their members may find themselves in sympathy with the complaints of dissenting minorities in other societies, and may even feel moral pressure to assist them, for instance, in promoting democracy or greater equality. Such assistance might be permitted without requiring the international community to support it.

The content of the human rights I have proposed is not unfamiliar.[38] But I believe my proposal adds a new angle in thinking about their justification. What it adds is this: a narrow conception of human rights is justified not only or simply because it expresses an area of overlap among a range of reasonable conceptions of justice. Its narrowness is also justified by the role that decent societies can agree it should play within foreign policy. Human rights are foreign policy imperatives. They generate moral obligations – for non-engagement, aid, or intervention – to be represented within foreign policy as priorities, insofar as a society is in a favorable position to be able to implement the policy or has incurred a special debt. I have stressed that all societies have duties of non-engagement with unjust regimes that flout human rights, and some societies have positive duties, generated by their causal responsibility for human rights abuses or by their wealthy status, to aid or intervene for the sake of human rights. An advantage of treating human rights as generating these duties is that it becomes more difficult to justify weighing-off considerations of human rights against other foreign policy objectives, such as promoting domestic economic gain or non-urgent security interests. This should make it more difficult generally for human rights policy to be compromised. Human rights rhetoric that does not acknowledge the proper priority of concern about human rights distorts the policy role that the moral priority of human rights necessitates – and amounts to no genuine human rights policy at all.

The idea that human rights should function as foreign policy imperatives shows why even societies with relatively similar conceptions of justice, such as liberal societies, would find it appropriate to adopt a pared-down conception of human rights. I have proposed that human rights represent a threshold below which a foreign policy response of some sort is morally required. These are matters about which societies are apt to be cautious. Accordingly, they will be drawn to a narrow construal of the content of human rights.

We ought to think of human rights as generating foreign policy imperatives. This view expresses an idea of international responsibility. The principle of International Responsibility for Human Rights, however, is defensible only on a narrow conception of human rights. Given the foreign policy stakes involved and room for significant and not unreasonable disagreement about the requirements of domestic justice, only a narrow conception of human rights could be collectively endorsed.

NOTES

This paper was presented to the Program on Ethics and Public Life at Cornell University, at the Eastern Division of the American Philosophical Association and also at Libera Università Internazionale degli Studi Sociali, Rome. I am grateful for the critical feedback I received and to my commentator at Cornell, Henry Shue. For their comments and helpful suggestions, I would also like to thank Arthur Applbaum, Deen Chatterjee, David Estlund, James Nickel, Judith Jarvis Thomson, Stephen White, and especially Lionel McPherson.

1 I first defended a version of this principle in "La Responsabilita Internazionale per i Diritti Umani," *Paradigmi*, 18 : 1 (Jan.–Apr. 2000), 43–57.

2 I take human rights violations to cover deprivations through neglect as well as deliberate abuses.

3 See, for example, James W. Nickel, *Making Sense of Human Rights* (Berkeley: University of California Press, 1987), and Fernando R. Tesón, *A Philosophy of International Law* (Boulder, CO: Westview Press, 1998), ch. 4.

4 For a more skeptical view, see, for example, Carl Wellman, *Welfare Rights* (Totowa, New Jersey: Rowman and Littlefield, 1982). Wellman writes, "Our most fundamental welfare rights are at best civic rights, moral rights of the individual as a citizen holding against his or her state. Only in this way can the problem of scarce resources and pointless duplication be solved in theory and the responsibility for meeting human need fixed in practice."(181) A more qualified skepticism can be found in Onora O'Neill, "Transnational Economic Justice," in her *Bounds of Justice* (Cambridge: Cambridge University Press, 2000); see also Onora O'Neill, *Faces of Hunger* (London: Allen and Unwin, 1986), ch. 6.

5 The ideas in this paragraph are discussed at length in my "Personal Concern," *Canadian Journal of Philosophy*, 30: 1 (March 2000), 115–36.

6 See Peter Singer, "Famine, Affluence, and Morality," *Philosophy & Public Affairs*, 1: 3 (Spring 1972), 229–43.

7 There is, in effect, a global basic structure. See Allen Buchanan, "Rawls's Law of Peoples: Rules for a Vanished Westphalian World," *Ethics*, 110: 4 (July 2000), 705–6.

8 See Samuel Scheffler, "Individual Responsibility in a Global Age," *Social Philosophy and Policy*, 23: 1 (Winter 1995), 219–36.

9 This is a term used by John Rawls in his "Law of Peoples," in *On Human Rights*, ed. Stephen Shute and Susan Hurley (New York: BasicBooks, 1993). See also John Rawls, *The Law of Peoples* (Cambridge, Mass.: Harvard University Press, 1999).

10 See Rawls, *The Law of Peoples*. See also John Rawls, "The Idea of Public Reason Revisited," *The University of Chicago Law Review*, 64:3 (Summer 1997), 765–807.

11 It presupposes what Joel Feinberg calls a "community of interest." See his "Collective Responsibility," in *Collective Responsibility: Five Decades of Debate in Applied Ethics*, ed. Larry May and Stacey Hoffman (Savage, MD: Rowman and Littlefield, 1991), p. 62.

12 These imperatives may include the objective of securing compliance with agreements a society has already entered into, agreements that bear on the protection of human rights. This would only make the case for human rights stronger, since it would be part of international law enforcement. But the foreign policy imperatives that stem from human rights have moral force even when a non-compliant state has not signed any agreement.

13 I do not wish to deny that the cost to better-off states of protecting human rights globally could be substantial, even when distributed broadly across the international community. But I believe that human rights can be protected without morally objectionable cost, given reasonable proposals for solving entrenched problems over time. For discussion of what counts as an unreasonable burden, see Richard W. Miller, "Cosmopolitan Respect and Patriotic Concern," *Philosophy & Public Affairs* 27: 3 (Summer 1998), 202–24.

14 The threshold of a decent minimum would appear to be considerably weaker than what would be required by redistributive schemes favored by those who argue for a global "difference principle." See Charles R. Beitz, *Political Theory and International Relations* (Princeton: Princeton University Press, 1979), 136–53; Thomas Pogge, "An Egalitarian Law of Peoples," *Philosophy & Public Affairs*, 23: 3 (Summer 1994), 195–224; and Kok-Chor Tan, "Critical Notice of John Rawls, *The Law of Peoples*," *Canadian Journal of Philosophy*, 31: 1 (March 2001), 113–32.

15 Still, this criterion of responsibility may well fall short of desert as the basis for moral blame. We might better use the concept of liability rather than blameworthiness. For further discussion, see Erin Kelly, "The Burdens of Collective Liability," in *Ethics and Foreign Intervention*, ed. Deen Chatterjee and Don Scheid (Cambridge: Cambridge University Press, 2003). See also Erin Kelly, "Doing without Desert," *Pacific Philosophical Quarterly*, 83: 2 (2002), 180–205. For criticism of the idea of rejecting the concept of desert as fundamental to morality and justice, see Samuel Scheffler, "Responsibility, Reactive Attitudes, and Liberalism in Philosophy and Politics," *Philosophy & Public Affairs*, 21: 4 (Fall 1992), 299–323.

16 See T. M. Scanlon, "Preference and Urgency," *The Journal of Philosophy*, 72: 19 (November 1975), 655–69.

17 I am not assuming, however, that what makes a person's life go best is determined by what satisfies her preferences. Distinguishing a category of urgent needs can be done without embracing any particular theory of what makes a person's life go best.

18 Rawls, *The Law of Peoples*, pp. 32–3.

19 Ibid., p. 37.

20 See, Charles R. Beitz, "Rawls's Law of Peoples," *Ethics*, 110: 4 (July 2000), 669–96. For further discussion of Rawls' view as insufficiently cosmopolitan, see Kok-Chor Tan, "Liberal Toleration in Rawls's Law of Peoples," *Ethics*, 108: 2 (1998), 276–95; and his "Critical Notice of John Rawls, *The Law of Peoples*." See also Thomas Pogge, "An Egalitarian Law of Peoples."

21 Beitz, "Rawls's Law of Peoples", 677.

22 Ibid., 681.

23 Ibid., 685.

24 Ibid., 685.

25 See Martha C. Nussbaum, *For Love of Country: Debating the Limits of Patriotism*, ed. Joshua Cohen (Boston: Beacon Press, 1996); Thomas Pogge, "Cosmopolitanism and Sovereignty," *Ethics*, 103: 1 (October 1992), 48–75; and Beitz, "Rawls's Law of Peoples."

26 See Rawls, *The Law of Peoples*, pp. 61–2.

27 I cannot here address the difficult question of whether cultural claims can give rise to group rights. See Buchanan, "Rawls's Law of Peoples: Rules for a Vanished Westphalian World," 716–21. See also Allen Buchanan, *Secession* (Boulder, CO: Westview Press, 1991), pp. 74–81. I am suggesting, however, that persons whose basic human rights are protected may have no urgent claims to group rights.

28 See, for instance, Martha Nussbaum, "Non-Relative Virtues: An Aristotelian Approach," in *The Quality of Life*, eds. Martha C. Nussbaum and Amartya Sen (Oxford: Oxford University Press, 1993), pp. 242–69, and also her *Women and Human Development: The Capabilities Approach* (Cambridge: Cambridge University Press, 2000).

29 The categories I use were suggested to me by James Nickel.

30 For extensive discussion of the nature of subsistence and security rights, see Henry Shue, *Basic Rights: Subsistence, Affluence, and U.S. Foreign Policy*, 2nd edn. (Princeton: Princeton University Press, 1980).

31 This right will be subject to certain qualifications. It is also not a right to open borders, and does not imply a right to immigrate into the society of one's choice.

32 This need not take the form of a democratic government. See, for instance, Rawls' discussion of a "decent consultation hierarchy," in *The Law of Peoples*, pp. 71–8. Nevertheless, it is a strong requirement, as my remarks in note 36 suggest. Political authority cannot be forced on any group as a mere system of domination.

33 On the interconnectedness of rights, see Nickel, *Making Sense of Human Rights*, p. 104.

34 Amartya Sen has demonstrated that famines do not occur in countries with democratic voting rights and a free press. See *Development as Freedom* (New York: Alfred A. Knopf, 1999), chs. 6–7.

35 See Tesón, *A Philosophy of International Law*, pp. 109–15.
36 If rejection of these values is not supported by a substantial majority, including at least some of those denied the rights in question, we would have reason to suspect that some persons' basic political rights are not protected.
37 See Rawls, *The Law of Peoples*, pp. 71–85.
38 Shue presents a narrow conception of rights in *Basic Rights*. See also Rawls, *The Law of Peoples*. An even narrower conception is presented in Michael Ignatieff, *Human Rights as Politics and Idolatry*, ed. Amy Gutmann (Princeton: Princeton University Press, 2001).

Chapter 10

Human rights and the law of peoples

CHARLES R. BEITZ

One of the many contributions to international thought of *The Law of Peoples* is a distinctive and unorthodox view about human rights.[1] In this essay, I would like to explore the prospects for a political theory of human rights suggested by certain features of this view. I do not pretend to offer an interpretation, or even a variant, of Rawls' view, since in some respects I differ from it. But I believe the conception of human rights in *The Law of Peoples* poses an instructive challenge to adherents of more familiar philosophical views and I want to concentrate here on what might be learned from it.

HUMAN RIGHTS IN POLITICAL PRACTICE

Philosophical conceptions of human rights can go wrong by failing to take seriously the idea of a human right as we find it in international law and politics. We need a political theory of human rights because the international *practice* of human rights is problematic – it is unclear, for example, how these objects called "human rights" should be conceived, why certain values but not others should count as human rights, and what responsibilities, and for whom, attach to human rights. Any theory aiming to shed light on these problems should take account of the elements of international practice that give rise to them.

The contemporary practice of human rights originated during World War II and achieved its first and defining public expression in the Universal Declaration of 1948.[2] The aim was to establish common minimum standards for the legal, political and economic institutions and practices of states, whose achievement could be regarded as a matter of international concern. The manner in which this concern might justifiably be expressed has been a subject of dispute from the outset and international practice has evolved. For example, the original Human Rights Commission discussed and then abandoned a proposal that the UN be authorized to use military force against states in cases of egregious violations.[3] Yet in the last decade human rights violations have been accepted as justifications of ("humanitarian") intervention in cases ranging from Bosnia to East Timor. One should not, however, be misled by the dramatic character of military intervention; more often, and usually less controversially, human rights have justified less momentous forms of international action. For example, human rights have served as standards of public evaluation of the domestic performance of regimes by international organizations. Adherence to human rights has been imposed as a condition of membership in some international organizations and as a qualification for participation in aid and development schemes. Concerns about human rights abuses have also motivated and shaped the work of a growing number of non-governmental organizations devoted to standard-setting and monitoring of domestic government performance, advocacy of political change, public education, and coordination of transnational political activity.[4]

Within the human rights community, international efforts to protect against violations are typically referred to as "enforcement." The modes of action I have just listed are "political enforcement." There is also "judicial enforcement," which can occur at both the domestic and international levels. Many of the framers of modern international human rights doctrine believed that enforcement would ideally take place through national courts, perhaps applying provisions in national constitutions for which the international declarations would function as models and stimulants. But of course, local judicial enforcement may not take place, and from the outset, both global and regional mechanisms have also been envisioned. So, for example, in Europe, Africa and Latin America, regional human rights regimes enable individuals to hold states accountable for infringements of human rights and prescribe sanctions for non-compliance (the regional codes tend to be narrower in scope than the principal UN instruments). There is, relatedly, the rise of the idea that because human rights abuses constitute violations of a state's legal responsibilities to all ("*erga omnes*"), they may be enforceable by all (not only by the victims of abuses or their fellow citizens).[5]

Abstracting from the details about enforcement, we might say that the role of human rights in international political discourse has two aspects: first, human rights violations may serve to justify interference in the internal affairs of states or other local communities; second, they may argue for various external agents, such as international organizations and other states, to commit the resources required for effective interference. Often they do both.

This formula may seem excessively simple when we reflect on the substantive breadth of human rights doctrine. International doctrine recognizes a surprisingly wide range of values as human rights. A crude, initial classification would include rights against certain forms of mistreatment of the person (for example, torture), rights to institutions with certain desirable features (periodic elections), and rights to have access to certain goods (an adequate standard of living). The simple idea that human rights violations provide reasons for outsiders to interfere in a society on behalf of its own members might appear to conceal the diversity of moral issues that can arise in practice. For example, some forms of interference, which aim to change the conduct of local authorities, are unwanted by them and may require the use of force to succeed. Both the use of force and the violation of local political autonomy require a justification. Other forms of interference aim to promote institutional reform, and although not overtly coercive, might employ modes of influence aimed at changing local political preferences over time, without the consent of those acted upon. Here a different problem of justification arises. And still other forms of interference consist of providing assistance to a receptive local government. Here there is neither coercion nor a violation of local autonomy; the main ethical problem is to determine the amount of assistance owed and the appropriate distribution of the cost of providing it.

It would be a mistake, of course, to believe that there is any very neat mapping of forms of political action on to categories of rights. Not implausibly, for example, the industrial countries could do more to promote economic development in poor societies by changing world trade rules that allow agricultural protection than by increasing direct development assistance. So we should not simply assume that rights of access to certain goods are associated with duties on others to provide those goods. Nevertheless, it has to be acknowledged that international human rights doctrine embraces a diversity of values and that the protection of these values under a variety of political and social circumstances could call for many different kinds of political action – and indeed, by many different political actors (not only states and international organizations). I do not believe these facts argue against our earlier description of the role of human rights so much as complicate it. They emphasize that a realistic understanding of contemporary human rights practice must work with a broader interpretation of the ideas of "interference" and "enforcement" than the conventional meanings of those words might suggest.

TWO APPROACHES TO HUMAN RIGHTS

Most philosophers who have written about human rights adopt one or another variant of what I shall call the "orthodox" conception. In contrast, I shall say that the view of human rights in *The Law of Peoples* represents a "practical" conception.[6] In this section, I try to explain the difference.

John Simmons recently described human rights as follows:

Human rights [his emphasis] are rights possessed by all human beings (at all times and in all places), simply in virtue of their humanity . . . . [They] will have the properties of universality, independence (from social or legal recognition), naturalness, inalienability, non-forfeitability, and imprescriptibility. Only so understood will an account of human rights capture the central idea of rights that can always be claimed by any human being.[7]

These remarks occur in an essay devoted to human rights in the political theories of Locke and Kant. Although there is no explicit reference to modern international doctrine, Simmons writes that a comparison of these theories "should help us to see more clearly the range of options available to contemporary defenders of human rights."[8] Simmons's characterization of these rights represents with unusual clarity the view I believe is orthodox among philosophers.

The distinguishing feature of this conception is the idea that human rights have an existence in the moral order that is independent of their expression in international doctrine. Typically, they are thought to reside at a deep, perhaps even a fundamental, level of our moral beliefs and to be discoverable by reason or rational intuition. Thus, human rights are sometimes said to be "natural" or to belong to persons "as such" or "simply in virtue of their humanity." On such views, international human rights – that is, the rights of the declarations and covenants – derive their authority, to whatever extent they have authority, from these underlying values that constitute their foundation. The task of the theorist of international human rights doctrine is to describe or discover these objects properly called "human rights" and then to say which of the entitlements alleged to be human rights in international doctrine pass muster.

The practical view, by contrast, takes the doctrine and discourse of human rights as we find them in international political practice as basic. Questions like What are human rights?, What human rights do we have?, and Who has duties to act when human rights are violated? are understood to refer to objects of the sort called "human rights" in contemporary international life, however these are best conceived. There is no assumption of a prior or independent layer of fundamental values whose nature and content can be discovered independently of reflection about the international realm and then used to interpret and criticize international doctrine. Instead, the functional role of human rights in international discourse and practice is regarded as definitive of the idea of a human right, and the content of international doctrine is worked out by considering how the doctrine would best be interpreted in light of this role.

The distinction between orthodox and practical views of human rights is not the same as that between foundationalist and non-foundationalist (or "sentimentalist") conceptions suggested by Rorty.[9] It is true that orthodox views are foundationalist in an obvious sense: they interpret international human rights as the public, doctrinal expression of a distinctive underlying (or foundational) order of moral values conceived as rights. It does not follow, however, that practical views are non-foundational, if by this is meant that such views must deny that there are intelligible moral grounds for international human rights. It would be better to put the contrast as follows. Orthodox views treat the justification of international human rights as internal to the conception of a human right: once we understand the nature of a human right, we shall understand what must be said to justify claims about the legitimate content of international doctrine. By contrast, practical views treat the question of the justification of human rights as separable from the question of their nature. It is comprehensible, on such a view, that people might agree about the nature of international human rights but disagree about the kinds of considerations that ground them. It is hard to see how adherents of the orthodox view could make sense of this prospect.

HOW ORTHODOX VIEWS MISLEAD

Orthodox views can yield skeptical results. For example, Maurice Cranston famously held that the only rights worthy of the adjective "human" were the contemporary descendants of (what he thought were) the classical natural rights to life, liberty, and property. The rest – in particular, so-called "economic and social rights" – were elements of a political ideal without either the universality or the preemptory force he believed should attach to genuine human rights.[10] Cranston wrote at the height of the Cold War, and his position has often been criticized on substantive grounds. But his critics have seldom disputed the premise he shares with other adherents of the orthodox view.

But I believe the premise is suspect. Orthodox conceptions tend to distort rather than illuminate international human rights practice and therefore produce unjustifiably skeptical conclusions about international doctrine. Perhaps there are objects of the kind that orthodoxy considers to be "human rights," but those objects, if they exist, are to be distinguished from the objects referred to in international doctrine and practice as "human rights." Orthodoxy about international human rights seems to me, finally, dogmatic.[11]

According to the orthodox view, human rights – that is, the underlying moral values that international human rights seek to express – share several distinguishing characteristics with "natural rights." First, human rights are pre-institutional – that is, they are rights one would have in a pre-political "state of nature." Second, human rights belong to people "solely in virtue of their common humanity." They are grounded on characteristics that people might be said to possess when they are considered in abstraction from any social situation; therefore the reasons why we should care about them must not refer to aspects of people's merely contingent social relationships. Finally, human rights are timeless – all human beings at all times and places would be justified in claiming them.

A moment's reflection will show that the combined effect of these conditions is to limit severely the values that can be counted as genuine human rights. This is why adherents of the orthodox view tend to be skeptical that human rights should be construed as embracing the very wide range of political values found in international doctrine. But it is a serious question why international human rights should be interpreted in this way. Why not say that the assimilation of human rights (as found in international doctrine) to human rights (construed as fundamental moral values) is an elision?

Why, for example, conceive of human rights as pre-institutional? The idea simply would not occur to anybody not already in the thrall of the natural rights tradition. The reason is that natural rights and the human rights found in international doctrine do not fill the same conceptual space. Principles of natural right, at least in the more liberal variants (such as Locke's) that modern theorists typically have in mind, were attempts to formulate constraints on the use of a government's coercive power in circumstances of religious and moral diversity. They make sense only against a background assumption that a central problem of political life is the protection of individual freedom against a predictable threat of tyranny or oppression. But no disinterested reading of the historical and political record could represent the motivating concern of international human rights as this limited. To make sense of the human rights of the international declarations one must suppose they have a larger aspiration – for example, to describe social conditions conducive to the living of dignified human lives. They represent a more ambitious assumption of responsibility for the public sphere than was required by the motivating concerns of classical natural rights theories. One is entitled to believe this is wrong-headed, but such a belief would be a substantive position in political theory, not a deduction from a proper understanding of the idea of a human right.

Or consider the idea that human rights belong to people "solely in virtue of their common humanity" and without reference to their affiliations and memberships.[12] Philosophical acceptance of this idea owes a great deal to the influence of H. L. A. Hart's article, "Are There Any Natural Rights?"[13] Hart distinguishes between "general rights" and "special rights." Special rights arise out of "special transactions [or] special relationships" such as promises, contracts, or membership in a political society, whereas general rights belong to "all men capable of choice . . . in the absence of those special conditions which give rise to special rights."[14] Hart holds that natural rights must be "general" because they belong to men "*qua* men and not only if they are members of some society or stand in some special relation to each other."[15] Hart himself never mentions the phrase "human rights," but those influenced by Hart's distinction have thought that human rights, because they are supposed to be claimable by anyone, must be "general rights" in his sense.

This, again, is a highly restrictive premise. It would, for example, probably exclude the right to an adequate standard of living (Universal Declaration, art. 25.1) from the catalog of genuine human rights. We shall consider the grounds of such a right at greater length below. For now the question is: why accept an analytical premise that excludes such a right *tout court*? Human rights of the kind found in international doctrine, or at least some of them, might rather be conceived as a category of "special rights" – for example, rights that arise out of people's relationships as participants in a global political economy – or as political conclusions derived from an array of ethical considerations, including those of humanity, reciprocity, and perhaps compensation. These possibilities are obscured if one infers from the fact that human rights are supposed to be *claimable* by everyone, that they must be *general* in Hart's sense. But I can see no good reason for the inference. To hold that a right to an adequate standard of living cannot be a human right because it does not fit the paradigm of a "general right" seems, once again, to achieve a normative conclusion by conceptual fiat.

Finally, consider the thought that human rights are timeless. The idea is tempting as an inference from the condition of universality, and because the natural rights of the tradition were supposed to be timeless. But again I believe this encourages a misconception of the point of international human rights. It seems unlikely that its framers intended the doctrine of human rights to apply, for example, to the ancient Greeks or to China in the Ch'in dynasty or to European societies in the Middle Ages. International human rights, to judge by the contents of the declaration and covenants, are suited to play a role in a certain range of societies. Roughly speaking, these are societies which have at least some of the defining features of modernization: e.g., a minimal legal system (including a capability for enforcement), an economy with a portion of employment in industry rather than agriculture, some participation in global cultural and economic life, and the existence or prospect of a public institutional capacity to raise revenue and provide essential collective goods. The human rights of international doctrine are protections against a variety of threats to basic human interests which predictably arise in societies with these features.[16] This means it would be unrealistic to regard the catalog of internationally protected human rights as fixed or invariant across time. This fact would be troubling if there were some reason, external to international practice, to believe that human rights should be eternal. But what reason might that be?

These reflections do not amount to a refutation of orthodox views, but I hope to have accomplished two more modest results. The first is to show that the inferences drawn from any such conception about the scope and content of international human rights are normative conclusions requiring a defense; it is a sleight-of-hand to present them as analytic. The second is to raise doubt about the relevance of such an exercise to the main theoretical questions about international human rights. These questions pertain to a developing political and social practice which is in important respects historically novel. It is just dogmatic to hold that any adequate understanding of this practice should *begin* by identifying the objects of theoretical interest with objects that originated in a particular philosophical tradition and were constructed for quite different purposes.

TOWARD A PRACTICAL CONCEPTION:
RAWLS ON HUMAN RIGHTS

The account of human rights found in *The Law of Peoples* points toward a more constructive understanding of human rights. According to Rawls, human rights "express a special class of urgent rights" whose violation "is equally condemned by both reasonable liberal peoples and decent hierarchical peoples." Their political function is to "restrict the justifying reasons for war and its conduct, and they specify limits to a regime's internal autonomy."[17] The consistency of a regime's domestic law with human rights is necessary for the regime to be a member "in good standing in a reasonably just Society of Peoples" and "is sufficient to exclude justified and forceful intervention by other peoples."[18]

Although he holds that human rights "are binding on all peoples and societies,"[19] Rawls does not claim that they belong to human beings "as such" or "in virtue of their common humanity," nor that they are universal in the sense of being recognized by all significant cultural moral codes. They can be said to be common to all persons only in a special sense, internal to the Law of Peoples: they are compatible with all reasonable political doctrines, including those of both "liberal" and "decent" peoples.[20] This conception of human rights is self-consciously eclectic: for the purposes of the Law of Peoples, Rawls explicitly disowns an orthodox idea of human rights as based on "a theological, philosophical, or moral conception of the human person."[21]

What is going on here? Some light may be shed by considering Rawls' remarks, in *A Theory of Justice*, on the distinction between the role and the content of justice. He suggests that although people may disagree about the content of principles of justice – that is, they may hold different *conceptions* of justice – they may nevertheless agree about the role these principles should play in moral and political thought. The *concept* of justice is identified by the discursive role commonly presupposed by these conceptions. It is then left open to moral argument to settle on one of the rival conceptions as the best or most reasonable interpretation of the concept.[22]

The brief remarks on human rights in *The Law of Peoples* might reflect a similar line of thought. One might believe that although people disagree about the content of human rights, they can agree about the role that human rights play in practical reasoning about international affairs. Agreement about the role of human rights defines the kind of thing that particular conceptions of human rights are conceptions *of*; that is, of that about which normative disagreement typically occurs. Writing about the concept of justice, Rawls says that agreement about the role of principles does not settle any important questions about their content.[23] It does, however, give some structure to dispute about the attractiveness of the various alternative conceptions, since some of these will be better suited to the public role of justice than others. Similarly in the case of human rights, some views about the content of human rights may be more persuasive, once we understand what human rights are for, than others. And indeed, when he turns to consider the content of human rights doctrine, the reasons Rawls adduces to explain why some but not other values should count as human rights are of just this character: they refer to the capacity of a doctrine of human rights with a certain content to serve as a shared public basis of action for both liberal and decent societies committed to preserving a world in which such societies can prosper.[24]

I noted earlier that a practical conception would treat the justification of human rights as a distinct problem from that of their content. Rawls' view about human rights has this feature. Human rights "are a proper subset of the rights possessed by the members of a liberal constitutional democratic regime, or of the rights of the members of a decent hierarchical society."[25] Members of each type of society would presumably be drawn to human rights for their own reasons, taking into account the need for an international doctrine that could also be supported by societies of the other type. There is no need for a single, commonly agreed justification of human rights.[26] In this respect, Rawls' approach to human rights recalls the view taken by the framers of the Universal Declaration of 1948. They deliberately refrained from proposing any foundational theory, believing that adherents of diverse ethical traditions would find reasons of their own to support the standards set forth in the declaration.[27]

How accurate is Rawls' account of the role played by human rights in moral discourse about international affairs? The main point of similarity, of course, is the recognition of human rights as justifying grounds of interference by the international community in the internal affairs of states. There are also some differences. For example, Rawls does not describe human rights as enforceable entitlements, as they are regarded in the regional human rights courts. He notices but does not take into account the broad array of noncoercive political and economic measures that might be used by states and international organizations to influence the internal affairs of societies where human rights are threatened. These measures importantly include what might better be classified as assistance than interference. And he does not represent human rights as justifications for individuals and nongovernmental organizations to engage in reform-oriented political action. In all of these respects, Rawls' conception of the political role of human rights is narrower than what we observe in present practice (though it is not inconsistent). Rawls offers no account of the variations, and I believe it would be better, in a theory aimed at interpreting present practice, to adopt the broader and more realistic conception.

Rawls' view diverges more substantially from international doctrine in connection with the content of human rights. He distinguishes human rights in the Law of Peoples – for convenience, "human rights proper" (Rawls' phrase) – from a conception of human rights that "simply expands the class of human rights to include all the rights that liberal governments guarantee."[28] Human rights "proper" include rights to life (including "the means of subsistence"), personal liberty (including liberty, though not equal liberty, of conscience), personal property and equal treatment under law. These rights are essential to any "common good idea of justice" and therefore are not "peculiarly liberal or special to the Western tradition."[29] Among the rights included in international doctrine but omitted from Rawls' list are freedom of expression and association (beyond whatever is required for freedom of conscience and religious practice) and the rights of democratic political participation, as well as economic rights that cannot be understood as applications of the right to the means of subsistence. These rights distinguish liberal democratic societies from "decent hierarchical societies" as Rawls understands them. He observes that these and certain other rights of the declaration "seem more aptly described as stating liberal aspirations" or "appear to presuppose specific kinds of institutions."[30]

Rawls is certainly correct that any plausible theory of human rights should enable us to distinguish between genuine human rights and the objects identified as human rights in political practice. Otherwise, the theory would yield no critical leverage. His own account of the distinction relies on an idea of reasonable toleration among peoples – specifically, toleration by liberal societies of those non-liberal societies which he labels as "decent hierarchical peoples."[31] I have considered some objections to this account elsewhere.[32] Here, I would like to concentrate on the more abstract and constructive idea behind it, which would survive even if the objections were accepted.

This is the perception, which is essential to any practical conception, that the public role of a political doctrine of human rights constrains its content. The most important consequence of this is that the doctrine should be constructed so that appeals to human rights, under conditions to be specified, will suffice to justify interference by the world community or its agents in the internal affairs of states. This is one important respect in which a practical approach to human rights can be critical of existing practice.

I believe that this requirement will limit the content of a plausible doctrine of human rights in at least three ways. First, it will exclude from the catalog of genuine human rights those that protect interests that could not be seen as significant by most members of any existing society. I do not mean that genuine human rights should be restricted, as John Vincent once put it, to the "least common denominator" of the world's moral cultures.[33] Such a restriction makes human rights doctrine objectionably dependent on the range of actual agreement. A better way to state the condition would be that human rights should constitute principles of action that persons in any culture would have reason to accept. This is a complicated idea and I cannot offer an analysis of it here.[34] But if interference in defense of human rights is to be distinguished from an unwarranted imposition of alien values, then some such condition is essential.

Secondly, it should be possible for political agents to regard the doctrine, taken as a whole, as a reasonable basis for cooperation in international schemes to enforce its requirements. Whatever its form, cooperation to advance human rights will impose costs on some agents; the ends achieved by these enforcement schemes should be sufficiently urgent to provide a reason for agents to accept these costs. I put the point in this awkward way because the protection of human rights on a particular occasion is not best seen as a one-off affair; however incomplete, there is an international practice of human rights, and it is cooperation in the practice that should be reasonable for its participants. This means that human rights doctrine – that is, the set of standards that can trigger international action – should be appraised as a package of requirements. It is more than an arbitrary historical fact that human rights as we find them embody a negotiated compromise among states, and the 1993 Vienna Declaration's insistence that international human rights are "indivisible and interdependent and interrelated"[35] did not so much state a philosophical thesis as express a political logic.

A third consideration concerns the means of interference. Whatever its form – and as I have suggested we must read "interference" or "enforcement" broadly – interference in a society to protect human rights constitutes political action and therefore falls under ethical constraints that apply to any such action. These constraints have to do, broadly speaking, with economy of force and respect for innocent life. Here it may be suggestive to think of the *jus ad bellum*. So, for example, the means of interference should obey analogs of the conventional constraints of discrimination and proportionality, and there should be a reasonable expectation of success in accomplishing its aims. Values for which there are no means of interference realistically available satisfying these constraints could not count as human rights.

Obviously, these conditions need interpretation and defense. I cannot attempt that here. I state them as grounds for the conjecture that a practical theory could achieve some significant critical leverage on the practice as we observe it by taking seriously the interference-justifying role of human rights. Such a theory need not be, as one might have thought initially, simply an endorsement of present practice.

THE HUMAN RIGHT TO AN ADEQUATE STANDARD OF LIVING

So far I have described a practical conception of human rights and drawn the contrast with orthodox views. In this section I would like to explore how these relatively abstract ideas bear on some questions about a particularly important and controversial human right. This is the right, proclaimed in Article 25.1 of the Universal Declaration, to "a standard of living adequate for the health and well-being of [oneself] and of [one's] family." Here, as clearly as anywhere in the Declaration, the central concerns of this volume are brought into sharp relief.

Three questions are particularly important: Is the standard of living the kind of value that could qualify as the subject matter of a human right at all? What would it mean for there to be such a right? If such a right were violated, who would have obligations to act, and why?

How might a practical theory of human rights reply to these questions? We do not find much help in *The Law of Peoples*. It is true that

Rawls counts among genuine human rights a right to "the means of subsistence." But he says very little about the grounds of this right, aside from the (important) observation that "the sensible and rational exercise of all liberties, of whatever kind . . . always implies having general all-purpose economic means."[36] In particular, there is no explanation of the nature and extent of the duties associated with this right or the reasons why those who might be called upon to contribute to its satisfaction should believe themselves obligated to do so. Moreover, given Rawls' conception of human rights, it is unclear what could be the practical force of a human right to subsistence. He holds that human rights are conditions whose violation would justify coercive intervention by outsiders in a society's internal affairs, but it seems unlikely, except in rare cases (like that of Somalia), that failures to satisfy subsistence rights would yield to coercive intervention.[37]

So we are left to consider for ourselves how someone who takes a practical view might answer these questions. Let us ask first whether the standard of living is an appropriate subject-matter for a human right at all. On this point the most important conclusion from our earlier discussion is negative: if we give up the familiar forms of orthodoxy, we obviate the need to conform a conception of international human rights to the formal constraints of the foundational moral idea. We need not worry, for example, whether, given a philosophically defensible conception of *natural* rights, there could be natural *welfare* rights. That question simply does not arise.

On a practical view, the question whether the standard of living is an appropriate subject-matter for a human right is answered differently: by considering whether such a right could play the functional roles for which human rights are intended. In the previous section, I listed three conditions a human right should satisfy to qualify under this criterion. I cannot carry out the exercise here, but I believe brief reflection shows that a human right to an adequate standard of living would quality under all three conditions.

Or would it? Someone might object that international institutions are weak and dispose very limited resources of wealth and power. In view of this, the objection holds, it would be best to limit the possible causes of international action so that scarce resources can be sufficiently concentrated to have real effect. To do otherwise diverts attention from the most important deprivations and devalues the currency of human rights by reducing the chances that efforts to defend them will succeed.[38]

The objection cannot be dismissed as arising from a faulty conception of human rights; it takes seriously, as it should, the concern that a doctrine of human rights be suited for its intended public role. However, I believe the objection rests on an excessively pessimistic estimate of the available international capacity to protect human rights joined with a failure to register an accurate comparison of the relative urgency of protecting various categories of rights. On the first point, it should be remembered that interference to protect human rights can take many forms and that the resources needed for success may not be fungible. For example, there may not be any way to redeploy funds and technology devoted to agricultural development assistance so as to encourage respect for the rule of law or to discourage cruelty and political oppression. On the second point, it is hardly obvious that it would always be better or more urgent – assuming this were realistically the choice – to save some people from the cruelty of oppressive political rule than to save others from the depredations of malnutrition and preventable childhood disease. How, exactly, such an unhappy choice should be made is a complicated question, but there do not seem to be grounds for thinking that either alternative is categorically to be preferred.

The second question is: what would it mean for there to be a human right to an adequate standard of living? When we assert its existence, what are we asserting? To be clear: the question is not, What is an adequate standard of living? I assume for present purposes that we can give an analysis of this idea, following the views of Amartya Sen, in terms of the development of basic capabilities.[39] The question I mean to ask is different: What would it mean to have a *human right* to an adequate standard of living?

A plausible reply might go as follows. The primary responsibility to satisfy human rights rests with domestic-level societies, so the most elementary implication of the claim that people have human rights to an adequate standard of living is that states should take steps to ensure that their people have access to sufficient resources to achieve their basic capabilities. But human rights are supposed to state conditions whose satisfaction is a matter of global concern. So a human right to an adequate standard of living must have at least two further features, corresponding to two reasons why a government or society might fail in these responsibilities. First, a government might have the capacity to undertake policy measures aimed at securing the substance of the right, but fail to do so (or fail to do so effectively). The fact that there is a human right means that a government cannot object that external interference aimed at making good this failure, assuming this were to be feasible and likely to succeed, is a violation of its sovereign prerogatives. Second, a society might have the will but lack the capacity to achieve an adequate standard of living through indigenous efforts. In such cases, the human right to an adequate standard of living serves as the ground of a duty on appropriately placed outside agents to assist the society to satisfy the right.[40]

The relevant idea of assistance will plainly be fairly broad and will leave considerable room for quasi-empirical dispute about how it would be best accomplished. Among other things, this means that an individual whose human right is violated does not necessarily have a claim-right against any specific individual agent for direct provision of the substance of the right – for food, for example, or for shelter or health care. This seems to depart from the ordinary understanding of a right and might therefore prompt an objection. What could be the practical value of human rights if they cannot be depended on to serve as grounds of claims?

To reply: human rights do indeed serve as grounds of claims – just not, or not necessarily, claims against particular agents for direct provision of the substance of the right. Human rights are standards for law and public policy whose breach on a sufficient scale constitutes a pro tanto justification of remedial international action. If an individual whose human right is unsatisfied has a claim – that is, a moral claim – it is a claim, in the first instance, on her own society to undertake whatever public policies would be required to ensure the satisfaction of the right, and derivatively, on capable and appropriately placed external agents for political action to remedy the breach.[41] This is not odd, once we grasp the political role of human rights.

Finally, there is the question of responsibility for human rights. When the human right to an adequate standard of living is not satisfied at the domestic level, who is responsible to do what, and why? The first part of this question has been well discussed by Henry Shue in connection with subsistence rights and I believe substantially all of his account applies here.[42] The short of it is that a judgment about who is responsible to act depends on the intersection of considerations of causal responsibility for a deprivation and capacity to intervene effectively. Any such judgment is complicated by the fact that the world lacks a global institutional capacity to allocate and coordinate obligations. Agents often must decide how and when to act without knowledge or assurance about the plans of others. There are analogs of the familiar problems associated with providing public goods under anarchy. This means that judgments about responsibilities to act will have to be pragmatic (or, as Shue says, "strategic").

The second part of the question asks why an agent that is in a position to act has reason to do so. The most straightforward case is that of an agent that could avoid a deprivation by changing conduct that brings the deprivation about; here, the agent has, at least prima facie, a responsibility grounded on a general duty not to cause harm. It is important to observe, as Thomas Pogge argues, that the ethical implications will be more far-reaching than they may seem if the deprivations are the avoidable results of policies enforced by existing global institutions, for then it could be said that those who support and participate in these institutions thereby acquire responsibilities based on the duty not to cause harm.[43]

Considerations of this kind do not, however, exhaust the reasons to act in support of a human right to an adequate standard of living. If we take the focal case of wealthy countries that are in a position to contribute to international development efforts, then I believe that considerations of both humanity and international justice will provide independent reasons to contribute. The application of considerations of humanity will be obvious. There is a great deal that might be said about reasons of international justice. The point I would like to emphasize here is that one does not need an ambitiously cosmopolitan theory of global justice to explain obligations to contribute to the satisfaction of a right to an adequate standard of living.[44] Indeed, I believe an argument is available in the spirit of the political theory of *The Law of Peoples* (though, of course, Rawls himself does not offer such an argument).

Since I cannot develop the argument here, I simply offer it as a conjecture.[45] Imagine a global original position composed of representatives of peoples, with the interests of peoples interpreted as being sensitive to the interests of the individual persons who compose them. ("Sensitive to" need not cause the argument to collapse into some form of cosmopolitanism; a people's interests can be sensitive to the interests of individual persons without being constructed exclusively from them.) Suppose that the parties are deprived by a veil of ignorance of information about the economic circumstances of their societies. The conjecture is that under these circumstances the representatives would agree to a principle establishing a human right to an adequate standard of living with the elements described earlier (including, in relevant conditions, a requirement of international contribution to the costs of satisfying it).

The conjecture is motivated by two thoughts. First, the parties would understand, as Rawls observes in his account of subsistence rights, the central importance, for persons, of the means of life: having a threshold of material means is necessary for satisfying virtually any rational human interest. Second, the parties would see that acceptance of an international responsibility to ensure a material minimum is an essential element of a complete doctrine of human rights which, considered as a package, could constitute a basis of willing cooperation among (liberal and decent) peoples.

An argument along these lines would establish that the right to an adequate standard of living is an element of the Law of Peoples, or as we might say, a requirement of international justice.[46] It states a condition that anyone could reasonably expect social institutions to satisfy, and whose satisfaction in all societies represents a reasonable long-term goal of the international community. In this respect it fits the practical conception of a human right that we discussed earlier.

CONCLUDING COMMENT

Let me conclude by noting very briefly an objection to the general conception of human rights advanced in this essay. According to this view, the objection holds, human rights, or anyway those like the right to an adequate standard of living, seem to be no more than highly desirable social goals. But this omits what is really important about human rights. Rights have a preemptory quality – they demand immediate satisfaction, not simply efforts to satisfy them at some future time. This feature of rights is present in the orthodox view, as it was in traditional conceptions of natural right. A conception of human rights that cannot make sense of this quality, the objector might say, is radically incomplete.

In reply, two observations. First, according to a practical conception, human rights are not simply desirable goals; they are morally necessary ones. To say that something is a human right is to say that social institutions that fail to protect the right are defective – they fall short of meeting conditions that anyone would reasonably expect them to satisfy – and that international efforts to aid or promote reform are legitimate and in some cases may be morally required. To say this is to say something – in fact, it says quite a lot. Second, to the extent it must be conceded that human rights, unlike the familiar natural rights, do not always issue in directives for immediate remedial action when they are violated, one might wonder whether anything is lost in the concession. If we understand international human rights practically, what more might we reasonably wish to say?

NOTES

For comments on earlier drafts, I am grateful to Deen Chatterjee, Joshua Cohen, Thomas Pogge, Nick Rengger, Marion Smiley, and Andrew Williams, and to audiences at St. Andrews, Harvard, and Yale Universities.

1 John Rawls, *The Law of Peoples* (Cambridge: Harvard University Press, 1999) (henceforth, *LP*).

2 The declaration and other pertinent documents can be found in Ian Brownlie, ed., *Basic Documents on Human Rights*, 3d edn. (Oxford: Clarendon Press, 1992). I have discussed the political role of human rights in "Human Rights as a Common Concern," *American Political Science Review*, 95: 2 (June 2001), 269–82.

3 M. Glen Johnson, "A Magna Carta for Mankind: Writing the Universal Declaration of Human Rights," in *The Universal Declaration of Human Rights: A History of its Creation and Implementation*, ed. M. Glen Johnson and Janusz Symonides (Paris: UNESCO, 1998), p. 32.

4 This role of human rights doctrine is emphasized in William Korey, *NGOs and the Universal Declaration of Human Rights: "A Curious Grapevine"* (New York: St. Martin's Press, 1998) and Margaret Keck and Kathryn Sikkink, *Activists Beyond Borders: Advocacy Networks in International Politics* (Ithaca: Cornell University Press, 1998).

5 This idea first appeared in dicta in the International Court of Justice's opinion in *Barcelona Traction, Light and Power, Ltd.* (Belg. v. Spain), 1970 I. C. J. Reports. 3 (Feb. 5), paras. 33–4. For its general acceptance, see American Law Institute, *Restatement (Third) of the Foreign Relations Law of the United States* (St. Paul, Minn.: American Law Institute, 1987), sec. 702.

6 A similar – although perhaps not the same – distinction is described by Peter Jones in his illuminating article, "International Human Rights: Philosophical or Political?," in *National Rights, International Obligations*, eds. Simon Caney, David George, and Peter Jones (Boulder: Westview, 1996), pp. 183–204.

7 A. John Simmons, "Human Rights and World Citizenship," in *Justification and Legitimacy: Essays on Rights and Obligations* (Cambridge: Cambridge University Press, 2001), p. 185.

8 Ibid., p. 180.

9 Richard Rorty, "Human Rights, Rationality, and Sentimentality," in *On Human Rights: The Oxford Amnesty Lectures 1993*, ed. Stephen Shute and Susan Hurley (New York: Basic Books, 1993), pp. 115–17. Rorty attributes the idea of human rights foundationalism to the Argentinian jurist Eduardo Rabossi.

10 Maurice Cranston, *What Are Human Rights?* (London: Bodley Head, 1973), pp. 65–71.

11 I explain why in "What Human Rights Mean," *Daedalus* 132: 1 (Winter 2003), 36–46, on which I rely for the argument in the next few paragraphs.

12 One might believe this characteristic follows from an understanding of human rights as "universal," but this would be a mistake. The Declaration holds that human rights are universal in the sense that everyone is entitled to claim them: human rights are universal in application. Nothing obviously follows about their justification.

13 H. L. A. Hart, "Are There Any Natural Rights?," *Philosophical Review*, 64: 2 (1955), 175–91.

14 Ibid., pp. 183, 188; on political society as a cooperative scheme, see p. 185.

15 Ibid., p. 175. Compare Peter Jones, *Rights* (New York: St. Martin's Press, 1994), p. 81.

16 Jack Donnelly, *Universal Human Rights in Theory and Practice* (Ithaca, NY: Cornell University Press, 1989), p. 26. On rights as guarantees against "standard threats," see also Henry Shue, *Basic Rights*, 2nd edn. (Princeton: Princeton University Press, 1996), pp. 13, 32; and T. M. Scanlon, "Human Rights as a Neutral Concern," in *Human Rights and U.S. Foreign Policy*, ed. Peter G. Brown and Douglas MacLean (Lexington, Mass.: Lexington Books, 1979), pp. 83–92.

17 "In this way," Rawls continues, "they reflect the two basic and historically profound changes in how the powers of sovereignty have been conceived since World War II. First, war is no longer an admissible means of government policy and is justified only in self-defense, or in grave cases of intervention to protect human rights. And second, a government's internal autonomy is now limited." Rawls, *LP*, p. 79.

18 Ibid., p. 80.

19 Ibid.

20 This idea of the "commonness" of human rights needs elucidation. I consider it in "Human Rights as a Common Concern," pp. 274–6.

21 Ibid., pp. 78, 81.

22 John Rawls, *A Theory of Justice*, rev. edn. (Cambridge: Harvard University Press, 1999), p. 5. Rawls' remarks, as he notes, are influenced by H. L. A. Hart's distinction between a concept and its conceptions in *The Concept of Law* (Oxford: Clarendon Press, 1961), pp. 155–9.

23 Rawls, *A Theory of Justice*, p. 5.

24 *LP*, p. 80 n. 23, and p. 81.

25 Ibid., p. 81.

26 To think about human rights in this way would be to regard human rights, in Rawls' phrase, as a "political doctrine" constructed for a certain role in world politics. See Jones, "International Human Rights: Philosophical or Political?," pp. 186ff. Rawls' reservations about Jones's interpretation of the view (*LP*, p. 81 n. 25) do not seem to go to this characterization. Rawls himself describes

the Law of Peoples as a "public political conception of justice" for the Society of Peoples (p. 123).

27 See Mary Ann Glendon's sensitive account of these deliberations which, among other things, challenges the widespread idea that the content of the declaration is simply the result of a political compromise between East and West. *A World Made New: Eleanor Roosevelt and the Universal Declaration of Human Rights* (New York: Random House, 2001), ch. 3.

28 Rawls, *LP*, p. 78.

29 Ibid., p. 65.

30 Ibid., p. 80, n. 23.

31 Ibid., pp. 62–70, 83–4.

32 See "Rawls' Law of Peoples," *Ethics* 110 (2000), pp. 684–8. The subject of international toleration deserves more extensive consideration on another occasion.

33 R. J. Vincent, *Human Rights and International Relations* (Cambridge: Cambridge University Press, 1986), pp. 48–9.

34 T. M. Scanlon's remarks about the identification of "a system of moral goods and bads" that any reasonable person would recognize are instructive. See "Value, Desire, and Quality of Life," in *The Quality of Life*, ed. Martha Nussbaum and Amartya Sen (Oxford: Clarendon Press, 1993), pp. 195–9.

35 United Nations, "Vienna Declaration and Programme of Action," adopted by the World Conference on Human Rights, June 25, 1993 (A/CONF.157/23) (www.unhchr.ch/huridocda/huridoca.nsf/-(Symbol)/A.CONF.157.23.En).

36 *LP*, p. 65 n. 1.

37 Perhaps Rawls recognizes that human rights play a more complex role in international relations than is reflected in his official view about their political significance. In a discussion about the development of poor societies, he emphasizes the importance of an "insistence on human rights." But he does not say what this might mean for political action. *LP*, p. 109.

38 See Ignatieff, *Human Rights as Politics and Idolatry*, p. 90. Compare Cranston: "[T]he effect of a universal declaration that is overloaded with affirmations of economic and social rights is to push the political and civil rights out of the realm of the morally compelling and into the twilight world of utopian aspirations." "Are There Any Human Rights?," p. 12.

39 See Amartya Sen, *The Standard of Living*, ed. Geoffrey Hawthorn (Cambridge: Cambridge University Press, 1987), and "Capability and Well-Being," in *The Quality of Life*, ed. Martha Nussbaum and Amartya Sen (Oxford: Clarendon Press, 1993), esp. pp. 40–2.

40 Rawls himself does not ground the duty to assist burdened societies on considerations about human rights. His account of this duty refers, instead, to the "long-term goal" of liberal and decent societies to bring "burdened societies" into the "Society of Peoples." *LP*, pp. 109, 106.

41 This is in accord with Thomas Pogge's "institutional understanding of human rights," described in "How Should Human Rights Be Conceived?" *Jahrbuch für Recht und Ethik*, 3 (1995), 103–20.

42 Shue, *Basic Rights*, pp. 35–64 and 153–66 (in the 1996 Afterword). See also Shue's contribution to this volume, p. 225 below. See also James Nickel, *Making Sense of Human Rights* (Berkeley: University of California Press, 1987), pp. 54–5, on which Shue's remarks in the Afterword rely.

43 Thomas Pogge, "A Global Resources Dividend," in *Ethics of Consumption: The Good Life, Justice, and Global Stewardship*, eds. David A. Crocker and Toby Linden (Lanham, Md.: Rowman and Littlefield, 1998): 501–36. The point is emphasized in Pogge's contribution to this volume, pp. 260–88 below. For similar reasons, rich countries may have responsibilities to desist from internal policies that have the predictable effect of imposing economic costs on poor countries; consider, e.g., farm subsidies in the United States and European Union which artificially reduce prices of domestically grown crops and deprive poor countries of export markets.

44 For an outline of one such theory, see my *Political Theory and International Relations*, rev. edn. (Princeton: Princeton University Press, 1999), part III.

45 Compare Thomas Pogge, "An Egalitarian Law of Peoples," *Philosophy & Public Affairs*, 23 (1994), esp. parts III–IV, pp. 208–14.

46 But not "global justice," if that phrase is understood to invoke cosmopolitan considerations.

PART IV

Rights, responsibilities and institutional reforms

Chapter 11

Thickening convergence: human rights and cultural diversity

HENRY SHUE

> Every substantive account of distributive justice is a local account.
> Michael Walzer[1]

> The human rights of women and of the girl-child are an inalienable, integral and indivisible part of universal human rights. The full and equal participation of women in political, civil, economic, social and cultural life, at the national, regional and international levels, and the eradication of all forms of discrimination on grounds of sex are priority objectives of the international community. Gender-based violence and all forms of sexual harassment and exploitation, including those resulting from cultural prejudice and international trafficking, are incompatible with the dignity and worth of the human person, and must be eliminated.
> *Vienna Declaration and Programme of Action*, I, 18[2]

Running from at least as far back as Hegel, through Marx's trenchant "Zur Judenfrage," and into such diverse contemporary pieces as Charles Taylor's "Atomism" and Catharine MacKinnon's "Crimes of War, Crimes of Peace," is the concern that moral conceptions (including conceptions of rights) will, because of their reach for universality, lose their grasp upon the rich concreteness of actual social life. Since "Zur Judenfrage" a standard, if not the primary, criticism of conceptions of human rights has been that universality has been gained at the price of abstraction, abstraction from any concrete form of social life.[3] Charles Taylor's formulation of one problem in "Atomism" as being about the "primacy of rights" has been influential.[4] More recently, in prose worthy of a Young Hegelian, Catharine MacKinnon has charged against conceptions of universal human rights that "what happens to women

217

is either too particular to be universal or too universal to be particular, meaning either too human to be female or too female to be human."[5] As Marx saw the concrete Jewish question as a critical test for conceptions of rights, MacKinnon sees concrete women's questions, like how to comprehend, and deal with, the astounding number of cases of rape in the war against Bosnia, as similar tests.[6]

These critiques of theories of rights are not all the same.[7] Marx alone, as Jeremy Waldron has shown, was offering four analytically separable lines of criticism, and various subsequent critics have selected various particular strands to develop, each in their own ways.[8] I want quickly to sketch only what I take to be one element of this rich mix without in any way suggesting that it corresponds precisely with any one of the views so far mentioned.

Un-moored from both the subtlety and the substantiveness of any particular form of life, moral conceptions succumb, one criticism can go, to the twin dangers of abstraction and atomism, different but mutually reinforcing. By trying to ground, say, a conception of rights in human life in general – human life as such – theorists cut their conceptions off from any grounding in any recognizable kind of human life and leave their conceptions ungrounded anywhere, adrift in the imaginations (and computer disks) of individual theorists. The initial result is excessive abstraction. And the individual humans, un-dressed through abstraction of all distinguishing garb down to their bare bones, are look-alike skeletons, not recognizably male or female, African or Scandinavian, senile or infantile. Stripped of all particular attachments – emotional, political, sexual – the individuals lack all individuality and are deprived of all the specific interests, projects, and loves and hates that might define some distinguishable identity. They are too undifferentiated to find each other either attractive or repulsive. So they bounce around, coupling and uncoupling in various combinations, but without much effect or affect. In other words, a further result of abstraction can be atomism. And so on – I am simply trying to invoke one element of a well-known, general cry, now often labeled "communitarian."

Now since the world actually consists of Serbian Christians raping and murdering Bosnian Muslims, Rwandan Hutus massacring Rwandan Tutsis, Turks hunting down Kurds, Russians hunting down Chechnyans, Americans and Germans trying to pretend that none of this is actually happening, and very particular others, the thought naturally occurs that the solution to abstraction and atomism is to start from some level of actual human society or culture, in all its sometimes-frightening and sometimes-inspiring specificity. If humanity is never found culturally naked – even the physically naked starving children speak some particular language, believe some specific fairy-tales, and pray to identifiable if equally silent Gods – we are well advised to begin in appreciation and comprehension of the involuted forms in which humanity is always embodied. We are still free to look for similarities as well and to try to generalize and to argue that different structures are serving the same function, but we cannot posit a cross-cultural core unless we find one. And to find it we must begin with the contingent and messy practices actually shared within a living, breathing, functioning human community. One might well consider an example of this kind of alternative offered by a critic of abstract universality already mentioned. I shall, however, attend here to a recent essay by Michael Walzer, who has long and consistently devoted his efforts to formulating a position that takes the diversity of functioning cultures seriously.

CONVERGENCE ON CONCRETE CASES

I shall in the end be, generally speaking, exploring some of the broad middle ground between what Walzer defends and (his account of) what he attacks (and, I think but will not try to show, between what Marx, Taylor, and MacKinnon each defend and attack). What Walzer attacks is the argument that attempts to abstract from specific, substantive moral argument, "richly referential, culturally resonant, locked into a locally established symbolic system or network of meanings."[9] In particular, Walzer targets "proceduralism" as typified for him by the work of Jürgen Habermas and Bruce Ackerman, and, in a less critical way, Stuart Hampshire.[10] I want later to look at how argument about rights can be richly referential and can lock into symbolic systems and networks of meaning, as Walzer wishes, but without those systems and networks being local or being resonant with only one culture, as Walzer assumes they must. The choice we face, I will suggest, is far more subtle than one within a dichotomy of "thick" localism and "thin" universalism. First, however, I want to set out briefly what we might call Walzer's localist turn.

Walzer writes: "Morality is thick from the beginning, culturally integrated, fully resonant, and it reveals itself thinly only on special occasion . . ."[11] His example of a special occasion is his watching on the United States television news in 1989 pictures of people marching in the streets of Prague with signs saying "Truth" and "Justice" and realizing both (1) that while the signs were, in effect, tips of moral/ intellectual icebergs with fuller outlines he did not fathom [my image], because he did not know the deep, thick meanings of truth and justice in Czech society, (2) he "also recognized and acknowledged the values that the marchers were defending . . . The marchers shared a culture with which I was largely unfamiliar . . . And yet, I could have walked comfortably in their midst. I could carry the same signs."[12] It is Walzer's ability to carry the same signs as the Prague marchers that Walzer takes to show that there is a "thin," cross-culturally shared, element of "truth" and "justice" in addition to the "thick," culturally specific element of each.[13]

Walzer operates with a sharp distinction between concrete cases, on which there is "thin" cross-cultural agreement, and theoretical justifications, on which there is "thick" disagreement. I want briefly to jump ahead in his essay to look at an argument he sketches about theoretical justification, which I take to be the reference of "substantial account" in the first sentence that follows (and of "substantive account" in the quotation from *Spheres of Justice* at the very beginning of this paper), and then come back to his remarks about concrete cases:

It is possible, nonetheless, to give some *substantial account* of the moral minimum [emphasis added]. I see nothing wrong with the effort to do that so long as we understand that it is necessarily expressive of our own thick morality. A moral equivalent of Esperanto is probably impossible – or, rather, just as Esperanto is much closer to European languages than to any others, so minimalism when it is expressed as Minimal Morality will be forced into the idiom and orientation of one of the maximal moralities. There is no neutral (unexpressive) moral language.[14]

The implied argument seems roughly like the argument of a philosopher of science who says that there is no theory-neutral language of observation because indispensable observational terms are themselves theory-laden (so that one cannot have a neutrally described "critical experiment" to adjudicate between two incompatible theories). The different theoretical justifications, or moral theories, that for each different culture constitute that culture's "thick" morality and stand behind the (often cross-culturally shared) judgments about concrete cases are, in effect, not inter-translatable. The picture suggested is of a society-level equivalent of the philosophical problem of other minds, or of private languages that were private to cultures rather than to individuals.

I see no reason at all to accept this picture of hard-shelled monadic cultures, and I think our practice simply belies it.[15] No doubt many of the subtleties and involutions of a particular culture, including some of its most sophisticated moral reflections, do not translate well, or perhaps even at all. Nevertheless, any general thesis of non-translatability seems greatly exaggerated, even leaving aside the serious difficulties in specifying how one is supposed to individuate cultures in the first place.

Concrete cases, by contrast, are where we can and do, at least sometimes, understand and agree, according to Walzer. When a Prague marcher's sign said "Truth," it meant "the marchers wanted to hear true statements from their political leaders; they wanted to be able to believe what they read in the newspapers; they didn't want to be lied to anymore"; when a sign said "Justice," it simply meant "an end to arbitrary arrests, equal and impartial law enforcement, the abolition of the privileges and prerogatives of the party elite – common, garden variety justice."[16] The subjects of shared understanding are (relatively) concrete cases: eliminate this and that privilege, stop lying here and there. The overlapping tips of the cultural icebergs are cases, perhaps even paradigm cases.

That Walzer believes that it is concrete cases toward which cross-cultural convergence moves is made especially clear in his discussion of the Old Testament prophet Isaiah's condemnation of those who "grind the faces of the poor":[17]

What they say about these issues will be part and parcel of what they say about everything else, but some aspect of it – its negativity perhaps, its rejection of brutality ('grinding the face') – will be immediately accessible to people who don't know anything about the other parts and parcels. Pretty much anybody looking on will see something here that they recognize. The sum of these recognitions is what I mean by minimal morality . . . This is morality close to the bone.[18]

"Every *substantive account* of distributive justice is a local account" [emphasis added] had been a theme of *Spheres of Justice*. Walzer still takes this to be, not necessarily, but only contingently, true:

Societies are necessarily particular because they have members and memories, members *with* memories not only of their own but also of their common life. Humanity, by contrast, has members but no memory, and so it has no history and no culture, no customary practices, no familiar life-ways, no festivals, no shared understanding of social goods . . . The value of minimalism lies in the encounters it facilitates, of which it is also the product. But these encounters are not – not now, at least – sufficiently sustained to produce a thick morality.[19]

If there are no shared culture and no shared practices, there can be no shared morality except the consensus cases that are "close to the bone."[20]

And finally, but tellingly:

I want to stress again that the moral minimum is not a free-standing morality. It simply designates some reiterated features of particular thick or maximal moralities.[21]

As an account of how things are, this seems to me misleading at best; and as political and moral counsel, it seems positively misguided, for reasons to come below.

In *Thick and Thin*, then, Walzer portrays a relativism, or localism, of theories and a non-relativism of, or convergence upon, (at least some) cases. This two-tiered portrayal I take to be, among other things, Walzer's way of attempting to avoid the general relativism charged by Ronald Dworkin against *Spheres of Justice* without abandoning his sense of deep moral and cultural difference.[22] In having two tiers, Walzer is, at the international level, somewhat like John Rawls, at the domestic level, with his notion of an overlapping consensus reached from divergent origins.[23] However, for Rawls the consensus is upon fundamental principles of justice, while for Walzer it is upon a variety of concrete cases, including some cases of justice. Nor does Rawls presuppose the diverging views that lie behind the convergence upon principles as literally non-translatable, although, since Rawls sees no way to adjudicate between the diverging views that he calls liberal and hierarchical, they might as well be non-translatable – the disagreements appear un-decidable in any case.[24] The main difference is that Walzer appears to see the un-decidable disagreements as coming even closer to the ground than Rawls does; for Walzer members of different societies/cultures agree on cases only.[25] As enticing as it is, however, I must resist the temptation to carry through in this short paper this hinted additional comparison between Walzer and Rawls in their handlings of convergence and divergence.

SPRINGS OF ABSTRACTION

While I do not find Walzer's positive account of the situation persuasive, I want to acknowledge his negative point that theories of rights have sometimes been much too abstract, but offer in this section an alternative diagnosis of one source of this tendency toward abstraction in some accounts of rights.[26] Then in the following section I will note a picture of the international situation that contrasts sharply with Walzer's and suggests an alternate route away from excessive abstraction, through a cross-cultural, not a localist, turn. I believe that the indeterminate character of some of the literature about rights actually results from a fairly straightforward failure to engage tasks inherent to rights theory. The troublesome problems are not those alleged by external critics, but central ones set by the internal logic of rights themselves. The unfinished parts of rights theory are difficult parts, but they are what can move it farther away from excessive abstraction.

The difficulty seems to me now to go considerably deeper than I used to think it did. I have argued from the beginning of my concern with rights that the duties constitutive of the implementation of rights have been greatly over-simplified and under-analyzed.[27] Much more remains to be done to produce a sophisticated elaboration even at the abstract level. Yet our not taking duties seriously enough now seems to me to be, not a relatively peripheral failure to complete a few final details on an otherwise sound structure, but a reflection of a failure to confront issues central to rights theory.[28]

Hordes of contemporary "communitarian" critics of rights theory have, sometimes consciously but often unconsciously, re-echoed pieces of the critique of rights in Marx's "Zur Judenfrage," which, as already observed, was to some extent already an echo of Hegel.[29] The charge of abstract atomism – or, one might better say, coupled charges of abstraction and atomism – leveled by Marx against one account of rights he had encountered are still endlessly repeated. Against many accounts of rights, the charge is of course perfectly applicable. Yet, as Waldron also noticed, Marx himself saw differences among approaches to rights and was more unrelentingly critical of "the rights of man" than of "the rights of citizen," because Marx judged the latter, unlike the former, to be compatible with, and even in part expressive of, the "social being" and solidarity with (at least some) others that is the opposite of the abstract atomism he was condemning in the universalizing theory.[30]

While Marx himself was of course not interested in exploring the possibilities for the construction of theories of rights that would be expressive of the ties constituting human community, his implicit recommendation to rights theorists was what I have in the case of Michael Walzer called the localist turn: turn away from attempts to formulate universal rights, which will impel you into empty abstractions divorced from the rich specifics of social life, and instead focus upon the rights of the members of a single community. Ironically, this localist turn has become a central methodological dogma of "communitarians," who always want to begin from the given features of one actual society or culture, from existing social practices. We have seen a subtler version of it in Michael Walzer.

Another mantra of popular "communitarian" doctrine is: "too many rights, not enough responsibilities."[31] If applied to the most abstract theoretical accounts of rights, "not enough responsibilities" would be a considerable understatement. Theories of rights often do not provide a systematic account of the generation or the assignment of the duties, or responsibilities, necessary to give reality to the rights set out. Indeed I want to suggest that this complaint correctly points toward the heart of the problem.

At the extreme are theories of rights that say or assume that the only content that a right can have is a liberty: all rights are rights to liberty. Or, as Hart argued, a right to liberty is somehow the closest thing there is to a natural right. If one adds into this a relatively negative concept of liberty, it is easy to convince oneself that no interesting theoretical problems arise about the generation of the analysis of implementing duties, much less the assignment of the responsibility of carrying the (unseen) variety of duties among people in the (unseen) variety of different kinds of relationships to the bearers of the rights to liberty. The content of the right is non-interference, so obviously, it may seem, the full content of the implementing duties is non-interference. Now I do not want to devote much space to this extreme position, according to which the only rights are rights to negative liberty. It is, however, worth noting that even on these extreme assumptions a more complex account of implementing duties is unavoidably called for. While it is not a logical necessity, actual claims of rights are always pleas for protection. Even if the content of the right is as purely negative as being left entirely alone, people do not announce rights to be left alone simply as a means of informing all second parties who, it is naively believed, will somehow automatically act accordingly as soon as they gain the information about what is wanted. On the contrary, one declares a *right* to be left alone as a means of appealing to some third parties for protection against those second parties who will in fact not choose to leave others alone. If even this meagre appeal for protection against violators is to be granted, then, besides a duty to leave others alone that must fall upon everyone – a universal duty of non-interference – a duty to protect right-bearers against second-parties who violate their universal duty of non-interference must fall upon at least some third parties.

The absolute minimum structure for the implementation among human beings of any right, including a right whose own content is totally negative, is, then, at least two kinds of duties, which are ordinarily also differently assigned or distributed: (1) a duty not to violate the right (e.g., a duty of non-interference where the content of the right is a negative liberty), normally assigned universally; and (2) a duty to protect right-bearers against violations of duty (1), normally assigned non-universally, often assigned, according to current conventions, to the state.[32]

Now this is all quite tedious, since I am so far in this section merely repeating myself from other occasions. However, two theses, both of which I have in the past defended in close conjunction with each other, need to be kept distinct, because neither depends upon the other even if both are correct. Their independence of each other was certainly not always evident to me. The thesis that is less relevant at the moment is that the content of most rights that people are actually interested in is far from accurately describable as "negative." The contemporary international consensus upon even the minimum package of rights includes, as John Rawls eventually acknowledged, "at least certain minimum rights to means of subsistence and security" – "certain general all-purpose economic means."[33] The minimum includes "welfare," or economic and social, rights. This is also increasingly entrenched in international law.[34]

The unavoidability of genuinely positive duties, on the other hand, can be established entirely separately from the centrality of rights with positive content. Indeed, the point of the preceding paragraph was that even if, contrary to fact, there were no rights with positive content, there would still be genuinely positive duties. Positive duties, like the duty to protect people against the violation of their rights, are ineliminable from any adequate structure of rights, irrespective of the content of the rights.[35] Positive duties are embedded in the structure of the implementation of any right.[36] The only exception would be a "right" that did not need any protection. And unless those who provide the protection can be expected to do so entirely out of generosity or exuberance, those third parties will need to be compensated, the provision of which will involve the performance of yet other positive duties, like tax payment to provide the compensation. And so on.

Now, while I believe that elaborating an adequate account of duties is an essential task facing theorists of rights, I want to step back from that analysis itself and look at its significance for the overall project of constructing adequate theories of rights. The argument made so far would be compatible with seeing the completion of the analysis of the generation and allocation of duties as a necessary but peripheral task, but I promised earlier to try to show that its importance is considerably greater than that. As long as it was possible for us theorists to convince ourselves that for any given right there was only one, and the same, all-purpose duty – namely, do not violate Right X – there seemed to be nothing to discuss about the implementing duties, certainly not about which duties were required. And with the one simplistic duty tacitly assumed, there were no questions about its assignment: obviously the duty was universal (it did not ask much in any case). Now two critical points emerge.

Incorporating empirical understanding. First we now realize that serious theorists of rights need political, sociological, historical, and economic understanding. [If we as individual theorists cannot have it all, we must collaborate with other individuals who have what we are ignorant of.] An analysis of implementing duties is an analysis of adequate institutions.[37] Rights theory becomes much more difficult, because one cannot offer only conceptual analyses. The conceptual analyses, which of course remain essential and perhaps fundamental, must be given in conjunction with an analogue of what the social scientists call "operationalization." One must spell out, at least a little bit, what it would actually mean for a certain right to be fulfilled and enjoyed. This entails analyzing which tasks must be performed (generation of the analysis of duties) and which kinds of people can reasonably be expected to perform them (principles for the assignment of duties, or principles of responsibility). These remain normative, philosophical tasks, so they cannot merely be dumped into the laps of social scientists. On the other hand, they require knowledgeable judgments about the workings of actual and possible social practices and institutions, so social scientific knowledge is indispensable.

The bad news, then, is that theorizing about rights becomes much more difficult and demanding, especially in the level of empirical knowledge required. The good news, which brings us full circle, is that theories of rights cease to be guilty of the abstraction from social practice of which they have long, and sometimes rightly, been accused, from Hegel through Marx to Walzer. My point is not merely that the critics can be answered, but that one has no choice whether to answer them. One must answer them because an analysis of duties is inherently needed for the completion of even a minimal theory of rights. As soon as one sees that any right involves a wide spectrum of duties on the part of other persons – some relatively positive and some relatively negative, some relatively formal and some relatively informal, some relatively local and some fully global – one sees that the philosophical work is barely begun until one provides a systematic generation of the variety of duties, which extends well beyond the "purely" philosophical, if pure entails non-empirical.

And once the variety of duties is clear, the need for principles for assigning different types of duty to persons with different types of re-lations to the bearer of the rights becomes virtually undeniable – and intellectually very exciting. One begins, for example, to need to confront questions about the proper role of incentives and the relation between what a person can reasonably be expected to do and what that person can be provided with incentives to do, or deprived of incentives not to do – how much sacrifice can be expected of which people for the sake of the fulfillment of which rights?[38] One must learn something about the life-cycle of social norms: how they are created, nurtured, and destroyed.[39] For a theory of rights is a theory about which social norms various groups ought to have, and this must depend in part on how norms actually operate psychologically and politically, within and across cultures. One needs then, among other things, to talk with mem-bers of other cultures.

Creating social solidarity. More important still, conversation about the responsible allocation of duties can itself actually build solidarity and community, although this result is of course not guaranteed. This is precisely the opposite of Marx's picture of the "rights of man" pitting individuals against each other. For a system of rights and duties is a pact among people saying that those who, as luck will have it, turn out to be relatively fortunate and secure will protect, in certain specific ways, those who turn out to be threatened and vulnerable, in certain specific ways. I do not mean that anyone has only the rights or the duties that she has herself voluntarily agreed to. I mean something more along the lines of what could reasonably be agreed to by reasonable people – this now-popular kind of standard seems to me to be an unobjectionable, if not very useful, formula. A system of rights and duties needs to be rea-sonable looked at from either side: a list of rights may appear attractive until one considers how burdensome the implementing duties would have to be, and a list of duties may seem burdensome until one consid-ers how much one would want the protection provided by the rights in question if one were vulnerable to the threats. But to determine what is reasonable, and who is reasonable, one needs to attend to, and explore thoroughly, specific reasons.[40]

Serious concrete discussion of duties inherent in rights, as well as the rights themselves, can, then, take the form of a real conversation among people about what they consider it sensible to guarantee to each other in various particular ways. Of course this can in fact lead to disputes, disagreements, and misunderstandings. But insofar as such a conversation constitutes a genuine expression of concern for the interests of the other participants, a genuine attempt to understand their conception of their interests, and an energetic and imaginative effort to arrive at a mutually acceptable arrangement, we have some reason to hope.[41] Or, so it seems, at least within a single culture.

CROSS-CULTURAL SOCIAL PRACTICE

In order to indicate clearly the relation between the section just completed and the section about to begin, I would like to summarize the overall structure of this essay. Michael Walzer has, in effect, presented us with a dilemma about rights (and morality more generally): an account of rights must be either abstract or local. If one tries to provide an account of universal rights, the account must be thin, or abstract. If instead one attempts an account of thick, or richly concrete, rights, the account must be local. Accounts of rights must be either universal and abstract or local and concrete. This is the dilemma of rights.

In the preceding section I have just argued that abstraction is every bit as objectionable as Walzer assumes and that it is fatally objectionable for reasons inherent to accounts of rights: an abstract account of rights is a failed account. Its failure is lack of specification of what must be done to honor and implement rights.[42] No one who is morally serious about rights can settle for the emptiness of merely abstract accounts of them. The dilemma's evaluative assumption that *exclusive* abstraction – abstraction unbalanced by concrete specification – is bad is indeed correct.

In this section I return to the alleged dilemma itself and argue that Walzer is not correct that the only route to the concrete follows a localist turn. I shall present a picture that contrasts sharply with Walzer's, that seems to me much more accurate, and that has the political merit of pointing us outward rather than inward. To suggest in general that there can be some middle way or other between abstract universalism

228

and cultural specificity is hardly a new idea – see Hegel! What I hope might be useful here is a constructive characterization, from among the variety of possible middle ways currently available, of a particular middle way that the human rights movement may actually be taking in reality.

The fundamental error in the implicit portrayal of the international situation by Walzer is the insularity attributed to the cultural blocs that only so tentatively reach toward each other. This picture of insularity has two aspects: intra-bloc homogeneity and inter-bloc passivity. Both these attributed characteristics are increasingly inapplicable descriptively and inappropriate politically to the international situation.

Intra-bloc homogeneity. Since pursuit of the issues about how the units in question are individuated would take us into so many tangles, I use "bloc" simply as a place-holder for whatever Walzer means. Roughly, the many blocs that Walzer seems to have in mind are nation-states treated as if they were single cultures. It is difficult to gain a sufficiently vivid and sharp picture of the internal complexity of the blocs, especially of "them," as distinguished from "us." Concerning us, it is comparatively harder to forget that we are not all liberals and that, for instance, racism that challenges liberalism's commitment to equal respect and concern for all persons is flourishing in the United States, Europe, and Australia, for example. Concerning "them," by contrast, homogenizing stereotypes are more difficult to resist. Writing at the end of the 1970s specifically about the universality of human rights, T. M. Scanlon warned of this danger:

The main argument that I want to consider against acting to defend human rights . . . holds that while human rights have a special place in "our" moral and political tradition they are not universally shared. Many countries have different notions of political morality, and it is therefore inappropriate for us to bring pressure to bear on them to conform to our conception of human rights. To do so is a kind of moral imperialism. I believe this argument to be seriously mistaken. It puts itself forward as a kind of enlightened and tolerant relativism, but this masks what is in fact an attitude of moral and cultural superiority. Like many forms of relativism, this argument rests on the attribution to "them" of a unanimity that does not in fact exist. "They" are said to be different from us and to live by different rules. Such stereotypes are seldom accurate, and the attribution of unanimity is particularly implausible in the case of human rights violations. These actions have victims who generally resent what is done to them . . .[43]

Ann Elizabeth Mayer has provided a politically important current instance. Much of the strongest opposition to the declaration of the universality of human rights that was finally adopted in Vienna in 1993 came from Muslim *governments*, notably including both the Iranian clerical dictatorship and the Saudi monarchical dictatorship, each of which considers the other to be heretical and therefore illegitimate. With their joint support, the Organization of the Islamic Conference had issued in August 1990 the *Cairo Declaration on Human Rights in Islam*, put forward as an Islamic countermodel to what is generally known as the "International Bill of Rights," including the two *International Covenants* that are widely ratified and in force, and is what John Rawls above and Louis Henkin below are treating as definitive.[44] As Mayer notes, Harvard's Samuel P. Huntington subsequently weighed in at the time of the Vienna Conference with the explosive idea that the planet-dominating successor to the Cold War is turning out to be a "clash of civilizations" between "Western and Islamic" conceptions, in which human rights turns out to be a "Western" concept unsuitable for "Islamic" cultures.[45] Quite a few different things are going on here – most of them, in my judgment, not good – but I want only to note Mayer's main thesis: that it is only non-democratic governments in power which are unanimous that there is a distinctively Islamic conception of human rights that is incompatible with what is otherwise the international consensus:

An examination going beyond the official rhetoric about Islamic human rights reveals that there is no real consensus on the part of Muslims that their religion mandates a culturally distinctive approach to rights or that it precludes the adoption of international human rights norms. In fact, the relationship of Islamic culture to the positions that Muslims inside and outside governments are currently articulating on human rights is neither a simple nor a direct one, and the range of Muslims' attitudes on human rights defies Orientalist stereotypes and facile generalizations about a supposedly monolithic Islamic culture.[46]

This is a beautiful instance of Scanlon's general point. Even someone like Walzer, who is inclined to see an intra-cultural consensus, need not accept the official state account of what the consensus is, as Huntington appears to have done, but Mayer's case of Huntington and the dictatorship-promoted "Islamic conception of human rights" shows how easily it can happen.

Inter-bloc passivity. If anything, the other aspect of the misleadingly pictured insularity is even more of a problem. One gets the sense that even if cultures are not literally non-intertranslatable, the difficulties in the way of serious intellectual exchange are formidable. However, Jeremy Waldron has aptly outlined the structure of the process through which we can and, I will shortly suggest, sometimes actually do, find a middle way:

Even if it is true that moral judgement cannot take place in a vacuum but always in relation to some shared practice, *our evaluations themselves* – when we are confident that we are making them in the company of others – *can constitute the background practice* that gives them sense and substance [emphasis added]. The process may go something like this. The members of a given society, S_1, find themselves holding views about the practices of a neighbouring society, S_2. These views are not just reflex applications of their own mores, for in S_1, as in any complex culture, the idea that circumstances may sometimes make a moral difference will be understood in a sufficiently sophisticated manner in local evaluations to justify its wider application in the case of differences between societies. Moreover, views like these may sometimes be not only held out but also reflected on, as members of S_1 ask each other whether their reaction to S_2 is appropriate, whether there is not some aspect of S_2 they are missing, and so on. And if they are aware, as again sophisticated people will be, that people in S_2 are having thoughts of a similar kind about S_1 (including the thought that people in S_1 are having thoughts of a similar kind about them . . .), it may occur to them to include in their reflections the question of whether there is anything in common between the external evaluations they are making and the external evaluations that they are aware are being made from S_2. And so it goes on. Where there is close and intimate contact between two societies, the line between the internal and external evaluations will blur (or at least the line between internal and external *reflective* evaluations will) [emphasis original].[47]

It is of course true, as relativists often insist, that agreement reached must rest upon something else shared prior to the agreement – but, the point is, not necessarily prior to the conversation that leads to the agreement![48] Even the shared "premise" on which new-found agreement rests need not have existed *ex ante*, before the conversation occurred. A conversation that began with S_1s thinking that a practice of the S_2s (say, female genital mutilation) was reprehensible, and with the S_2s thinking that the S_1s were simply ignorant or contemptuous of their culture and religion, *could* end with the S_2s realizing something about their own convictions (say, that even if permanent physical mutilation were appropriate as the most severe form of punishment for the worst kind of flagrant offense against religion and family committed by a competent adult, it would still not be appropriate as a routine measure inflicted upon uncomprehending children by adults who had involuntarily suffered it themselves long before they understood anything about it) that would provide them a ground for doubting the necessity for the dubious practice. One could also say that the S_2s had discovered at least a little corner of a premise about protecting the bodily integrity of children against assault by adults causing irreversible damage that they shared with the S_1s, but what would count, for the S_2s, about this bit of premise concerning protection for the bodies of children would be, not the fact that their belief in it happened to be shared with the S_1s, but simply that it was indeed their belief. Yet they might not previously have realized that they had this belief because, perhaps, they had not articulated it exactly this way prior to this conversation with the S_1s. Or they might not previously have recognized that what they conceived as a solemn ritual of religious devotion was also the mutilation of a child's body, just as a Christian taking communion might not think of herself as violating the grape boycott by the farmworkers' union.[49]

One of the main points that Waldron is making, however, is that it is not necessary to, and at some stage it becomes quite inaccurate to, try to assign every belief to one or the other group, like His and Her towels. If the conversation is sustained, shared views – and of course disagreements as well – emerge. There may be a stage that is well characterized by the Rawlsian notion of an overlapping consensus which Rawls unfortunately tends to restrict to individual societies: ultimate premises differ but certain intermediate premises serve all equally well. Many possibilities are actually available, but the one that Waldron is highlighting, and that I think Rawls sometimes obscures with his taxonomy of types of national societies, is that after a time the matters on which there is consensus may come to have more significance than the matters that were originally considered ultimate.[50] One can certainly think that if different premises lead to the same conclusions, it is the conclusions, not the premises, to which one should devote one's attention. This shift may sometimes be misguided, but we have no reason to think it always is.

Indeed, the core international consensus upon human rights is precisely such a case in which people appear to have chosen to focus upon the shared conclusions about which rights there are and, for the most part, forget the fact that various people's original motivations were marxian, liberal, Christian, Islamic, and so on. John Rawls was exactly right when he observed in "The Law of Peoples" that human rights as

now generally understood "do not depend on any particular comprehensive moral doctrine or philosophical conception of human nature,
such as, for example, that human beings are moral persons and have
equal worth, or that they have certain particular moral and intellectual
powers that entitle them to these rights."[51] The accuracy of Rawls's description of the situation is confirmed by, for example, the following
account written a few years earlier by one of the most distinguished
scholars of international law, specializing in human rights:

The idea of rights here distilled from contemporary international instruments
responds, I believe, to common moral intuitions and accepted political principles. Those intuitions and principles have not been authoritatively articulated.
Developed during the decades following the Second World War, international
human rights are not the work of philosophers, but of politicians and citizens,
and philosophers have only begun to try to build conceptual justifications for
them. The international expressions of rights themselves claim no philosophical
foundation, nor do they reflect any clear philosophical assumptions; they artic-
ulate no particular moral principles or any single, comprehensive theory of the
relation of the individual to society.[52]

For better or for worse, one of the most powerful political forces of
the latter half of the twentieth century, the international human rights
movement, has proceeded without a widely shared philosophical account of itself. The international consensus on human rights not only is
not the incomprehensible tip of an untranslatable iceberg of theory but
is a remarkably free-floating cross-cultural social practice. Any justifi-
catory theory that emerges may be constructed from the beginning as
a cross-cultural consensus. Practice now is far ahead of theory, and the
owl of Minerva responsible for human rights evidently still dozes in her
tree.

Yet the kind of conversation sketched by Jeremy Waldron shows one
route by which this practice could develop theoretical depth. The well-
established and widespread practice of activism for human rights could
generate an accompanying practice of evaluation that took on a life of
its own and became progressively richer and, in Walzer's general sense,
thicker.[53] Contrary to what has emerged as Walzer's pessimistic picture,
we need not merely compare the respective cases about which we are
each confident in order to see where we happen already to agree, and
then stop. We can construct together institutions specifying a division of
the necessary moral labor that we are all willing to live with. By turning
to concrete institutional embodiments of the duties correlative to rights

233

we escape the abstraction of free-floating rights. It may be helpful to think of this as a process designed to find a division of moral labor that no one can reasonably reject, but judgments about what can and cannot reasonably be rejected must be made about specific proposals for specific circumstances.[54] The now-popular general formula, "cannot reasonably be rejected," is by itself, however, no decisive touchstone for determining what specifically is reasonable, and we must examine what is reasonable in concrete contexts, many of which will in fact be cross-cultural.

Cross-cultural conversations can not only answer questions that need answering but build both wider international consensus on principle and solidarity of commitment that is itself instrumentally and intrinsically valuable.[55] In order to find already existing rich and deep vocabularies of morality, we may at present have to turn inward. Many of our most urgent problems, however, require us to turn outward, and there too moral consensus can be created, enriched, and deepened. We may at last find specificity and universality of rights together.

NOTES

This chapter was originally written for a symposium at the Freie Universitat Berlin organized by Stefan Gosepath and Georg Lohmann, and an earlier version of it was published in German as "Menschenrechte und kulturelle Differenz," in *Philosophie der Menschenrechte*, ed. Stefan Gosepath and Georg Lohmann (Frankfurt am Main: Suhrkamp Verlag, 1998), pp. 343–77. It has not previously appeared in English.

For helpful criticisms and suggestions I am grateful to the participants in the original conference in Berlin, especially Henry S. Richardson, as well as to the participants in a Columbia University Seminar on Human Rights in New York, to James Griffin, and to John Tasioulas. Remaining confusions are uniquely my own.

1 Michael Walzer, *Spheres of Justice: A Defense of Pluralism and Equality* (New York: Basic Books, 1983), p. 314. While the sentence quoted is specifically about conceptions of justice, Walzer clearly believes that moral conceptions generally, including conceptions of rights, have the same feature, namely that only the local can (properly) attain richness. For a provocatively different reading of Walzer from my own, see John Tasioulas, "Between Tradition and Critique: Michael Walzer on Justice and Interpretation," in *Law, Justice and the State*, ed. Aleksander Peczenik and Mikael M. Karlsson (Stuttgart : Franz Steiner Verlag, 1995), pp. 59–71. For a broader critique of Walzer, see Brian Orend, *Michael Walzer on War and Justice* (Montreal and Kingston: McGill – Queen's University Press, 2000).

2 United Nations, *World Conference on Human Rights*, New York: UN Department of Public Information 1993, [DPI/1394–39399–August 1993], pp. 33–4. The *Vienna Declaration and Programme of Action* of the World Conference on Human Rights was "adopted by consensus" by representatives of 171 States on 25 June 1993, p. 1.

3 Marx/Engels, *Werke*, Bd. 1, Berlin: Dietz Verlag 1972, pp. 347–77; the essay was originally published in 1844. An abridged text, but with substantive commentary, is in Jeremy Waldron, ed., *'Nonsense upon Stilts': Bentham, Burke and Marx on the Rights of Man* (London and New York: Methuen, 1987).

4 Charles Taylor, *Philosophy and the Human Sciences, Philosophical Papers*, vol. 2 (Cambridge and New York: Cambridge University Press, 1985), pp. 187–210. "Theories which assert the primacy of rights are those which take as the fundamental, or at least a fundamental, principle of their political theory the ascription of certain rights to individuals and which deny the same status to a principle of belonging or obligation, that is a principle which states our obligation as men to belong to or sustain society . . ." (188). "Atomism" was first published in 1979. Taylor has revisited the issue more recently in "Cross-Purposes: The Liberal-Communitarian Debate," in Nancy Rosenblum, ed., *Liberalism and the Moral Life* (Cambridge, Mass.: Harvard University Press, 1989).

5 Catharine MacKinnon, "Crimes of War, Crimes of Peace," in *On Human Rights*, Oxford Amnesty Lectures 1993, ed. Stephen Shute and Susan Hurley (New York: BasicBooks, 1993), p. 85. Since I am noting only the conceptual framework, not the specific content, I ought to mention that this essay is an eloquent plea on behalf of the women of Bosnia, and women who are victims of war generally, based on an appeal to the ideal of equality.

6 Carol C. Gould made the connection between Marx's critique of abstract universality and philosophers' treatment of women earlier, and much more systematically, in a paper that had, ironically, been presented in Yugoslavia: "The Woman Question: Philosophy of Liberation and the Liberation of Philosophy," *The Philosophical Forum*, vol. v, nos. 1–2 (Fall–Winter, 1973–4), pp. 5–44. Also relevant to the issues in this essay is Carol C. Gould, "Cultural Justice and the Limits of Difference: Perspectives on Ethnicity and Nationality," photocopy.

7 I am grateful to Blain E. Neufeld for emphasizing to me the importance of the differences.

8 Jeremy Waldron presents a valuable four-way division of the general criticism into excessive abstraction, rationalism, individualism, and egoism – see *'Nonsense upon Stilts'*, p. 166.

9 Michael Walzer, *Thick and Thin: Moral Argument at Home and Abroad* (Notre Dame and London: University of Notre Dame Press, 1994), p. xi, n. 1. Walzer notes that he has borrowed the term "thick" from his colleague Clifford Geertz's influential notion of "thick description," emphasizing that the

Walzerian modifier applies to people's own moral arguments, not to accounts of other people's moral arguments by social scientists. Pp. 1–19, from which I shall be quoting below, were originally published as Michael Walzer, "Moral Minimalism," in *From the Twilight of Probability: Ethics and Politics*, ed. William R. Shea and Antonio Spadafora (Canton, Mass.: Science History Publications, 1992), pp. 3–14. Also see the following useful volume containing critical essays about Walzer's views and a reply to criticisms by Walzer: David Miller and Michael Walzer, eds., *Pluralism, Justice, and Equality* (Oxford and New York: Oxford University Press, 1995).

10 On Habermas, *Thick and Thin*, pp. 12–13; on Ackerman, pp. 13–14. The reference to Hampshire, which may be less evident than the others, is to his suggestion of "a thin notion of minimum procedural justice" in *Innocence and Experience* (Cambridge, Mass.: Harvard University Press, 1989), pp. 72–8.

11 Walzer, *Thick and Thin*, p. 4.

12 Ibid., p. 1.

13 I take it, for our purposes, that someone might have had a sign saying "human rights" and everything would still apply.

14 Walzer, *Thick and Thin*, p. 9.

15 Onora O'Neill made this same observation in *Constructions of Reason: Explorations of Kant's Practical Philosophy* (Cambridge and New York: Cambridge University Press, 1989).

16 Walzer, *Thick and Thin*, p. 2.

17 Isaiah 3:15.

18 Walzer, *Thick and Thin*, pp. 5–6.

19 Ibid., pp. 8 and 18–19. Minimal morality would be the product of the cross-cultural encounters only if it were lowest common denominator abstractions, not consensus upon concrete cases – unless the product were the realization that there is a consensus on the cases.

20 To be fair to Walzer, one should note that the "thin" universal morality does have considerable practical bite: "perhaps the end product of this effort will be a set of standards to which all societies can be held – negative injunctions, most likely, rules against murder, deceit, torture, oppression, and tyranny" (10). [No justification at all is offered for the assertion that all the standards will likely be negative.] Military intervention will even sometimes be justified on the basis of some of these standards (15); this appears to be generally consistent with the influential view about intervention developed in *Just and Unjust Wars*, pp. 51–63; 86–108; and 339–42.

21 Walzer, *Thick and Thin*, p. 10.

22 For the exchange at the time of publication, see Ronald Dworkin, "To Each His Own," *New York Review of Books*, April 14, 1983, pp. 4–6, repr. as "What Justice Isn't," in Ronald Dworkin, *A Matter of Principle* (Oxford: Clarendon Press, 1986); and Letters by Michael Walzer and Ronald Dworkin, *New York Review of Books*, July 21, 1983, pp. 43–6. For an instructive subsequent commentary,

see William A. Galston, *Liberal Purposes: Goods, Virtues, and Diversity in the Liberal State*, Cambridge Studies in Philosophy and Public Policy (Cambridge and New York: Cambridge University Press, 1991), pp. 42–54.

23 John Rawls, *Political Liberalism*, John Dewey Essays in Philosophy, vol. 4 (New York: Columbia University Press, 1993), Lecture IV, pp. 133–72. For particularly relevant reviews, see Susan Moller Okin, *American Political Science Review*, vol. 87, no. 4 (December 1993), pp. 1010–11; and Brian Barry, "John Rawls and the Search for Stability," *Ethics*, 105 (July 1995), 874–915.

24 In "The Law of Peoples," his initial foray into international questions, Rawls seems to me in practice to "black-box" liberal society and hierarchical society, as if they were at that level impenetrable to each other, as fully as Walzerian theory would require – see John Rawls, "The Law of Peoples," in *On Human Rights*, ed. Shute and Hurley, pp. 41–82 and 220–30; and John Rawls, *The Law of Peoples with "The Idea of Public Reason Revisited "* (Cambridge, Mass. and London: Harvard University Press, 1999). On the other hand, he does see a shared commitment to a package of basic rights among "well-ordered" hierarchical and liberal societies.

25 Insofar as the principles covering the cases were what Rawls long ago called "summary rules," which are simply extensionally equivalent to the cases covered, Walzer would of course have to grant that [summary] principles were shared. This is utterly trivial, however, and no one – certainly neither Walzer nor Rawls – is interested in summary rules. For the concept of a summary rule, see John Rawls, "Two Concepts of Rules," *Philosophical Review*, 44 (1955), 3–32.

26 Onora O'Neill has distinguished abstraction, which selectively omits, from idealization, which selectively adds: "Abstraction, taken literally, is a matter of selective omission, of leaving out some predicates from descriptions and theories. Selective omission can hardly be objected to. It is unavoidable . . . An idealized account or theory not merely omits certain predicates that are true of the matter to be considered but adds predicates that are false of the matter to be considered . . . 'Omission' of a predicate in abstracting merely means that nothing is allowed to rest on the predicate's being satisfied or not satisfied. By contrast, when we idealize, we add a predicate to a theory, and the theory applies only where that predicate is satisfied . . . Many of the complaints leveled at abstraction in ethical and political reasoning are in fact complaints about reliance on idealized conceptions of agency." Onora O'Neill, "Ethical Reasoning and Ideological Pluralism," *Ethics*, 98: 4 (July 1988), 705–22; quotations are from pp. 711–12. While I agree that idealization brings its own problems, inveterate abstraction can nevertheless omit from an account elements that are vitally needed.

27 Henry Shue, *Basic Rights: Subsistence, Affluence, and U.S. Foreign Policy*, 2nd edn. (Princeton, NJ: Princeton University Press, 1996), ch. 2.

28 This realization was beginning to dawn in Henry Shue, "Mediating Duties," *Ethics*, 98 (July 1988), 687–704; and "Negative Duties Toward All, Positive Duties Toward Some," in *Human Rights for the 21st Century: Foundations for Responsible Hope*, ed. Peter Juviler and Bertram Gross, with Vladimir Kartashkin and Elena Lukasheva (Armonk, NY and London: M. E. Sharpe 1993), pp. 266–74. Onora O'Neill has done me one better, arguing that duties are so important that our theories should be duty-based, not rights-based. For two different responses to O'Neill on this point, as well as references to her arguments, see Thomas Pogge, "O'Neill on Rights and Duties," *Grazer Philosophische Studien*, 43 (1992), 233–47; and James W. Nickel, "How Human Rights Generate Duties to Protect and Provide," *Human Rights Quarterly*, 15 (1993), 77–86.

29 In fairly crude form it appears in, for example, Mary Ann Glendon, *Rights Talk: The Impoverishment of Political Discourse* (New York: The Free Press, 1991). Glendon credits Marx with Hegel's critical point and embraces it wholeheartedly: "The eighteenth-century rights of life, liberty, and property, as Karl Marx was the first to note, are preeminently rights of separated, independent, individuals" (p. 47). Glendon headed the Vatican's delegation to the 1995 Beijing Conference on Women's Rights.

30 Jeremy Waldron, " 'Nonsense upon stilts'? – A reply," in *'Nonsense upon Stilts'* pp. 129–32.

31 This is, I think, a popularization of the charge made in "Atomism" by Charles Taylor.

32 I say that duty (2), the duty to protect, is "ordinarily" assigned differently from duty (1); it is, on the other hand, logically possible for duty (2) to be universal as well. If one were trying to implement a certain sort of anarchism, for example, one might, instead of having a state, police forces, and so on to do the protecting of rights – the professionalization of protection, as it were – try to make every individual responsible not only for not violating a right [duty 1], but for interceding to protect anyone threatened by a failure in performance of the duty not to violate the right. Given the contemporary professionalization, and internationalization, of crime, I see little to be learned from this line of speculation, however.

33 John Rawls, "The Law of Peoples," in *On Human Rights* ed. Shute and Hurley, p. 62 and p. 225 (note 26); and compare Rawls, *The Law of Peoples*, p. 65.

34 See, for example, Philip Alston, "International Law and the Right to Food," in *Food As A Human Right*, ed. by Asbjorn Eide, Wenche Barth Eide, *et al.* (Tokyo: United Nations University, 1984), pp. 162–74; and Philip Alston, "International Law and the Human Right to Food," in *The Right to Food*, ed. P. Alston and K. Tomasevski, International Studies in Human Rights (Dordrecht: Martinus Nijhoff for Netherlands Institute of Human Rights, 1984), pp. 9–68.

35 The next step in the argument, of course, is: since the implementation of every right, including so-called negative rights, necessitates the performance of positive duties, the terminology of "negative rights" and "positive rights" is grossly misleading and ought to be abandoned – see *Basic Rights*, ch. 2.

36 This thesis continues to be challenged forcefully by Thomas W. Pogge, *World Poverty and Human Rights: Cosmopolitan Responsibilities and Reforms* (Cambridge: Polity Press, 2002), ch. 2, "How Should Human Rights be Conceived?" Also see Thomas W. Pogge, *Realizing Rawls* (Ithaca and London: Cornell University Press, 1989), pp. 32 and 238; Pogge suggests that a "negative duty not to make others the victims of unjust institutions" (238) accounts for all relevant requirements. Onora O'Neill made a fundamentally similar move in "Lifeboat Earth," *Philosophy & Public Affairs*, 4: 3 (Spring 1975), 273–92, arguing that, in the case of famines, a "right not to be killed and a corresponding duty not to kill" will perform all the crucial work otherwise believed to require more positive duties, once one understands the background of institutions lying behind famines. A valuable recent discussion is in Brian Orend, *Human Rights: Concept and Context* (Peterborough, Ontario: Broadview Press, 2002), pp. 139–47.

37 However much one may wish to fault John Rawls for not progressing far beyond ideal theory, he did realize that even ideal theory needs to be about "basic structure," the institutions that embody the normative principles.

38 Again, whatever one thinks of the Rawlsian solutions, the consideration of political stability in (the rarely read) Part Three of *A Theory of Justice*, as well as the central role played in the argument in the original position by the psychological strains of commitment, are admirable examples of attempts to integrate empirical matters of motivation, incentive, and social structure, with matters of reasonable normative demands.

39 Highly promising work is now being done on functioning international norms. See, for example, Christian G. K. Reus-Smit, *The Moral Purpose of the State* (Princeton, NJ: Princeton University Press, 1999); Neta C. Crawford, *Argument and Change in World Politics: Ethics, Decolonization, and Humanitarian Intervention* (Cambridge: Cambridge University Press, 2002) and Nina Tannenwald, *The Nuclear Taboo* (Cambridge: Cambridge University Press, 2003).

40 I have tried to illustrate how one might begin to assess the reasonableness of duties to implement a right to food in "Solidarity among Strangers and the Right to Food," in *World Hunger and Morality*, ed. William Aiken and Hugh LaFollette, (Upper Saddle River, NJ: Prentice-Hall 1996), pp. 113–32.

41 I am struggling here to come up with a far less "ideal" version of something resembling the Scanlon/Barry criterion – see T. M. Scanlon, "Contractualism and Utilitarianism," in *Utilitarianism and Beyond*, ed. Amartya Sen and Bernard Williams (Cambridge and New York: Cambridge University Press,

1982), pp. 103–28; and Brian Barry, *Justice as Impartiality, A Treatise on Social Justice*, vol. II, (Oxford: Clarendon Press, 1995), ch. 3.

42 For attempts to characterize how specification proceeds, see Henry S. Richardson, "Specifying Norms as a Way to Resolve Concrete Ethical Problems," *Philosophy & Public Affairs*, vol. 19, no. 4 (Fall 1990), pp. 279–310; and "Beyond Good and Right: Towards a Constructive Ethical Pragmatism," *Philosophy & Public Affairs*, vol. 24, no. 2 (Spring 1995), pp. 108–41.

43 Thomas M. Scanlon, "Human Rights as a Neutral Concern," in *Human Rights and U.S. Foreign Policy: Principles and Applications*, ed. Peter G. Brown and Douglas MacLean (Lexington, Mass. and Toronto: Lexington Books, 1979), pp. 87–8. Scanlon applied this point directly to Walzer's views in his review of *Spheres of Justice* – see T. M. Scanlon, "Local Justice," *London Review of Books*, September 5, 1985, p. 17.

44 Ann Elizabeth Mayer, "Universal Versus Islamic Human Rights: A Clash of Cultures or A Clash with a Construct," *Michigan Journal of International Law*, 15: 2 (Winter 1994), 307–404, at p. 327. Also see Ann Elizabeth Mayer, *Islam and Human Rights: Tradition and Politics*, 2nd edn. (Boulder, Col.: Westview Press, 1995; and London: Pinter Publishers, 1995).

45 See Samuel P. Huntington, "The Clash of Civilizations?" *Foreign Affairs*, 72: 3 (Summer 1993), 22–49; and Nathan Gardels, "The Islamic–Confucian Connection: Interview with Samuel P. Huntington," *New Perspectives Quarterly*, 10: 3 (Summer 1993), 19–23. The "World Conference on Human Rights" in Vienna was in June 1993. Huntington's response to critics was: "If Not Civilizations, What? Paradigms of the Post-Cold War World," *Foreign Affairs*, 72: 5 (November/December 1993), 186–94.

46 Ann Elizabeth Mayer, "Universal Versus Islamic Human Rights," p. 309.

47 Jeremy Waldron, " 'Nonsense upon stilts'? – A reply," in *'Nonsense upon Stilts'*, p. 170.

48 I do not intend to invoke any "magic of conversation," as Martin Hollis tellingly and skeptically referred to it in discussion at Columbia University. Actual conversations lead to misunderstandings and disagreements as well as to understandings and agreements. I intend to assert only that it is groundless to assume that agreement is somehow in principle out of reach because of unbridgeable chasms between cultures. It would be a valuable, but heavily empirical, project to spell out all the constraints and conditions that do most to promote agreement. Nevertheless, it would manifestly be helpful if the participants in a conversation were motivated by a commitment to formulating principles that they can indeed agree upon, as specified in Scanlon, "Contractualism and Utilitarianism," and Barry, *Justice as Impartiality*.

49 One could have a kind of how-many-angels-on-the-head-of-a-pin debate about whether some belief of the S_1s had been transferred, via the conversation, to the S_2s or the S_2s had just seen a new wrinkle in one of their existing

beliefs. Does one already believe everything entailed by what one believes? This matters for analyses of knowledge, but not here.

50 I have briefly explored some of the complexities of what for Rawls would count, I think, as international public reason in Henry Shue, "Rawls and the Outlaws," *Politics, Philosophy & Economics*, 1: 3 (2002), 307–23.

51 John Rawls, "The Law of Peoples," in *On Human Rights*, p. 68.

52 Louis Henkin, *The Age of Rights* (New York: Columbia University Press, 1990), p. 6.

53 I believe that this is not merely possible but is actually happening. It is, however, beyond my competence and the scope of this article to attempt to establish the empirical point. Significant work on the evolution of transcultural norms about human rights is being done by specialists in international relations. Kathryn Sikkink has documented the depth of cooperation on human rights between IOs (international organizations) and NGOs (nongovernmental organizations), many of the latter operating chapters within rights-violating states and helping crucially to bring international pressure to bear upon their own governments – see "The Power of Principled Ideas: Human Rights Policies in the United States and Western Europe," in *Ideas & Foreign Policy: Beliefs, Institutions, and Political Change*, ed. Judith Goldstein and Robert O. Keohane (Ithaca, NY: Cornell University Press 1993), pp. 139–70; and other work by Sikkink, especially on Latin America, referenced there. Christian Reus-Smit has argued that the connections between international and domestic go even deeper and that it is now an essential element in the identity of a modern state that it display some type of commitment to human rights – see *The Moral Purpose of the State*.

54 A splendid example of the specificity recommended is the Global Resources Tax (GRT) advocated by Pogge – see Thomas W. Pogge, "An Egalitarian Law of Peoples," *Philosophy & Public Affairs*, 23: 3 (Summer 1994), 195–224, esp. 199–205. Strictly speaking, Pogge is discussing justice, but the same tax mechanism – often now called the Tobin tax (for economist James Tobin) – could be employed in the name of subsistence rights. My attempt to be similarly concrete, on a different subject, is: Henry Shue, "Avoidable Necessity: Global Warming, International Fairness, and Alternative Energy," in *Theory and Practice*, NOMOS 37, edited by Ian Shapiro and Judith Wagner DeCew (New York: New York University Press, 1995), pp. 239–64. In the same NOMOS volume Susan J. Brison notes the concreteness of Ronald Dworkin's method in *Life's Dominion* – see "The Theoretical Importance of Practice," p. 234.

55 See Thomas W. Pogge, *Realizing Rawls* (Ithaca, NY: Cornell University Press, 1989), pp. 227–38. "An intercultural conversation about the validity of human rights is now taking place among people with different cultural assumptions" – Xiaorong Li, "'Asian Values' and the Universality of Human Rights," *Philosophy and Public Policy*, 16: 2 (Spring 1996), 18–23 (23).

Chapter 12

Global justice: whose obligations?

ONORA O'NEILL

COSMOPOLITAN RIGHTS AND STATE OBLIGATIONS

Many respected and prominent accounts of justice have cosmopolitan aspirations yet provide a poor basis for thinking about the demands of justice in a globalizing world, and especially for thinking about economic justice. Typically they endorse some account of cosmopolitan principles of justice, then assume without argument, or without sufficient argument, that the *primary agents of justice* must be states. Other agents and agencies are seen as *secondary agents of justice*, whose contribution to justice is regulated, defined and allocated by states. These approaches to justice are cosmopolitan in assuming that justice is owed to all human beings, wherever they live and whatever their citizenship, yet anti-cosmopolitan in assuming that many significant obligations stop or vary at state or other boundaries.

There are tensions, and perhaps incoherences, in thinking that anti-cosmopolitan institutions such as bounded states and their subordinate institutions can shoulder primary obligations of cosmopolitan justice. On the surface, states are fundamentally ill-suited and ill-placed to secure or strengthen justice beyond their own borders. Their primary responsibilities are to their own maintenance and to their inhabitants. Historically the states that have secured a measure of justice beyond their borders – *pax Romana, pax Britannica, pax Americana* – have generally been imperial states that exercised power beyond their borders, or obliterated certain borders, or made them more porous in certain respects. These facts are so obvious that it is remarkable that anyone should see the pursuit of justice for those beyond their borders as a primary task of states. And, of course, many have made no such assumptions. Unlike cosmopolitans, would-be realists about international relations have always argued that states should do nothing about injustice beyond their borders, except where it is important to their own survival and interests.

The lamentable but strong evidence that states have failed to secure justice, and in particular economic justice, beyond their borders, should not surprise us. Although "humanitarian interventions" to curb major violations of human rights have become more numerous since the ending of the Cold War, even massive violations do not always lead to intervention (and there can be good prudential reasons for refraining: non-intervention in Chechnya or in China is wholly realistic).[1] Even when there has been intervention it has often been late or ineffective, or both (consider former Yugoslavia or Somalia). And the supposed attempts of richer states and of international agencies to reduce poverty in less developed countries have also been ineffective. In the 1990s the gap between rich and poor has grown rather than shrunk.[2] Assigning obligations to secure justice beyond their borders to states may be no more sensible than assigning obligations to supervise hen houses to foxes.

It is not only practitioners who combine cosmopolitan and anti-cosmopolitan rhetoric. Many prominent political and philosophical approaches to justice also combine cosmopolitan aspirations with statist assumptions. One example is the *Universal Declaration of Rights* of 1948, which demands "the promotion of universal respect for and observance of human rights,"[3] then assumes that this noble goal can be pursued by assigning to states the counterpart obligations to respect these rights. The poor drafting of the *Declaration* obscures this hiatus: the text refers promiscuously to "countries," "member-states" and "nations." However a careful reading makes it quite plain that obligations to secure universal rights are assigned to states, almost always to the state of which an individual is a citizen or member.[4] Rights against states of which an individual is not a citizen or member, if any, are far less extensive. For example, the *Declaration* distinguishes the rights to freedom of movement and association that states should guarantee their citizens or members from those they should guarantee non-members (Consider: "the right to freedom of movement and residence within the borders of each state" Art. 13, "the right to leave any country, including his own, and to return to his country" Art. 13 and "the right to seek and enjoy in other countries asylum from persecution" Art. 14).

John Rawls' theory of justice offers a more philosophical account of principles of justice of universal scope that links them to a substantially statist view of agents of justice. Rawls gives priority to an account of "domestic" justice: he aims initially to "formulate a reasonable conception of justice for the basic structure of society conceived for the time being as a closed system isolated from other societies."[5] This initial assumption recurs constantly in his writings; it is not discarded even in his late writings on justice beyond borders. Many commentators think that a latent statism marks even Rawls' most explicit attempts to arrive at a wider account of justice. His account of global justice remains an account of "international" justice, in which the supposed legitimacy of assigning control of bounded territories to "peoples" is presupposed, and limits and perhaps undermines his arguments for justice beyond borders.[6]

COULD ABSTRACT COSMOPOLITANISM BE ENOUGH?

Looked at with hindsight, the gigantic costs of assuming that states (or even Rawlsian "peoples") are the primary agents of justice may seem obvious. Yet what are the alternatives? One possibility would be to offer an account of international justice that says *nothing* about the allocation of obligations, assuming only that all agents and agencies are bound by the same basic principles of justice. Cannot an abstract account of universal rights of cosmopolitan scope be matched by an equally abstract account of universal obligations of cosmopolitan scope? Indeed, could we not adopt an abstract account of universal obligations and then forget about any account of universal rights? The latter approach was adopted by Peter Singer in his still much discussed 1972 article on famine, affluence, and morality, which argues that anybody with more than he or she needs ought to give the surplus to the relief of poverty.[7] Utilitarian and similar consequentialist positions subsume justice in generalized beneficence, obliging each to do whatever is likely to contribute most to aggregate happiness or welfare. Judgments about what is likely to contribute most to happiness or welfare will, of course, always be made against complex background assumptions and evidence about others' action, about institutions and about resources, about the effects of possible action, and about the value of those effects. Such judgments will not, however, be derived from or presuppose any independent views about rights: they may or may not support the rights promulgated in the *Universal Declaration*, or in other manifestos and charters; they will regard distance and borders, hence states, as lacking intrinsic moral significance.

Utilitarian and other consequentialist approaches to global justice have notable weaknesses. In placing all conclusions at the beck and call of claims about the value of outcomes and about the vastly complex causal connections that determine outcomes, they gain a spurious precision. Such reasoning may seem to anchor moral requirements in empirical calculation, but when evidence, data and calculations (not to mention units of account) are all hazy, those requirements will be elastic, if not indeterminate. They may foster a rhetoric of cosmopolitan justice, yet fail to determine *who* ought to do *what* for *whom*. Of course, Utilitarian reasoning can also be deployed more circumspectly – or possibly more ambitiously – to work out which institutions should be constructed and how obligations should be allocated among them, leaving the resolution of particular cases to the normal functioning of these institutions. But here too very demanding calculations are needed to see just who should do what to help "rear the fabric of felicity by the hands of reason and of law".[8]

So if we think that ethical requirements are universally important, we have reason to look for accounts of rights and obligations that have firmer anchoring than Utilitarian thinking or alternative forms of abstract cosmopolitanism can provide. Moreover, we will have strong reasons to think that it will not be possible to anchor an account of rights without offering an account of obligations. The abstract cosmopolitanism that Declarations of Rights favour has practical import only when we can determine *who* ought to do or provide *what* for *whom*.

This may look unproblematic: surely universal rights are secured by universal performance of obligations. If all agents and agencies have the same obligations why should any further allocation of obligations be needed? However this neat parallel is illusory. Although all agents and agencies can be bound by the same *underlying* obligations of justice, many of more specific forms of action required to implement the rights promulgated in the Declaration and subsequent documents have to be discharged by specific agents and agencies. This may not be the case for the core obligations corresponding to liberty rights, but is generally true of obligations to provide goods and services, of obligations to construct institutions that may be relevant for poverty reduction, and also of obligations to enforce the obligations corresponding to liberty rights.

Up to a point, statist approaches to anchoring the obligations of justice may, it seems, be on the right track. They do not leave rights claims floating free, or rely on a merely abstract claim that obligations are universal, leaving it entirely open *who* is obliged to meet or secure *which* rights for *which* others. In viewing states as *primary agents of justice* realists recognize that rights are mere rhetoric unless there are counterpart obligations, and take seriously the need to assign specific tasks to institutions and individuals.

Despite these merits, statist approaches to cosmopolitan justice are now implausible. The initial assumption that states alone are *primary agents of justice* views states, and states alone, as having the will and the capabilities to discharge, delegate, or assign all obligations of justice. The problem with statist approaches is not that they seek to allocate the obligations that are the counterparts to human rights, but that they allocate them in ways that may not work. Despite the supposed realism of those who assign obligations to states, their approach to international justice – and above all to development issues – is often quite unrealistic.

There are at least three quite different reasons for thinking that it is not enough to view states as primary agents of justice, which allocate and determine the obligations of other, secondary agents of justice. One reason that has been much discussed – it was all too evident in 1948 – is that many states are unjust: they lack the will to shoulder the obligations proclaimed in the Declaration and other documents. Although such states may have the competence and capacity to be primary agents of justice, they abuse that role and inflict and institutionalize forms of injustice. Tyrannies and rogue states constantly violate the rights of their inhabitants (it is often misleading to speak of them as *citizens*). They quite often violate the rights of outsiders. Even when the United Nations and "the international community" seek to impress on such states the importance of respecting human rights, the sanctions that can be brought to bear are always limited, and often risk provoking or causing further harm to the very inhabitants whose rights are being violated. If rogue states could be reformed they would deliver justice, and only their reform can deliver full political justice. But as things are they deliver not only political but other forms of injustice.

A second reason for thinking that states are not always appropriate primary agents of justice is that many states are incapable of securing justice for their citizens or members: even if they have the will, they lack the capabilities to shoulder the obligations assigned them by the Declaration and other international documents, so cannot effectively assign obligations to secondary agents of justice or secure their compliance. Like rogue states and tyrannies, weak states and failing states (sometimes labelled "quasi states") fail to secure the supposed rights of their inhabitants. But they typically do so in quite different ways. They may fail to enforce the law rather than enforce unjust laws or policies; they may leave individuals without redress in the face of corruption and banditry; they may fail to challenge unjust and criminal activities; they may fail to provide elementary infrastructure or health or educational services; they may fail to provide the basic conditions for economic activity, let alone prosperity or economic justice. Sometimes they cannot even exercise effective control of central state institutions, such as the police, the customs or the armed services.

A third reason for thinking that states cannot be the sole agents of justice is that even states with some capacities to secure rights, and in particular the rights of their own citizens, often find that processes of globalization require them to make their borders more porous, thereby weakening state power and allowing powerful agents and agencies of other sorts to become more active within their borders. For example, weak states often cannot do much to control the activities of transnational corporations or of international crime within their borders, and may not succeed in regulating legitimate business either.

Given that there are many bad states, many weak states and many states too weak to prevent or regulate the activities of supposedly external bodies within their borders, the thought that justice must always begin by assigning primary obligations to states implausible. Yet we have seen the thought that we might say *nothing* about who holds these obligations, hence *nothing* about the allocation of specific tasks needed for justice is, is also implausible. This should I think leave both political philosophers and thoughtful citizens with a strong feeling of unease: yet often it does not. It is not obvious why there is so little unease, but I shall offer a suggestion on that point before going on to consider briefly which agents and agencies other than states might carry obligations of justice beyond borders.

PRACTICAL QUESTIONS AND RETROSPECTIVE QUESTIONS

Discussions of the moral agency of states, as of other institutions, have sometimes been viewed as implausible on the grounds that neither states nor other institutions can be held responsible or blamed for moral failures. Moral blame and fault, it is said, can be ascribed to individuals but not to institutions and collectivities. For example, individuals can feel guilt and remorse, states or groups cannot. Taken neat, this "realist" view queries not only specific claims about the appropriate allocation of obligations, but the underlying view of agency needed for accounts of justice.

There are indeed large differences in the ways that individuals and institutions can respond to their own past failings. But a retrospective focus on past failings is not the same as a prospective focus on present and future obligations. It conflates questions about past and about future responsibility. *Practical questions* about what a given agent or agency should do are quite different from *retrospective questions* about failure and the proper response to failure.

Forward and backward looking ethical questions may seem inseparable if one takes a rather specific, complex and hostile view of obligations, such as the one Bernard Williams criticizes in *Ethics and the Limits of Philosophy*, in a chapter where he discusses a construct that he calls "the morality system."[9] "The morality system" is a way of looking at ethical requirements that links them closely to issues about blame and other retrospective attitudes. This way of looking at ethics deliberately lumps together *forward-looking practical questions* – "what ought I, or we, or this institution do?" and judgmental, *retrospective questions* – "what view should we take of those who fail to do what they ought?" The conflation is often made by those who (unlike Williams) speak mostly of *responsibilities* rather than *obligations*, who often implicitly privilege a retrospective stance.

It seems to me unfortunate to conflate these two types of questions. There may be a lot to be said about moral requirements that does not entail anything much about retrospective attitudes or action. In particular, claims about the requirements of justice may be quite distinct from claims about what should be done when these are flouted. Blaming and shaming, punishing and rewarding and other retrospective attitudes and action may be out of place, or need to take distinctive forms, when institutional agents are concerned. We evidently take quite different views of punishing states and punishing individuals, and do not generally ascribe the full range of retrospective attitudes to past moral failure of states or of other institutions. We do not expect them to feel guilt, or regret or remorse, although we may sometimes think that they should compensate, or even apologize. Of course, it may be that these retrospective issues have also loomed too large in personal ethics. Williams may be right in holding that questions about blame and other reactive attitudes should have a more limited place in personal ethics than some suppose.

Even if retrospective questions have very little part in an account of justice, practical questions are not out of place in thinking about institutional agents: like individuals, institutions can have obligations. Most political philosophers would hold that states have obligations of justice ranging from obligations not to conduct aggressive wars to obligations to honour treaties, from obligations not to commit crimes against humanity to obligations to protect their citizens. Yet we are curiously diffident in speaking about the obligations, including the obligations of justice, of institutions other than states and those bodies that represent or derive from them (governments, international agencies). In thinking of states as the *primary agents of justice*, many would-be advocates of justice cosmopolitan maintain positions that are less distant from the realist positions they reject than one might imagine. They view non-state institutions as having only *secondary obligations of justice*, defined by their required compliance with state requirements. It is as if they viewed states alone as active global citizens and all other institutions as passive global citizens.

AGENTS AND AGENCIES

There is nothing very unusual or surprising about ascribing obligations to institutions, including states. Institutional agents and agencies, like individual agents, bring cognitive and decision-making capacities and capabilities to bear on choices that initiate action and affect what happens. The fact that institutional capabilities exist only with the support and participation of individuals does not show that institutions have no moral obligations. For it is equally true that many individual capabilities arise only through the action of others and through participation in institutions and practices (there is a sense in which *natural persons* have *artificial capabilities*). Both individual and institutional capabilities are determined not only by the intrinsic abilities of the agent or agency, but also by the capabilities that are constituted when intrinsic abilities are deployed using determinate resources and institutional powers. Individual and institutional capabilities can be exercised in many specific areas of life, although little is gained by trying to classify them into types of agency such as "moral agency," "legal agency," "political agency" and the like. It is probably more useful to replace these ways of talking with less reifying modes of speech, and to distinguish types of constraint and capability, rather than types of agency.

We can, I suggest, ask of any agent or agency – an individual, an institution, or a collectivity – whether he or she or we, it or they, can be bound by specific constraints or principles, such as economic constraints, or moral constraints, or prudential constraints, or professional constraints. In particular we can ask whether an agent or agency of a specified type could be bound by certain sorts of normative requirements, such as those that correspond to securing or respecting aspects of a conception of justice. The answers we can plausibly give will depend on the relationship between the propositional content of principles of justice and the actual capabilities of the putative agent or agency. Agents and agencies can only be obliged to act in ways for which they have an adequate set of capabilities. Where there is an effective primary agent of justice, the allocation of specific obligations to other agents and agencies with coherent and effective capabilities to discharge them is feasible.

So, for example, we may think that a child of fifteen could be required to study a second language, but hardly that a financial services company could be so required; that a corporation could be required to demonstrate compliance with health and safety legislation, but hardly that a five-year-old could be so required; that a university could be required to comply with a complex financial memorandum, but hardly that a market stall holder could be so required. And so on with banal specificity. Only if we conclude that an agent – individual, institution, or collectivity – *can* carry a certain obligation does the further question arise as to whether it *ought* to carry that obligation. Of course, where we can establish that a specific obligation – say, an obligation not to obstruct free speech – is held by every competent agent, no *further* argument is needed to show that it falls on all agents and agencies with the capability to avoid obstructing free speech. But, as we have noted, some specific obligations that are important for justice can be discharged only by specific agents and institutions, with the competence to carry parts of the relevant task. Assuming falsely that the primary obligation of allocating other obligations of justice can always be assigned to states, even if they are weak and incompetent, indeed incapable of making and enforcing an effective allocation of the tasks of justice, is an inadequate approach to justice.

It is not enough merely to *assume* that there will always be an effective and decent state to assign obligations of justice to other institutions. Any adequate assignment must allocate specific obligations to those with the necessary powers, skills and resources (other considerations may also be relevant). Police forces with adequate resources and ordinary degrees of freedom from intimidation can be required to keep order and prevent torture: they cannot be required to provide health care. Hospitals and medical practitioners can be required not to deceive patients: they cannot be required to maintain national security. States and the governments that represent them at a given time can be required to live up to undertakings made in treaties: they cannot be required to farm the land. Individuals can be required not to assault or defraud others: they cannot be required to secure world peace. In these and other cases, obligations cannot be coherently ascribed to agents or agencies that are incapable of carrying them.

OUGHT AND CAN

I have argued so far that both institutions and individuals can have obligations *if but only if* they have adequate capabilities to fulfil or discharge those obligations. This is a more guarded thought than the adage "*ought* implies *can*," which can be misinterpreted as suggesting that having used money for frivolous purposes I now am released from a debt I could otherwise have repaid. The thought that obligations presuppose capabilities for their discharge, so lapse when agents and agencies do not have and cannot acquire the requisite capacities needs a lot of further explication. Nevertheless, I think there are robust links between obligations and capabilities for action: in particular lack of capability always counts against an ascription of obligations, except where the lack is chosen. Individuals cannot be obliged to resolve the problems of world hunger, or to grow wings and fly; institutions cannot have obligations to perform tasks for which they lack capabilities.

If this is convincing, then weak states cannot coherently be required to carry tasks for which they are not competent. Nor can weak international institutions. Yet we are constantly tempted to assume that weak states and weak international bodies can carry obligations that exceed their capabilities. We often hear claims that states and the governments that represent them should solve a wide range of social problems, or that the United Nations or "the international community" should deal with an even wider range of requirements of justice. And yet we know that weak states and the UN, and all their respective subordinate institutions, often have inadequate resources and capabilities for these tasks. The UN has not been designed or resourced to have effective powers to deal with large ranges of problems that commentators commonly suggest it should solve. The traditional conception of states as sovereign is wholly at odds with the multiple and real limitations on the powers of many states, including the multiple ways in which (like other agents) they are dependent on other more powerful institutions that may oppose, prevent or demand certain uses of state power. Weak states are always ill-equipped to enforce or secure respect for central human rights, even for their own citizens.

Conventional responses to these points often stress the need to build up weak states and to reform international institutions. Both strategies are important. However, such reform is evidently taking a long time, and in the meantime many lives are lived and lost. Supplementary strategies may be needed. States are not the only institutional agents that can make a difference to respect for human rights. Some powerful non-state actors have capabilities that can make a difference to some aspects of justice. For example, some religious groups and institutions, some professions, some transnational corporations and some non-governmental organizations may *in certain circumstances* be able to help secure respect for certain aspects of justice, even within failing states. This is significant because some non-state actors are powerful. For present purposes I shall set religious institutions and professions aside, and consider very briefly some tasks that certain other non-state actors, in particular TNCs and NGOs, might take on.

I select these examples because TNCs and NGOs are numerous and sometimes influential in weak states, and because their activities may be important for global justice or injustice. The *United Nations Conference on Trade and Development* estimates that there are now over 60,000 transnational corporations compared with 37,000 in 1990. These transnational corporations have around 800,000 foreign affiliates, compared with some 170,000 foreign affiliates in 1990, and millions of suppliers and distributors.[10] A census of non-governmental organizations would also run into many tens and probably hundreds of thousands.[11] Although many NGOs have limited powers and objectives, indeed many are single issue organizations, and although many are highly dependent on funders and founders, some have considerable power and resources, and a few have structures of governance that allow them to act on a wide range of issues.

But here is the rub. Where states are weak, who is to allocate obligations to particular non-state actors? Where there are no (adequate) primary agents of justice, how can there be any (adequate) secondary agents of justice? An alternative view would be that, if they have the relevant capabilities, non-state actors *need not, indeed ought not, hold back on meeting their basic obligations.* In exploring this thought I am not suggesting that either TNCs or NGOs can wholly supplant states. In particular, they are unlikely to be able to assign obligations of justice across a society (any that can do this have become states within a (weak) state). They are, however, quite likely to be able to find specific ways of carrying *some* of the underlying obligations of justice that fall on all agents and agencies; and they may even sometimes find ways of taking up some tasks that are usually carried by primary agents of justice. There is no reason for thinking that the underlying obligations of justice should be neglected by non-state actors simply because no effective state enforces legal requirements or allocates specific tasks.

In powerful states with effective legislation and institutions, non-state actors may reasonably view obligations of justice as a matter of conforming to laws and requirements established and enforced by those states. They can rightly see themselves merely as *secondary agents of justice.* Not so in weak states. Where states are too weak to allocate obligations, some relatively powerful non-state actors may be able to contribute to – or to damage – aspects of justice. Attention is often given to the ways in which non-state actors may take advantage of a lack of state power to inflict injustice: those who accuse some TNCs of lack of respect for human rights clearly take it that they are potential agents of justice, and actual agents of injustice. But there are other possibilities. For example, TNCs can contribute to justice by instituting economic and social polices that bear on human rights, on environmental standards or on labour practices, and even on wider areas of life. They may introduce local accounting and tendering practices that move a business culture away from corruption and towards accountability. They bear down on a culture of bribery by making it known that any "facilitation fees" will be made public in their accounts. They may institute environmental and safety standards that go beyond local legal requirements. They may publicly refuse to take part in customary forms of nepotism and cronyism. They may strive for labour relations that meet high standards. They may make demands in these areas on their suppliers and employees. Because TNCs are often major powers in weak economies, with which many local businesses want connections, these standards can ripple beyond the contexts in which they are introduced. Some TNCs might argue that setting standards and influencing local practice has little to do with the bottom line and shareholder value; others, in particular those whose business is long term, may judge matters differently. In any case, these are not unrealistic ideas: in the last few years they have been affirmed in a growing dialogue between international business and the UN, and in the policies of certain TNCs.[12]

NGOs are often less powerful than major TNCs, although the largest have considerable powers, and some administer programmes funded by (richer) states and international organisations. It is conventional to assume that NGOs can contribute to justice more readily than TNCs, because TNCs have shareholders. Realities may be more differentiated. Some NGOs have ideological commitments, or specific agendas that can hamper their contributions to justice. As noted some TNCs have found ranges of action where they can contribute. Where either sort of institution is capable of acting to improve justice, obligations of justice come into play.

Like TNCs, some NGOs can deploy good employment and environmental policies. More importantly, in a weak state an NGO whose funding is not local may be able to pursue employment and purchasing policies that implement standards that the government does not, indeed cannot, institute or achieve. Some NGOs may take responsibility for aspects of welfare and educational provision, even for constructing infrastructure and providing health care. Even when they acquire a major role in these and similar areas, they will not become primary agents of justice: they are unlikely to take on the task of allocating obligations to other institutions, or of enforcing compliance with that allocation. Equally they will not simply be secondary agents of justice, pursuing policies set by government and working under the authority of the relevant ministries. Rather they can use the area of discretion that lack of state power opens up to support changes that may lead towards more just and effective policies.

Where power is dispersed and in part privatized, in the sense that it is in large part non-statal, the distinction between primary and secondary agents of justice falters. Non-state actors, who in other contexts would be secondary agents of justice, may find themselves able to carry more aspects of those obligations of justice that hold for all agents and agencies, which well functioning states orchestrate. Their contribution to justice can and ought then to take advantage of opportunities before them. They can choose to support and promote justice, to wash their hands, or to take advantage of the situation to by acting unjustly. We need only think that they are obliged not to act unjustly to see that only the first of these options is acceptable.

When no available state agency can carry significant obligations of justice it can be destructive, even deluded, to assume that they will do so. It does not follow that those who think justice important should or can wait for the construction of more effective state institutions, and of a more just polity. Lives, indeed generations, may pass before that transformation is achieved. A more realistic view may be to accept that in the meanwhile some tasks *may be and should be* taken on by institutions that statist views of justice would regard merely as secondary agents of justice, lacking clear obligations in the absence of an adequate primary agent of justice. In some circumstances certain obligations of justice, and in particular of economic justice may, may be carried by TNCs and NGOs. Although TNCs and NGOs cannot take on *all* the tasks that states, international agencies or political institutions might carry if they had the capabilities, they may be adequately placed to deliver *some* of them.

Is it risky for institutions like TNCs and NGOs to step beyond the roles that they would have in relatively effective states, in which they would be only secondary agents of justice? One danger might arise because many obligations of justice require exemptions from certain standard ethical requirements. We traditionally accord states and other institutions a partial exemption from certain other obligations, when they need this for discharging their obligations. A police force may be exempt *to a limited degree* from a prohibition on coercion, or a peace-keeping force exempt *to a limited degree* from a prohibition on seizure of property, but only because these exemptions are needed if their broader obligations are to be met. A government may be exempt *to a limited degree* from a general prohibition on hoarding in a food emergency, but only because it has to look to the equity and feasibility of maintaining food distribution. Could we accept that a TNC or an NGO should have any exemption from such requirements where they shoulder obligations of justice?

It may be helpful to consider why we allow exemptions from certain moral constraints. In general we do so *if, but only if* those exemptions are needed for carrying obligations. For example, we allow parents certain powers over their children *because* they are required to care for them (absentee parents lose these powers). We allow the state certain exemptions from obligations not to coerce *because* it is responsible for enforcing law. Entitlement to exemptions is related to task, not to status. Where non-state actors take on certain obligations of justice the same standards are relevant. An NGO that is organising food distribution need be no less exempt from restrictions on hoarding than a government that is handling food delivery itself.

Non-state actors, including TNCs and NGOs, are in practice likely to rely more on negotiation and persuasion, backed by the real threat of withdrawing business or benefits, rather than on replication of the ordinary structure of state powers. Both sorts of non-state actor often adapt work in tandem with weak states. Although there will always be some aspects of justice, including political justice, to which they can contribute rather little, there will others, including economic justice, to which they often can and ought to contribute a lot.

RECONFIGURING REALISM

Political philosophers and others who assign extensive obligations to states have often done so in the name of *realism*. Their thought is often that states enjoy sovereignty, hence states and states alone have the power and the obligation to deliver justice, at least within their own boundaries, and to ensure that others respect rights within those boundaries. In international affairs, the thought has often been parallel. States and states alone have the power to establish and maintain a social and political order that lives up the demands of the Universal Declaration, or an economic system that secures adequate food, water, shelter, and basic health care for all: non-state actors are powerless. This is a most unrealistic form of realism, and increasingly unrealistic as globalization reconfigures power.

If we are to be seriously realistic, we need to think about the full range of agents and agencies that can carry obligations, and can *if they choose* contribute to securing wider respect for certain rights. The obligations that institutions and individuals carry can never exceed their capabilities. Those capabilities are seldom adequate to secure the full range of rights proclaimed in the Universal Declaration. If states alone could initiate an increase in justice, then the situation of those in weak states would often be profoundly depressing: where institutions and individuals are weak there will be few competent obligation-bearers, few obligations will be secure, and few rights will be respected. In a weak state whose revenue raising institutions are inadequate there will be no effective rights to tax-supported welfare systems; in a failing state where the rule of law is fragile there will be no effective obligations to bring criminals to justice – and so on.

But we need not take this passive view of state capability failure as making entitlement failure for others inevitable. It is often beside the point – a reversion to retrospective thinking about blame rather than practical thinking about obligations – to respond to such cases simply by reasserting that rights have been violated. In these cases neither individuals nor institutions had the requisite ranges of capabilities to carry these obligations. There may be a future time at which institutions with more extensive and reliable capabilities are established, when more extensive obligations can be discharged, and when wider ranges of rights can be respected and even secured. Persistent ascription of obligations to meet rights to an institutional structure that lacks the capabilities to discharge them replaces forward looking practical reasoning with blame: it is wholly unrealistic.

A more realistic approach might be to raise questions about obligations to construct, improve and strengthen the capabilities of institutions and of individuals, and in particular about the need to think about the allocation of obligations among individuals and institutions. Many distinguished approaches to this topic have been exclusively statist or quasi-statist, often because they have looked mainly at questions of political justice. It may, I believe, be more convincing – and more realistic – to look at matters more opportunistically. If we allow that whatever capabilities there are, including those held by non-state actors such as TNCs and NGOs, may be and should be deployed not only to avoid injustice, but to contribute where possible to a more just social order, then there may be much to be done even where states are weak and failing and cannot (in the short run) achieve either definitive allocations of the obligations of justice or any adequate form of political justice.

The realism about international justice – realism with a rather small "r" – that I am commending does not mean that those whose lives are led in weak states that cannot secure their rights have fewer rights *in the abstract* than those in strong states. They have exactly and only those rights for which sound arguments can be given, as do those in strong states. (There is little reason for expecting sound arguments to support all and only those rights that have been promulgated in the Universal Declaration or any other document.)[13] What those in strong states have, and those in weak states lack, is justiciable rights, where obligations to respect and enforce are allocated to agents with the necessary capabilities. What those in weak states need is a process of institution building by which justiciable rights are increasingly secured. Much of this process may indeed aim to strengthen state institutions, and to secure a greater degree of political justice, which in turn may deliver economic justice. But the task does not have to await the emergence of competent and politically just states. There may be additional routes towards greater justice if obligations of justice can be discharged without waiting for a definitive allocation or enforcement of tasks. Where non-state actors can contribute to justice, fundamental obligations that in other circumstances are secured by compliance with state requirements demand that they do so. If we take the universalism of obligations as seriously as we have often taken the universalism of rights, we need to look realistically at actual agents and agencies, with their actual powers and vulnerabilities. We do not need to assume that non-state actors will be paralysed in weak states, or that all progress to justice must be endlessly postponed until more competent and just states emerge.

NOTES

1 Michael Doyle, "The New Interventionism," *Metaphilosophy*, 32 (2000), 212–35.
2 See Thomas Pogge, "Priorities of Global Justice," *Metaphilosophy*, 32 (2001), 6–24 and "'Assisting' the Global Poor" in this volume for summaries of stark evidence of the paucity of serious efforts by richer states to reduce global poverty even during the prosperous decade following the ending of the cold war, and of the increase of deep poverty during that period. See also Charles Beitz, "Does Global Inequality Matter?", ibid., 95–112. For current facts and major programs see World Bank, World Development Report 2000/1: Attacking Poverty, www.worldbank.org/poverty/wdrpoverty/report/ch2.pdf.
3 *Universal Declaration of Human Rights* (1948), reprinted in Ian Brownlie, ed., 1981, *Basic Human Rights Documents* (Oxford: Clarendon, 1981), pp. 21–7, preamble.
4 For detail see Onora O'Neill, *Bounds of Justice* (Cambridge: Cambridge University Press, 2000) and "Agents of Justice," *Metaphilosophy*, 32 (2001), 180–95.
5 John Rawls, *A Theory of Justice* (Cambridge, Mass., Harvard University Press, 1971), p. 8.
6 See John Rawls, The *Law of Peoples* (Cambridge, Mass., Harvard University Press, 1999). Rawls maintains that his account of justice is designed for *peoples* not *states*. However his conception of a people is not cultural but political. It builds on notions of territoriality, boundaries and a monopoly of coercive power: most political philosophers would deem anything with these properties a state. See Andrew Kuper, "Rawlsian Global Justice: Beyond the Law of Peoples to a Cosmopolitan Law of Persons," *Political Theory* (2000); Onora O'Neill, "Political Liberalism and Public Reason: A Critical Notice of John Rawls, *Political Liberalism*," *The Philosophical Review*, 106 (1997), 411–28.
7 Peter Singer, "Famine, Affluence and Morality," *Philosophy & Public Affairs*, 1 (1972), 229–43.

8 Jeremy Bentham, *Introduction to the Principles of Morals and of Legislation*, ch 1, para 1, in *A Fragment on Government and Introduction to the Principles of Morals and of Legislation*, ed., Wilfred Harrison (Oxford: Blackwell, 1967), p. 125.

9 Bernard Williams, *Ethics and the Limits of Philosophy* (London: Fontana, 1985), ch 10.

10 See Mary Robinson, UN High Commissioner for Human Rights, *BP Lecture*, 29.11.01, www.bp.com/centres/press/s_detail.asp?id=142.

11 For some thoughts on the diversity of institutions that may contribute – positively or negatively – see Thomas Risse-Kappen, ed., *Bringing Transnational Relations Back in: Non-State Actors, Domestic Structures and International Institutions* (Cambridge: Cambridge University Press, 1995); Robert O'Brien et al., *Contesting Global Governance: Multilateral Economic Institutions and Global Social Movements*; Onora O'Neill "Agents of Justice," *Metaphilosophy*, 32 (2001), 180–95 and "Bounded and Cosmopolitan Justice," *Review of International Studies*, 26 (2000), 45–60.

12 This is now accepted UN policy: see the 1999 Global Compact initiative which asks corporations to sign up to 9 principles covering support for human rights, good labour relations and care for the environment, www.un.org/partners/business/fs1.htm. For a corporate response to the initiative see British Petroleum's policies as set out at www.bp.com/key_issues/social/human_rights.asp.

13 James Griffin, "Discrepancies between the Best Philosophical Account of Human Rights and the International Law of Human Rights," Presidential Address, *Proceedings of the Aristotelian Society*, 2001, 1–28.

Chapter 13

"Assisting" the global poor

THOMAS W. POGGE

We citizens of the affluent countries tend to discuss our obligations toward the distant needy mainly in terms of donations and transfers, assistance and redistribution: how much of our wealth, if any, should we give away to the hungry abroad? Using one prominent theorist to exemplify this way of conceiving the problem, I show how it is a serious error – and a very costly one for the global poor.

In his book *The Law of Peoples*, John Rawls adds an eighth law to his previous account: "Peoples have a duty to assist other peoples living under unfavorable conditions that prevent their having a just or decent political and social regime."[1] The addition is meant to show that Rawls' proposal can give a plausible account of global economic justice, albeit a less egalitarian one than his cosmopolitan critics have been urging upon him.[2] This newly added duty is, however, more than Rawls' account can justify and less than what is needed to do justice to the problem of world poverty.

It is doubtful that the new amendment would be adopted in Rawls' international original position, which represents liberal and decent peoples only. Each such representative is rational[3] and seeking an international order that enables his or her own people to be stably organized according to its own conception of justice or decency.[4] Such representatives may well agree to assist one another in times of need. But why is it rational for them to commit to assisting poor peoples that never had a liberal or decent institutional order?

This challenge highlights how Rawls' international original position is too strongly focused on safeguarding the well-orderedness of liberal and decent societies and therefore triply implausible: first, peoples neither liberal nor decent are not represented in the international original position, and the interests of their members are thereby discounted completely.[5] Second, because (liberal and decent) *peoples* count equally, the interests of their individual members (in the viability and stability of their domestic order) are represented unequally to the detriment of those who belong to more populous peoples.[6] Third, other important interests of members of liberal or decent peoples are not represented – for example, their interest in their socio-economic position relative to that of other societies.[7]

Though more demanding than what his international original position can justify, Rawls' duty of assistance is not demanding enough. This duty stipulates only an *absolute* target: no people should be prevented by poverty from organizing itself as a liberal or decent society. Rawls opposes any *relative* target: above the absolute threshold, international inequalities are unconstrained and hence a matter of moral indifference.

Rawls suggests why he opposes any relative target: once a people has attained the modest economic capacities necessary to sustain a liberal or decent institutional order, it is morally free to decide whether to make further net savings. If it does not, then its per capita income may fall further and further behind that of other peoples who save and invest more. It has a right to make this decision. But it also must then accept responsibility for the consequences. It cannot plausibly complain later about the evolved discrepancy in affluence – let alone demand a share of the much greater incomes other societies have become able to generate.[8]

One might adduce against this argument that the effects of crucial decisions made for a society are often borne by persons who had no role in this decision – by later generations, or by persons at the bottom of a "decent hierarchical society."[9] Both parts of Rawls' second principle of domestic justice forbid social institutions that impose the burdens (above some absolute threshold) of costly decisions made for a family upon members of this family alone. Decent societies, as Rawls describes them, may well be committed to similar domestic burden sharing. So it is unclear why liberal and decent societies should be categorically opposed to any analogous scheme of *international* burden sharing, even to a scheme that demands little from the wealthier societies and is adjusted according to the actual impact of perverse incentives and moral hazards.[10]

In keeping with the topic of this volume, I focus on another respect in which Rawls' new "duty of assistance" falls short: on the suggestion that the causes of severe poverty lie within the poor countries themselves. Rawls stresses repeatedly that this is true of the world as it is: "the causes of the wealth of a people and the forms it takes lie in their political culture and in the religious, philosophical, and moral traditions that support the basic structure of their political and social institutions, as well as in the industriousness and cooperative talents of its members, all supported by their political virtues . . . the political culture of a burdened society is all-important . . . Crucial also is the country's population policy."[11] When societies fail to thrive, "the problem is commonly the nature of the public political culture and the religious and philosophical traditions that underlie its institutions. The great social evils in poorer societies are likely to be oppressive government and corrupt elites."[12]

These passages suggest that poverty is due to domestic factors, not to foreign influences. This empirical view about poverty leads rather directly to the important moral error to be exposed: to the false idea that the problem of world poverty concerns us citizens of the rich countries mainly as potential helpers. I will therefore examine in detail the empirical view of the domestic causation of severe poverty, showing why it is false and also why it is so widely held in the developed world.

It is well to recall that existing peoples have arrived at their present levels of social, economic and cultural development through an historical process that was pervaded by enslavement, colonialism, even genocide. Though these monumental crimes are now in the past, they have left a legacy of great inequalities which would be unacceptable even if peoples were now masters of their own development. Even if the peoples of Africa had had, in recent decades, a real opportunity to achieve similar rates of economic growth as the developed countries, achieving such growth could not have helped them overcome their initial 30:1 disadvantage in per capita income. Even if, starting in 1960, African annual growth in per capita income had been a full percentage point above ours each and every year, the ratio would still be 20:1 today and would not be fully erased until early in the twenty-fourth century.[13] It is unclear then whether we may simply take for granted the existing inequality as if it had come about through choices freely made within each people. By seeing the problem of poverty merely in terms of assistance, we overlook that our enormous economic advantage is deeply tainted by how it accumulated over the course of *one* historical process that has devastated the societies and cultures of four continents.

But let us leave aside the continuing legacies of historical injustice and focus on the empirical view that at least in the post-colonial era, which brought impressive growth in global per capita income, the causes of the *persistence* of severe poverty, and hence the key to its eradication, lie within the poor countries themselves. Many find this view compelling in light of the great variation in how the former colonies have evolved over the last forty years. Some of them have done quite well in economic growth and poverty reduction while others exhibit worsening poverty and declining per capita incomes. Isn't it obvious that such strongly divergent national trajectories must be due to differing *domestic* causal factors in the countries concerned? And isn't it clear, then, that the persistence of severe poverty has local causes?

This reasoning connects three thoughts: there are great international variations in the evolution of severe poverty. These variations must be caused by local (country-specific) factors. These factors, together, fully explain the overall evolution of severe poverty worldwide. To see the fallacy, consider this parallel: there are great variations in the performance of my students. These variations must be caused by local (student-specific) factors. These factors, together, fully explain the overall performance of my class.

Clearly, the parallel reasoning results in a falsehood: the overall performance of my class also crucially depends on the quality of my teaching and on various other "global" factors as well. This shows that the second step is invalid. To see this more precisely, one must appreciate that there are two distinct questions about the evolution of severe poverty. One question concerns observed *variations* in national trajectories. In the answer to this question, local factors must play a central role. Yet, however full and correct, this answer may not suffice to answer the second question, which concerns the *overall* evolution of poverty worldwide: even if student-specific factors fully explain observed variations in the performance of my students, the quality of my teaching may still play a major role in explaining why they did not on the whole do much better or worse than they actually did. Likewise, even if country-specific factors fully explain the observed variations in the economic performance of the poor countries, global factors may still play a major role in explaining why they did not on the whole do much better or worse than they did in fact.

This is not merely a theoretical possibility. There is considerable international economic interaction regulated by an elaborate system of treaties and conventions about trade, investments, loans, patents, copyrights, trademarks, double taxation, labor standards, environmental protection, use of seabed resources and much else. In many ways, such rules can be shaped to be more or less favorable to various affected parties such as, for instance, the poor or the rich societies. Had these rules been shaped to be more favorable to the poor societies, much of the great poverty in them today would have been avoided.

Let me support this point with a quote from the *Economist* which – being strongly supportive of WTO globalization and having vilified, on its cover and in its editorial pages, the protesters of Seattle, Washington, and Genoa as enemies of the poor[14] – is surely not biased in my favor:

Rich countries cut their tariffs by less in the Uruguay Round than poor ones did. Since then, they have found new ways to close their markets, notably by imposing anti-dumping duties on imports they deem "unfairly cheap." Rich countries are particularly protectionist in many of the sectors where developing countries are best able to compete, such as agriculture, textiles, and clothing. As a result, according to a new study by Thomas Hertel, of Purdue University, and Will Martin, of the World Bank, rich countries' average tariffs on manufacturing imports from poor countries are four times higher than those on imports from other rich countries. This imposes a big burden on poor countries. The United Nations Conference on Trade and Development (UNCTAD) estimates that they could export $700 billion more a year by 2005 if rich countries did more to open their markets. Poor countries are also hobbled by a lack of know-how. Many had little understanding of what they signed up to in the Uruguay Round. That ignorance is now costing them dear. Michael Finger of the World Bank and Philip Schuler of the University of Maryland estimate that implementing commitments to improve trade procedures and establish technical and intellectual-property standards can cost more than a year's development budget for the poorest countries. Moreover, in those areas where poor countries could benefit from world trade rules, they are often unable to do so. . . . Of the WTO's 134 members, 29 do not even have missions at its headquarters in Geneva. Many more can barely afford to bring cases to the WTO.[15]

Such effects of the going WTO rules show that the causes of the persistence of severe poverty do not, *pace* Rawls, lie solely in the poor countries themselves. The global economic order also plays an important role. It is not surprising that this order is shaped to reflect the interests of the rich countries and their citizens and corporations. In the world as it is, the 15.6 percent of humankind living in the "high-income economies" have 81 percent of global income while the other 84.4 percent of humankind share the remaining 19 percent.[16] It is of great importance for these other countries to be allowed access to the markets of the high-income economies, where per capita incomes are 23 times higher on average. This fact gives our governments greatly superior bargaining power. If our officials serve us well in intergovernmental negotiations about the ground rules of the world economy, they use this superior bargaining power, and their advantages in information and expertise, to shape each facet of the global order to our benefit, allowing us to capture the lion's share of the gains from economic interaction. In this way, large inequalities, once accumulated, have a tendency to intensify[17] – and this is happening, quite dramatically, on the global plane: "The income gap between the fifth of the world's people living in the richest countries and the fifth in the poorest was 74 to 1 in 1997, up from 60 to 1 in 1990 and 30 to 1 in 1960."[18]

If the global economic order plays a major role in the persistence of severe poverty worldwide and if our governments, acting in our name, are prominently involved in shaping and upholding this order, then the deprivation of the distant needy may well engage not merely positive duties to assist but also more stringent negative duties not to harm. Yet, this obvious thought is strangely absent from the debates about our relation to the distant needy. Even those who have most forcefully presented the eradication of severe poverty as an important moral task for us are content to portray us as mere bystanders. Thus, Peter Singer argues that we should donate most of our income to save lives in the poor countries. He makes his case by telling the story of a healthy young professor who, walking by a shallow pond, sees a small child in it about to drown. Surely, Singer says, the professor has a duty to save the child, even at the cost of dirtying his clothes. And similarly, he argues, we have a duty to send money to poverty relief organizations that can, for each few dollars they receive, save one more child from a painful hunger death.[19] It is, in one way, a virtue of Singer's argument that it reaches even those who subscribe to the Purely Domestic Poverty Thesis (PDPT), the view that the persistence of severe poverty is due solely to domestic causes. But by catering to this empirical view, Singer also reinforces the common moral judgment that the citizens and governments of the affluent societies, whom he is addressing, are as innocent in regard to the persistence of severe poverty abroad as the professor is in regard to the child's predicament.[20]

Having argued that the PDPT, though widely held in the developed countries, is nonetheless quite far from the truth, I should be able to give some reasons for its popularity. I can see four main such reasons. The first is that belief in this thesis is rather comfortable for people in the developed world. Most of us know at least vaguely of the horrendous conditions among the global poor. We confront poverty statistics such as these: out of a total of 6 billion human beings, some 2.8 billion live below $2/day, and nearly 1.2 billion of them live below the $1/day international poverty line.[21] 799 million are undernourished, 1 billion lack access to safe water, 2.4 billion lack access to basic sanitation, and 876 million adults are illiterate.[22] More than 880 million lack access to basic health services.[23] Approximately 1 billion have no adequate shelter and 2 billion no electricity.[24] "Two out of five children in the developing world are stunted, one in three is underweight and one in ten is wasted."[25] 250 million children between 5 and 14 do wage work outside their household – often under harsh or cruel conditions: as soldiers, prostitutes, or domestic servants, or in agriculture, construction, textile or carpet production.[26] Roughly one third of all human deaths, some 50,000 daily, are due to poverty-related causes, easily preventable through better nutrition, safe drinking water, vaccines, cheap re-hydration packs and antibiotics.[27] Severe deprivations on such a scale would be considerably more disturbing to us were we to see them as due, in part, to a global institutional order that also sustains our comparatively lavish lifestyles by securing our resources and economic dominance. The PDPT shields us from such discomfort.

A second reason for the popularity of the PDPT in the developed world is awareness of the great differences among developing countries' economic performance. These differences draw our attention to domestic factors and international differences and thus away from global factors. Many ignore the causal role of global factors completely, often falling prey to the fallacy discussed above. Others fall for a different fallacy by concluding from the success of a few developing countries that the existing global economic order is quite hospitable to poverty eradication. This reasoning involves a some–all fallacy: the fact that *some* persons born into poverty in the United States become millionaires does not show that *all* such persons can do likewise.[28] The reason is that the pathways to riches are sparse. They are not rigidly limited, to be sure, but the United States clearly cannot achieve the kind of economic growth rates needed for everyone to become a millionaire (keeping fixed the value of the currency and the real income millionaires can now enjoy). The same holds true for developing countries. The Asian tigers (Hong Kong, Taiwan, Singapore and South Korea), which together constitute well under two percent of the population of the developing world, achieved impressive rates of economic growth and poverty reduction. They did so through a state-sponsored build-up of industries that mass produce low-tech consumer products. These industries were globally successful by using their considerable labor-cost advantage to beat competitors in the developed countries and by drawing on greater state support and/or a better-educated workforce to beat competitors in other developing countries.[29] Building such industries was hugely profitable for the Asian tigers. But if many other poor countries had adopted this same developmental strategy, competition among them would have rendered it much less profitable. We cannot conclude then that the existing global economic order, though less favorable to the poor countries than it might be, is still favorable enough for all of them to do as well as the Asian tigers have done in fact.

A third reason for the popularity of the PDPT in the developed world is the prevailing research focus among social scientists who, like the rest of us, pay much more attention to the differences among national and regional developmental trajectories than to the overall evolution of poverty and inequality worldwide. Across several academic disciplines, there is a vast literature analyzing the causal roles of the local climate, natural environment, resources, food habits, diseases, history, culture, social institutions, economic policies, leadership personalities, and much else.[30] Advice dispensed by development economists and others is also overwhelmingly focused on the design of national economic institutions and policies. Thus, libertarian economists of the "freshwater" school (so dubbed because its leading lights have taught in Chicago) argue that a country's best way to expel human misery is economic growth and its best way to achieve economic growth is to foster free enterprise with a minimum in taxes, regulations, and red tape. A competing, more left-leaning school of thought, represented by Amartya Sen, contends that poverty persists because poor countries have *too little* government: public schools, hospitals and infrastructure. Sen's favorite poster child is the poor Indian state of Kerala whose socialist government has given priority to fulfilling basic needs and thereby achieved more for that population's health, education and life expectancy than the governments of other, more affluent Indian states.[31] These hot and worthwhile debates about appropriate economic policies and social institutions for the poor countries overshadow the far more important question what causal role the rules of our globalized world economy play in the persistence of severe poverty.

This research focus among social scientists is surely partly due to the first two reasons: they, too, and their readers, are overly impressed by dramatic international differentials in economic performance and feel emotionally more comfortable, and careerwise more confident, with work that traces the persistence of severe poverty back to local causes rather than to global institutions we are involved in upholding. But there is also a good methodological reason for the research bias toward national and local causes: There being only this one world to observe, it is hard to obtain solid evidence about how the overall incidence of poverty would have evolved differently if this or that global factor had been different. By contrast, solid evidence about the effects of national and local factors can be gleaned from many poor countries that differ in their natural environment, history, culture, political and economic system, and government policies.

A fourth reason for the popularity of the PDPT is the prevalence of brutal and corrupt governments and elites in the poor countries. It seems far-fetched, even preposterous, to blame the global economic order for the persistence of severe poverty in countries that are ruled by obvious thugs and crooks. It also seems that whatever benefits global institutional reforms might bring to such countries would be captured by their corrupt elites, bringing little relief to the general population while reinforcing the power of their oppressors. Many among us believe then that we should postpone reforms that would make the global order fairer to the poor countries until they will have put their house in order by making their national political and economic order fairer to the domestic poor.

This last reason, too, is a bad one, because the existing world order is itself a crucial causal factor in the prevalence of corruption and oppression in the poor countries. It was only in 1999, for example, that the developed countries finally agreed to curb their firms' bribery of foreign officials by adopting the OECD *Convention on Combating Bribery of Foreign Public Officials in International Business Transactions.*[32] Until then, most developed states did not merely legally authorize their firms to bribe foreign officials, but even allowed them to deduct such bribes from their taxable revenues, thereby providing financial inducements and moral support to the practice of bribing politicians and officials in the poor countries.[33] This practice diverts the loyalties of officials in these countries and also makes a great difference to which persons are motivated to scramble for public office in the first place. Developing countries have suffered staggering losses as a result, most clearly in the awarding of public contracts. These losses arise in part from the fact that bribes are priced in: bidders on contracts must raise their price in order to get paid enough to pay the bribes. Additional losses arise as bidders can afford to be non-competitive, knowing that the success of their bid will depend on their bribes more than on the substance of their offer. Even greater losses arise from the fact that officials focused on bribes pay little attention to whether the goods and services they purchase in their country's behalf are of good quality or even needed at all. Much of what developing countries have imported over the decades has been of no use to them – or even harmful, by promoting environmental degradation or violence (bribery is especially pervasive in the arms trade). Preliminary evidence suggests that the new *Convention* is ineffective in curbing bribery by multinational corporations.[34] But even if it were effective, it would be very hard to purge the pervasive culture of corruption that is now deeply entrenched in many developing countries thanks to the extensive bribery they were subjected to during their formative years.

The issue of bribery is part of a larger problem. The political and economic elites of poor countries interact with their domestic inferiors, on the one hand, and with foreign governments and corporations, on the other. These two constituencies differ enormously in wealth and power. The former are by and large poorly educated and heavily preoccupied with the daily struggle to make ends meet. The latter, by contrast, have vastly greater rewards and penalties at their disposal. Politicians with a normal interest in their own political and economic success can thus be expected to cater to the interests of foreign governments and corporations rather than to competing interests of their much poorer compatriots. And this, of course, is what we find: there are plenty of poor-country governments that came to power or stay in power only thanks to foreign support. And there are plenty of poor-country politicians and bureaucrats who, induced or even bribed by foreigners, work against the interests of their people: *for* the development of a tourist-friendly sex industry (whose forced exploitation of children and women they tolerate and profit from), *for* the importation of unneeded, obsolete, or overpriced products at public expense, *for* the permission to import hazardous products, wastes, or factories, *against* laws protecting employees or the environment, and so on.

To be sure, there would not be such huge asymmetries in incentives if the poor countries were more democratic, allowing their populations a genuine political role. Why then are most of these countries so far from being genuinely democratic? This question brings further aspects of the current global institutional order into view.

It is a very central feature of this order that any group controlling a preponderance of the means of coercion within a country is internationally recognized as the legitimate government of this country's territory and people – regardless of how this group came to power, of how it exercises power and of the extent to which it is supported or opposed by the population it rules. That such a group exercising effective power receives international recognition means not merely that we engage it in negotiations. It means also that we accept this group's right to act for the people it rules, that we, most significantly, confer upon it the privileges freely to dispose of the country's natural resources (international resource privilege) and freely to borrow in the country's name (international borrowing privilege).

The *resource privilege* we confer upon a group in power is much more than mere acquiescence in its effective control over the natural resources of the country in question. This privilege includes the power[35] to effect legally valid transfers of ownership rights in such resources. Thus a corporation that has purchased resources from the Saudis or Suharto, or from Mobuto or Sani Abacha, has thereby become entitled to be – and actually *is* – recognized anywhere in the world as the legitimate owner of these resources. This is a remarkable feature of our global order. A group that overpowers the guards and takes control of a warehouse may be able to give some of the merchandise to others, accepting money in exchange. But the fence who pays them becomes merely the possessor, not the owner, of the loot. Contrast this with a group that overpowers an elected government and takes control of a country. Such a group, too, can give away some of the country's natural resources, accepting money in exchange. In this case, however, the purchaser acquires not merely possession, but all the rights and liberties of ownership, which are supposed to be – and actually *are* – protected and enforced by all other states' courts and police forces. The international resource privilege, then, is the legal power to confer globally valid ownership rights in the country's resources.

This international resource privilege has disastrous effects in poor but resource-rich countries, where the resource sector constitutes a large segment of the national economy. Whoever can take power in such a country by whatever means can maintain his rule, even against widespread popular opposition, by buying the arms and soldiers he needs with revenues from the export of natural resources and with funds borrowed against future resource sales. The resource privilege thus gives insiders strong incentives toward the violent acquisition and exercise of political power, thereby causing coup attempts and civil wars. Moreover, it also gives outsiders strong incentives to corrupt the officials of such countries who, no matter how badly they rule, continue to have resources to sell and money to spend.

Nigeria is a case in point. It produces about two million barrels of oil per day which, depending on the oil price, fetch some $10–20 billion annually, one quarter to one half of GDP. Whoever controls this revenue stream can afford enough weapons and soldiers to keep himself in power regardless of what the population may think of him. And so long as he succeeds in doing so, his purse will be continuously replenished with new funds with which he can cement his rule and live in opulence. With such a powerful incentive, it cannot be surprising that, during 28 of the past 32 years, Nigeria has been ruled by military strongmen who took power and ruled by force.[36] Nor can it be surprising that even a polished elected president fails to stop gross corruption: Olusegun Obasanjo knows full well that, if he tried to spend the oil revenues solely for the benefit of the Nigerian people, military officers could – thanks to the international resource privilege – quickly restore their customary perks.[37] With such a huge price on his head, even the best-intentioned president could not end the theft of oil revenues and survive in power.

The incentives arising from the international resource privilege help explain what economists have long observed and found puzzling: the significant *negative* correlation between resource wealth (relative to GDP) and economic performance.[38] This explanation is confirmed by a recent regression analysis by two Yale economists, which shows that the causal link from resource wealth to poor economic performance is mediated through reduced chances for democracy.[39] Holding the global order fixed as a given background, the authors do not consider how the causal link they analyze itself depends on global rules that grant the resource privilege to any group in power, irrespective of its domestic illegitimacy.

The *borrowing privilege* we confer upon a group in power includes the power to impose internationally valid legal obligations upon the country at large. Any successor government that refuses to honor debts incurred by an ever so corrupt, brutal, undemocratic, unconstitutional, repressive, unpopular predecessor will be severely punished by the banks and governments of other countries. At minimum it will lose its own borrowing privilege by being excluded from the international financial markets. Such refusals are therefore quite rare, as governments, even when newly elected after a dramatic break with the past, are compelled to pay the debts of their ever so awful predecessors.

The international borrowing privilege makes three important contributions to the incidence of oppressive and corrupt elites in the developing world. First, this privilege facilitates borrowing by destructive rulers who can borrow more money and can do so more cheaply than they could do if they alone, rather than the whole country, were obliged to repay. In this way, the borrowing privilege helps such rulers maintain themselves in power even against near-universal popular discontent and opposition.[40] Second, the international borrowing privilege imposes upon democratic successor regimes the often huge debts of their corrupt predecessors. It thereby saps the capacity of such democratic governments to implement structural reforms and other political programs, thus rendering such governments less successful and less stable than they would otherwise be. (It is small consolation that putschists are sometimes weakened by being held liable for the debts of their democratic predecessors.) Third, the international borrowing privilege strengthens incentives toward coup attempts: whoever succeeds in bringing a preponderance of the means of coercion under his control gets the borrowing privilege as an additional reward.

By discussing several global systemic factors in some detail, I hope to have undermined a view that, encouraged by libertarian and more leftist economists alike, most people in the developed world are all too ready to believe: the persistence of severe poverty is due to causes that are indigenous to the countries in which it occurs and thus unrelated to the affluent societies and their governments. This view is dramatically mistaken. Yes, domestic factors contribute to the persistence of severe poverty in many countries. But these contributions often depend on features of the global institutional order, which sustain some of those factors and exacerbate the impact of others. In these ways, the non-indigenous factors I have discussed play a major causal role in the evolution of severe poverty worldwide. They are crucial for explaining the inability and especially the unwillingness of the poor countries' leaders to pursue more effective strategies of poverty eradication. And they are crucial therefore for explaining why global inequality is increasing so rapidly that substantial global economic growth since the end of the Cold War has not reduced income poverty and malnutrition[41] – *despite* substantial technological progress, *despite* a huge poverty reduction in China,[42] *despite* the post-Cold-War "peace dividend,"[43] *despite* a 32-percent drop in real food prices since 1985,[44] *despite* official development assistance (ODA), and *despite* the efforts of the international humanitarian and development organizations. If we are serious about eradicating severe poverty worldwide, we must understand the causal role of such non-indigenous factors and be willing to consider ways of modifying them or of reducing their impact.[45]

If the PDPT were true, the moral issues the distant needy raise for us might plausibly be considered under the assistance label alone.[46] But since the PDPT is seriously mistaken, this label may be misleading insofar as we may also be *contributing to*, or *profiting from*, social factors that exacerbate severe poverty abroad.

We can still deny that we are so contributing or profiting, even if we acknowledge the PDPT's collapse and accept our shared responsibility for the existing global order. We can say for instance that our imposition of this order benefits the global poor, or at least does not harm them by exacerbating their poverty. While such claims are often made, for the current WTO rules for example, it remains quite unclear what their meaning is supposed to be. Benefit, after all, is a comparative notion which implicitly appeals to some baseline scenario under which the global poor would be even worse off than they are now in the world as it is. What baseline might we adduce to show the global poor that they are benefiting from the present global order?

There are three options. We might invoke a *diachronic* comparison, appealing to the trend in the depth or incidence of severe poverty world-wide. But this argument fails for three independent reasons. Its premise is false: severe income poverty and malnutrition are not actually in decline globally (note 41). Moreover its inference is invalid: severe poverty might be declining, in China for instance, *despite* the fact that the global economic order tends to exacerbate such poverty. A diachronic comparison does not permit us to judge this possibility one way or the other and is therefore useless for judging the impact of any specific causal factor. Finally, we must not simply assume that the preceding situation was morally unproblematic. Otherwise we would have to conclude that a man is benefiting his wife if he beats her up ever less frequently, or that the United States economic order of the early nineteenth century benefited the slaves if their enslavement became less brutal during this period.

Our second option is to invoke a *subjunctive* comparison with an *historical* baseline. To judge whether the Israeli occupation reduced illiteracy in the West Bank, we should not ask diachronically whether illiteracy declined, but counterfactually whether illiteracy is lower than it would have been without the occupation. Adopting this idea, we might argue that the existing global order is benefiting the global poor insofar as they are better off than they would be if some preceding set of rules had remained in force. But this argument makes the – here inappropriate – assumption that those preceding rules were neutral, neither harming nor benefiting the global poor. By the same reasoning the military junta under Senior General Than Shwe could be said to be benefiting the Burmese people if merely they are better off than they would now be if the predecessor junta under General Ne Win were still in power.

Our third option is to invoke a *subjunctive* comparison with a *hypothetical* baseline – arguing perhaps that even more people would live and die even more miserably in some fictional state of nature than in this world as we have made it. But this option, too, is unpromising so long as we lack a precise and morally uniquely appropriate specification of that fictional world and a morally uniquely appropriate standard for comparing the two worlds in regard to severe poverty. You may think that these worries are merely academic, that our world is surely vastly better in this regard than any conceivable state of nature. And so it indeed appears from our vantage point. And yet: "Worldwide 34,000 children under age five die daily from hunger and preventable diseases."[47] Try to conceive a state of nature that can match this amazing feat of our globalized civilization![48]

None of our three options is suitable for explicating our question – whether the existing world order harms or benefits the global poor – in a way that is both clear and appropriate to the assessment of this order. This failure suggests the inverse strategy: instead of basing our justice assessment of this order on whether it does harm (independently defined), we can make our judgment of whether the imposition of this order does harm turn on an assessment of this order by some harm-independent criterion of justice.

To illustrate the idea, consider the institutional order of the US in its infancy, which greatly disadvantaged women vis-à-vis men. Our judgment of this order as unjust is not based on an historical comparison with how women had fared under British rule. It is not based on a comparison with how women would have fared had British rule continued. And it is not based on a comparison with how women would fare in some state of nature. (All these comparisons can be more plausibly invoked to just-ify than to criticize the institutional order under consideration.) Rather, it is because it assigned women a status inferior to men's that we judge this order to have been unjust to women and its imposition therefore a harm done to them.

Many harm-independent criteria might be proposed for assessing the justice of our global order. Such criteria differ in at least three respects. They differ in how they identify the relevant affected parties: as individual persons, households, social groups, nations, or states. They differ in their *absolute* demands – requiring, for instance, that affected parties must enjoy security of self and property or access to basic necessities. And they differ in their *relative* demands – requiring perhaps that basic rights or basic educational or medical opportunities must be equal or that economic inequalities must be constrained in certain ways.

Even if our global order fails to meet compelling absolute or relative requirements, it may still be defended on the grounds that this failure is unavoidable. An assessment of its justice must be sensitive then to information about what alternatives are feasible and about the conditions such feasible alternatives would engender. With regard to alternatives that diverge greatly from the existing global order, it may be impossible to establish such information in a rigorous way. It is quite possible, however, to estimate the impact of the existing global order relative to its nearby institutional alternatives. We saw such estimates in the *Economist* passage quoted above: the developing countries are missing out on some $700 billion annually in export revenues because the developed countries insisted on grandfathering heavy protections of their markets – through tariffs, quotas, anti-dumping duties and subsidies to domestic producers.[49] It is quite possible, though unseemly among economists, to extend this estimate to the number of poverty deaths that would have been avoided by a more symmetrical opening of markets.[50] The number is large, as $700 billion annually is nearly 12 percent of the gross national incomes of all developing countries, representing 84.4 percent of humankind.[51]

Many features of the existing global order embody similar trade-offs between the interests of the high-income countries and their citizens on the one hand and the global poor on the other. An unconditional resource privilege gives us access to a larger, cheaper and more reliable supply of foreign resources, because we can acquire ownership of them from anyone who happens to exercise effective power without regard to whether the country's population either approves the sale or benefits from the proceeds. Advantageous also to putschists and tyrants in the developing world, broad resource and borrowing privileges are much worse, however, for the global poor than would be narrower such privileges conditional on minimal domestic legitimacy. The existing TRIPs agreement is better for us and worse for the global poor than an alternative that would have required the rich countries to supply funds for shielding the global poor from exorbitant mark-ups on drugs and seeds.[52] The existing Law of the Sea Treaty is better for us and worse for them than an alternative that would have guaranteed the poor countries some share of the value of harvested seabed resources.[53] It is better for us and worse for the global poor that we do not have to pay for the negative externalities we impose on them: for the pollution we have produced over many decades and the resulting effects on their environment and climate, for the rapid depletion of natural resources, for the contribution of our tourists to the AIDS epidemic and for the violence caused by our demand for drugs and our war on drugs.

The cumulative impact of all these trade-offs upon the global poor is likely to be staggering. In the fourteen years since the end of the Cold War, some 250 million human beings have died prematurely from poverty-related causes, with 18 million more added each year (note 27). Had the developed countries shaping the global rules given more weight to the interests of the global poor, the toll in early deaths and deprivations would certainly and foreseeably have been vastly lower at negligible cost to our affluence. It is then very hard to see how we might defend the trade-offs manifested in our global order as compatible with justice. And if this order is unjust, then it follows, without appeal to any historical or state-of-nature baseline, that we are harming the global poor – by imposing on them an unjust global order under which the incidence of severe poverty, malnutrition, and premature death is much higher than it would be under any just alternative.

There are three ways of defending the trade-offs that our governments, often in collusion with corrupt and oppressive leaders in the developing world, have imposed. First we might say that it is permissible for us vigorously to promote our own interests in negotiations about how to fine-tune the various rules of the global order, even when doing so conflicts with the interests of the global poor. With our incomes 200 to 300 times larger than theirs[54] and 799 million living on the brink of starvation (note 22), this justification of the *status quo* is rarely voiced in public. To be sure, it is widely thought that our politicians and diplomats ought to represent the interests of their compatriots. But it is also widely thought that this mandate has its limits: even if they are able to do so, our representatives should not impose global rules under which we have unfair advantages that add millions of poverty deaths in the developing world. In the examples I have given, it looks like our politicians and diplomats have done exactly that in our name.

Our second defense avers that appearances are here deceptive, that the decisions reflected in the existing rules do benefit the global poor as well, at least in the long run. But in some important cases, such a defense strains credulity. It is very hard to deny that world poverty is exacerbated by the special prerogatives the rich countries gave themselves under WTO rules to favor their own firms through tariffs, quotas, anti-dumping duties, and subsidies. Still, career incentives do produce such denials which, in the more clear-cut cases of unfair rules, often take a weaker form: instead of claiming that certain prerogatives for the rich countries do not exacerbate poverty, economists merely claim that there are many complicating factors, methodological difficulties and other imponderabilia so that intellectual honesty precludes our drawing any firm conclusions.[55] If all else fails, we can fall back on the weakest claim: yes, the fine-tuning of some important rules was indeed worse for the global poor, but it was an honest mistake. When these rules were designed, development economics was less advanced and the relevant officials could not possibly have known that they were serving our interests at the expense of many additional premature deaths from poverty-related causes.

Boilerplate empirical defenses of this kind are easily produced and very well received. And it is quite unlikely that there will ever be a serious inquiry into what our politicians and diplomats and officials in the WTO, IMF and World Bank knew and should have known during their negotiations of international agreements. The possibility that these respectable gentlemen (very few women there) might be hunger's willing executioners, committing a rather large-scale crime against humanity in our name, will never be taken seriously in the developed world. And yet, nagging doubts remain. If our representatives did make honest mistakes to the detriment of the global poor, should we not at least make up for these mistakes through a real effort at reducing the (unexpectedly) large incidence of severe poverty today?

Similar questions are raised by our third defense, which asserts that the global rules we have imposed are not merely good for us, but also good for global efficiency, productivity and economic growth. These rules are Pareto-superior to their alternatives – not in the normal sense (better for some and worse for no one), but in this weaker ("Caldor-Hicks") sense: The rules are better for some and worse for others but so that the former can, out of their relative gains, fully compensate the latter for their relative losses. I doubt this argument can succeed for the grandfathering clauses in the WTO Treaty which still allow us, for many years to come, to favor our firms through tariffs, quotas, anti-dumping duties and huge subsidies. But it may well succeed in other cases such as the TRIPs Agreement. Still, even when it succeeds, there is the nagging question: given the vast economic inequality between gainers and losers (note 54), is the mere *possibility* of compensation sufficient to vindicate our decision? Or must there not rather be *actual* compensation, so that we may keep only such relative gains as *exceed* their relative losses?

The questions concluding the last two paragraphs indicate more precisely how, with the collapse of the PDPT, conventional discussions of world poverty under the assistance label are misleading. The label is not inaccurate: as affluent people and countries, we surely have positive moral duties to assist persons mired in life-threatening poverty whom we can help at little cost. But the label detracts from weightier, negative duties that also apply to us: We should reduce severe harms we will have caused; and we should not take advantage of injustice at the expense of its victims. These two negative duties apply to us if we (sometimes together with third world elites) are imposing a global order whose unfairness benefits us while exacerbating severe poverty abroad. We must then at least compensate the global poor. Failing to do this, we would be harming them and profiting from injustice at their expense. And insofar as we do compensate, we are not merely "assisting" the poor abroad, but reducing the impact of unfair rules that bring us unjust gains at their expense. We are not "redistributing" from the rich to the poor, but offsetting an unjust institutional redistribution from the poor to the rich – *re*-redistributing, if you like.

Let me illustrate the special weight these two negative duties are generally thought to have: imagine, by the side of a country road, an injured child who must be rushed to the hospital if her leg is to be saved. As a competent bystander who ignores her plight, you are subject to moral criticism for failing to assist. But if you are the driver who injured the child in the first place, then more is morally at stake: by leaving the child's needs unattended, you would greatly increase the harm you will have done her. As we judge such inaction of the driver more harshly than that of the bystander, we should judge our own inaction more harshly, too, if we are involved in upholding unjust rules that contribute to severe poverty we ignore.

Imagine further a society in which an aboriginal minority suffers severe discrimination in education and employment, reducing their wages far below those of their compatriots. As an affluent foreigner, you may think that perhaps you ought to do something to assist these people. But if you are profiting from the discrimination (by employing an aboriginal driver at half the wage other drivers receive, for instance), then more is morally at stake: we judge ourselves more harshly for taking advantage of an injustice by pocketing such gains than for failing to spend other assets we have on supporting the poor. As we do so, we should also judge ourselves more harshly insofar as assets we fail to use toward reducing severe poverty abroad constitute gains we derive from the unfairness of a global order that also contributes to the persistence of this poverty.

Negative duties not to support and not to pocket gains from an unfair institutional order that foreseeably contributes to severe deprivations are not only weightier than the positive duty to help relieve such deprivations. They are also much less sensitive to variations in community and distance. Duties to assist are strongest toward the near and dear and weakest toward foreigners in distant lands. But duties not to harm do not fade in this way. Consider again the driver who hits a child and then leaves her unattended by the side of the road. We do not upgrade our moral assessment of him when we learn that he did this far away from his home to a child with whom he had no communal bond of nationality, language, culture, or religion. If the unfairness of the global order we impose causes poverty to persist in the poor countries, then our moral responsibility for the associated deaths and deprivations is not diminished by diversity of nationality and geographical or cultural distance. It might be so diminished, perhaps, if harming foreigners were necessary to save ourselves from a comparable fate. But in the real world, the global poverty problem – though it involves one third of all human deaths – is quite small in economic terms: though 2,812 million persons are living below the higher ($2/day) international poverty line, and 43 percent below it on average, their collective shortfall amounts to only 1.13 percent of the incomes of the 955 million people in the high-income economies.[56] Clearly, we could eradicate severe poverty – through a reform of the global order or through other initiatives designed to compensate for its effects on the global poor – without "sacrificing" the fulfillment of our own needs or even mildly serious interests.[57]

It is widely believed in the developed world that we are already spending an inordinate amount on such initiatives. This belief is contradicted by the facts: the high-income countries have reduced their official development assistance (ODA) from 0.33 percent of their combined GNPs in 1990 to 0.22 percent, or $52.3 billion, in 2001.[58] Most ODA is allocated for political effect: only 23 percent goes to the 49 least developed countries;[59] and only $3.7 billion is spent on basic social services[60] – basic education, basic health, population programs, water supply, and sanitation – far less than the 20 percent agreed to at the 1995 World Summit for Social Development.[61] This is less than one percent of the developed countries' "peace dividend"[62] and comes to about $4 per year from each of us citizens of these countries, on average.[63]

When people like us die at a mature age, we can look back on a lifespan in which over a billion human beings, mostly children, have died from poverty-related causes. This massive death toll was and is foreseeable. And it is clear beyond any reasonable doubt that the developed countries could reduce this continuous death toll dramatically at little cost to ourselves (notes 56–7). And yet, very few citizens of the developed countries find these facts disturbing. This widespread unconcern can be explained, in large part, by a false view of why severe poverty persists. Most of us subscribe to the view that the causes of the persistence of severe poverty are indigenous to the countries in which it occurs. I am convinced that, with a better understanding of the role global institutional factors play in the persistence of severe poverty, many would take this problem much more seriously – including my esteemed teacher John Rawls.

NOTES

This chapter has been presented at the CUNY Graduate Center, the University of Hong Kong, Soochow University, the University of St. Andrews, Harvard's JFK School, the University of Sheffield, the University of North Carolina, and the Chinese University in Hong Kong. I am grateful to my audiences there, especially to Maria Alvarez, Liz Ashford, Sissila Bok, and Leif Wenar, as well as to Christian Barry, Daniel Bell, Chiara Bottici, and Ling Tong for very helpful written criticisms and suggestions.

1 John Rawls, *The Law of Peoples* (Cambridge Mass.: Harvard University Press, 1999), p. 37. For his earlier account, see John Rawls, "The Law of Peoples" in Stephen Shute and Susan Hurley, eds., *On Human Rights* (New York: Basic Books, 1993), p. 55.

2 See Rawls, *The Law of Peoples*, pp. 115–19, discussing Charles Beitz: *Political Theory and International Relations* (Princeton: Princeton University Press, 1979) and Thomas W. Pogge, "An Egalitarian Law of Peoples," *Philosophy & Public Affairs*, 23 (1994), 195–224.

3 Rawls, *The Law of Peoples*, pp. 32, 63, 69.

4 Ibid., pp. 29, 33, 34–5, 40, 63–7, 69, 115, 120. A society is well ordered if it has a stable institutional order that is either liberal or decent (ibid., pp. 4 and 63).

5 This feature renders problematic not only Rawls' asserted duty to assist burdened societies, but also his call for "forceful intervention" in the affairs of non-well-ordered societies that internally commit egregious offenses against human rights (ibid., p. 94 n. 6). Even if such interventions fall short of war (which must not be instigated for reasons other than self-defense – ibid., p. 37),

they may entail considerable risks for the interveners whose representatives would thus not rationally agree to more than a permission so to intervene.

6 Rawls recognizes this problem, in general terms at least, and is concerned to defend his use of an original position "that is fair to peoples and not to individual persons" (ibid., p. 17 n. 9).

7 See Pogge, "An Egalitarian Law of Peoples," 208–9.

8 See Rawls, *The Law of Peoples*, pp. 106–7 for the appeal to the just saving principle and ibid., pp. 117–18, for two invented stories illustrating such unjustified complaints about international inequality.

9 Rawls extensively discusses such societies, exemplified by an imaginary Kazanistan, as ones that liberal peoples should welcome as equal "members in good standing of a Society of Peoples" (ibid., p. 59).

10 As domestic institutions are to be so adjusted pursuant to the difference principle. See Thomas W. Pogge, *Realizing Rawls* (Ithaca: Cornell University Press, 1989), pp. 252–3.

11 Rawls, *The Law of Peoples*, p. 108.

12 Rawls, "The Law of Peoples," 77 – echoing Michael Walzer: "it is not the sign for some collective derangement or radical incapacity for a political community to produce an authoritarian regime. Indeed, the history, culture, and religion of the community may be such that authoritarian regimes come, as it were, naturally, reflecting a widely shared world view or way of life" (Michael Walzer, "The Moral Standing of States," *Philosophy & Public Affairs*, 9, 209–29, at 224–5).

13 In fact, this ratio has increased to 40:1, showing that average annual growth in per capita income was 0.7 percent *less* in Africa than in the developed world.

14 See, for instance, the *Economist* cover of December 11 (1999), showing an Indian child in rags with the heading "The real losers of Seattle." See also its editorial in the same issue (ibid., 15) and its flimsy "The case for globalisation," *Economist*, September 23 (2000), 19–20 and 85–7.

15 *Economist*, September 25 (1999), 89. The three cited studies are: Thomas W. Hertel and Will Martin, "Would Developing Countries Gain from Inclusion of Manufactures in the WTO Negotiations?" (www.gtap.agecon. purdue.edu/resources/download/42.pdf, 1999); UNCTAD (United Nations Conference on Trade and Development): *Trade and Development Report 1999* (New York: UN Publications, 1999); and J. Michael Finger and Philip Schuler, "Implementation of Uruguay Round Commitments: The Development Challenge," World Bank Research Working Paper 2215 (www.itd.org/wb/finger.doc), 1999.

16 World Bank, *World Development Report 2003* (New York: Oxford University Press, 2002), p. 235. Inequalities in wealth are significantly greater than inequalities in income. Well-off persons typically have more net worth than annual income, while the poor typically own less than one annual income.

The huge fortunes of the ultra-rich have been specially highlighted in recent reports by the United Nations Development Programme (UNDP): "the world's 200 richest people more than doubled their net worth in the four years to 1998, to more than \$1 trillion. The assets of the top three billionaires are more than the combined GNP of all least developed countries and their 600 million people" (UNDP: *Human Development Report 1999* (New York: Oxford University Press, 1999), p. 3. "The additional cost of achieving and maintaining universal access to basic education for all, basic health care for all, reproductive health care for all women, adequate food for all and safe water and sanitation for all is . . . less than 4 percent of the combined wealth of the 225 richest people in the world" (UNDP: *Human Development Report 1998* (New York: Oxford University Press, 1998), p. 30.

17 Rawls makes this point himself, quite forcefully, in the domestic context (John Rawls, *Political Liberalism* (New York: Columbia University Press, 1993), p. 267). In the international arena, he vaguely endorses "fair standards of trade" and writes that any "unjustified distributive effects" of cooperative organizations should be corrected (Rawls, *The Law of Peoples*, p. 43). But he gives no content to these evaluative terms and does not incorporate them into his law of peoples, which is compatible then with the imposition of a skewed global economic order that perpetuates the relative poverty of a large majority of humankind who are collectively unable to reform it by peaceful means (see Thomas W. Pogge, "Rawls on International Justice," *Philosophical Quarterly*, 51 (2001), 246–53, at 251–2). Such a global order is unjust even if it also requires the affluent societies to ride to the rescue (pursuant to their duty of assistance) whenever worsening poverty threatens the well-orderedness of any liberal or decent society. This said, the added duty of assistance does make the Society of Peoples Rawls envisions a significant improvement over the *status quo*. It entails, plausibly I believe, that most rich countries today are immoral or "outlaw states" on account of the severe poverty abroad that they tolerate and, I would add, contribute to. Denmark, Norway, Luxembourg, the Netherlands, and Sweden are possible exceptions – see UNDP: *Human Development Report 2003* (New York: Oxford University Press, 2003), pp. 228 and 290.

18 UNDP, *Human Development Report 1999*, 3, see 38. These ratios compare national average incomes *via* market exchange rates. The picture is bleak also when one compares the incomes of households worldwide *via* purchasing power parities: Over a recent five-year period, "world inequality has increased . . . from a Gini of 62.8 in 1988 to 66.0 in 1993. This represents an increase of 0.6 Gini points per year. This is a very fast increase, faster than the increase experienced by the US and UK in the decade of the 1980s . . . The bottom 5 percent of the world grew poorer, as their real incomes decreased between 1988 and 1993, while the richest quintile grew richer. It gained 12 percent in real terms, that is it grew more than twice as much as mean world

income (5.7 percent)" (Branko Milanovic: "True World Income Distribution, 1988 and 1993: First Calculation Based on Household Surveys Alone," *The Economic Journal*, 112 (2002), 51–92, at 88.

19 Peter Singer, "Famine, Affluence and Morality," *Philosophy & Public Affairs*, 1 (1972), 229–43; see also Peter Unger, *Living High and Letting Die: Our Illusion of Innocence* (Oxford: Oxford University Press, 1996).

20 Singer may not regard this reinforcement as regrettable. As a utilitarian, he believes that the stringency of our duty to combat world poverty is unaffected by whether the PDPT is true or false.

21 World Bank, *World Development Report 2000/2001* (New York: Oxford University Press, 2000), p. 23, and Shaohua Chen and Martin Ravallion: "How Did the World's Poorest Fare in the 1990s?" *Review of Income and Wealth*, 47 (2001), 283–300, at, 290. (Ravallion and Chen have managed the World Bank's income poverty assessments for well over a decade. These latest data are for 1998.) These two poverty lines are defined in terms of a monthly income with the same *purchasing power* as $65.48 and $32.74 had in the United States in 1993 (ibid., 285). Today, they correspond to $84 and $42 per person per month in the US (www.bls.gov/cpi/home.htm) and to about $20 and $10 per person per month in a typical poor country, where money has much greater purchasing power (Thomas W. Pogge, *World Poverty and Human Rights: Cosmopolitan Responsibilities and Reforms* (Cambridge: Polity Press, 2002), p. 97). Those below the higher line fall 43 percent below it on average, and those below the lower line fall 30 percent below it on average (Chen and Ravallion, "How Did the World's Poorest Fare in the 1990s?," 290 and 293, dividing the poverty gap index by the headcount index). The former are 47 percent of humankind with about one and one quarter percent of global income. The latter are 20 percent of humankind with about one third percent of global income.

22 UNDP, *Human Development Report 2003*, 87, 9, 6. Most of those suffering these deprivations are female (ibid. 310–30).

23 UNDP, *Human Development Report 1999*, 22.

24 UNDP, *Human Development Report 1998*, 49.

25 FAO (Food and Agriculture Organization of the United Nations), *The State of Food Insecurity in the World 1999* (www.fao.org/news/1999/img/sofi99-e.pdf), 11.

26 The UN International Labor Organization (ILO) reports that "some 250 million children between the ages of 5 and 14 are working in developing countries – 120 million full time, 130 million part time" (www.ilo.org/public/english/standards/ipec/simpoc/stats/4stt.htm). Of these, 170.5 million children are involved in hazardous work and 8.4 million in the "unconditionally worst" forms of child labor, "defined as slavery, trafficking, debt bondage and other forms of forced labour, forced recruitment of children for use in armed conflict, prostitution and pornography, and illicit

activities." ILO, *A Future Without Child Labour* (www.ilo.org/public/english/ standards/decl/publ/reports/report3.htm) 9, 11, and 18.

27 See FAO, *The State of Food Insecurity in the World 1999* and UNICEF (United Nations Children's Fund), *The State of the World's Children 2002* (New York: UNICEF, 2002). Two thirds of these are deaths of children. For the frequency of specific causes of deaths see WHO (World Health Organization): *The World Health Report 2001* (Geneva: WHO Publications, 2001), Annex Table 2, also available at www.who.int/whr/2001.

28 See G. A. Cohen: *History, Labour, and Freedom* (Oxford: Clarendon Press, 1988), pp. 262–3.

29 It also helped that the United States, eager to establish healthy capitalist economies as a counterweight to Soviet influence in the region, allowed the tigers free access to its market even while they maintained high tariffs to protect their own.

30 Some notable recent contributions are David Landes, *The Wealth and Poverty of Nations: Why Some Are So Rich and Some So Poor* (New York: Norton, 1998), Jared Diamond, *Guns, Germs, and Steel: The Fates of Human Societies* (New York: Norton, 1999), and Lawrence E. Harrison and Samuel P. Huntington, eds., *Culture Matters: How Values Shape Human Progress* (New York: Basic Books, 2001).

31 The leftist political coalition responsible for these policies was nevertheless soundly defeated in the last assembly elections, May 10, 2001, gaining only 40 seats out of 140.

32 The convention went into effect in February 1999 and has been widely ratified since (www.oecd.org/home).

33 In the United States, the post-Watergate Congress tried to prevent the bribing of foreign officials through its 1977 Foreign Corrupt Practices Act, passed after the Lockheed Corporation was found to have paid – not a modest sum to some third-world official, but rather – a US$2 million bribe to Prime Minister Kakuei Tanaka of powerful and democratic Japan. Not wanting its firms to be at a disadvantage vis-à-vis their foreign rivals, the United States was a major supporter of the Convention, as was the non-governmental organization Transparency International, which helped mobilize public support in many OECD countries.

34 "Plenty of laws exist to ban bribery by companies. But big multinationals continue to sidestep them with ease" – so the current situation is summarized in "The Short Arm of the Law," *Economist*, March 2 (2002), 63–5, at 63.

35 As understood by Wesley N. Hohfeld, *Fundamental Legal Conceptions* (New Haven: Yale University Press 1919), a power involves the legally recognized authority to alter the distribution of first-order liberty rights, claim rights and duties. Having *a* power or power*s* in this sense is distinct from having power (i.e., control over physical force and/or means of coercion).

36 See "Going on down," in *Economist*, June 8 (1996), 46–8. A later update says: "oil revenues [are] paid directly to the government at the highest level . . .

The head of state has supreme power and control of all the cash. He depends on nobody and nothing but oil. Patronage and corruption spread downwards from the top" (*Economist*, December 12 (1998), 19). See also www.eia.doe.gov/emeu/cabs/nigeria.html.

37 Because Obasanjo was, and is, a prominent member of the Advisory Council of Transparency International (see note 33), his election in early 1999 had raised great hopes. These hopes were sorely disappointed. Nigeria still ranks at the bottom of TI's own Corruption Perception Index (www.transparency.org/cpi/2003/cpi2003.en.html).

38 This "resource curse" or "Dutch disease" is exemplified by many developing countries which, despite great natural wealth, have achieved little economic growth and poverty reduction over the last decades. Here are the more important resource-rich developing countries with their average annual rates of change in real GDP per capita from 1975 to 2001: Nigeria −0.7 percent, Congo/Zaire −5.2 percent, Kenya +0.3 percent, Angola −2.3 percent, Mozambique +1.8 percent, Senegal −0.1 percent, Venezuela −0.9 percent, Ecuador +0.2 percent, Saudi Arabia −2.1 percent, United Arab Emirates −3.7 percent, Oman +2.3 percent, Kuwait −0.7 percent, Bahrain +1.1 percent, Brunei −2.2 percent, Indonesia +4.3 percent, the Philippines +0.1 percent (UNDP: *Human Development Report 2003*, 278–81; in some cases a somewhat different period was used due to insufficient data). Thus, with the notable exception of Indonesia, the resource-rich developing countries fell well below the annual rate in real per capita growth of their peers and of the developed countries (ibid., 281).

39 "All petrostates or resource-dependent countries in Africa fail to initiate meaningful political reforms . . . besides South Africa, transition to democracy has been successful only in resource-poor countries" (Ricky Lam and Leonard Wantchekon: "Dictatorships as a Political Dutch Disease" (www.nyarko.com/wantche1.pdf, 1999), 31). "Our cross-country regression confirms our theoretical insights. We find that a one percentage increase in the size of the natural resource sector [relative to GDP] generates a decrease by half a percentage point in the probability of survival of democratic regimes" (ibid., 35). See also Leonard Wantchekon, "Why Do Resource Dependent Countries Have Authoritarian Governments?" (www.yale.edu/leitner/pdf/1999-11.pdf, 1999).

40 The rulers of resource-rich developing countries have been especially adept at supplementing their income from resource sales by mortgaging their countries' future for their own benefit. As of 1998, Nigeria's foreign debt, run up by its succession of military dictatorships, stood at 79 percent of GNP. The 1998 ratios of foreign debt to GNP for other large resource-rich countries were: Kenya 61 percent, Angola 297 percent, Mozambique 223 percent, Venezuela 40 percent, Indonesia 176 percent, the Philippines 70 percent (UNDP: *Human Development Report 2000* (New York: Oxford University Press, 2000), 219–21).

The 1997 ratio for the Congo/Zaire is 232 percent (UNDP: *Human Development Report 1999*, 195). Needless to say, little of the borrowed funds were channeled into productive investments, e.g. in education and infrastructure, which would augment economic growth and thus tax revenues that could help meet interest and repayment obligations. Much was taken for personal use or expended on "internal security" and the military.

41 See the annual UNDP Reports for the number of undernourished, stuck around 800 million. The incidence of $1/day income poverty is reported to be flat and $2/day income poverty to be up about ten percent over the 1987–98 period (World Bank, *World Development Report 2000/2001*, 23, and Chen and Ravallion, "How Did the World's Poorest Fare in the 1990s?," 290). Severe flaws in the World Bank's method of calculating these numbers make it likely that the actual extent of severe income poverty is substantially greater. Among these flaws is the use of purchasing power parities based on the prices of all commodities rather than on the prices of basic necessities on which poor households are compelled to concentrate their expenditures. See Sanjay Reddy and Thomas W. Pogge, "How *Not* to Count the Poor" (www.socialanalysis.org, 2003) for a comprehensive critique.

42 The number of Chinese living below $1/day is reported to have declined by 30 percent, or 90 million, over the period (Chen and Ravallion, "How Did the World's Poorest Fare in the 1990s?," 290).

43 Thanks to the end of the Cold War, military expenditures worldwide have declined from 4.7 percent of aggregate GDP in 1985 to 2.9 percent in 1996 (UNDP: *Human Development Report 1998*, 197) – a savings of currently about $563 billion annually.

44 The World Bank Food Index fell from 124 in 1985 to 84.5 in 2000. These statistics are updated in "Global Commodity Markets," published by the World Bank's Development Prospects Group (www.worldbank.org/prospects/gcmonline/index.htm).

45 See Pogge, *World Poverty and Human Rights*, chapters 6 and 8, for concrete proposals toward modifying the international resource and borrowing privileges and toward reducing the impact of unfair global economic rules through a Global Resources Dividend, respectively.

46 Though it could still be argued that this label is inappropriate insofar as we are beneficiaries, and they are victims, of the historical injustices discussed earlier, such as colonialism.

47 USDA (United States Department of Agriculture): *U.S. Action Plan on Food Security* (www.fas.usda.gov/icd/summit/usactplan.pdf, 1999), p. iii. The United States government mentions this fact whilst arguing that the developed countries should *not* follow the FAO proposal to increase development assistance for agriculture by $6 billion annually, that $2.6 billion is ample (ibid., Appendix A).

48 See Pogge, *World Poverty and Human Rights*, 136–9.
49 In 2000, the rich countries spent $245 billion on subsidies to their farmers alone (Martin Wolf, "Broken Promises to the Poor," *Financial Times*, November 21 (2001), 13). In 2002, the United States imposed new tariffs against steel imports, with adverse effects in China, Brazil and Russia, and adopted a $173-billion farm bill that increases subsidies to domestic farmers some seventy percent over current levels and thereby greatly hurts farmers in poor countries. These and many other such examples render somewhat comical the endless polemics for and against free trade and open markets. These debates miss what is happening in the real world: The poor countries are not given access to free trade and open markets. They cannot take advantage even of the entitlements they do have under the slanted rules of the WTO, because they do not have the resources to bring and win cases against the US or EU. Moreover, a poor country would have far more to lose than to gain from imposing retaliatory countertariffs – as winning such a case would entitle them to do – against the US or EU.
50 Where such estimates are seemly, they are readily volunteered. After the terrorist attacks of September 11, 2001, the President of the World Bank publicized his estimate "that tens of thousands more children will die worldwide and some 10 million people are likely to be living below the poverty line of $1 a day . . . because the attacks will delay the rich countries' recovery into 2002" (www.econ.worldbank.org/files/2462_press-release.pdf).
51 World Bank, *World Development Report 2003*, 235.
52 The Trade-Related Aspects of Intellectual Property Rights (TRIPs) Treaty was concluded in 1995. For a discussion of its content and impact, see UNDP: *Human Development Report 2001* (New York: Oxford University Press, 2001), chapter 5; Carlos Correa: *Intellectual Property Rights, the WTO and Developing Countries: The TRIPs Agreement and Policy Options* (London: Zed Books, 2000); Calestous Juma: "Intellectual Property Rights and Globalization. Implications for Developing Countries" (www.ksg.harvard.edu/Trade_Workshop/jumaipr.pdf, 1999); Jayashree Watal, "Access to Essential Medicines in Developing Countries: Does the WTO TRIPS Agreement Hinder It?" (www2.cid.harvard.edu/cidbiotech/dp/discussion8.pdf, 2000); and www.cptech.org/ip/.
53 Such guarantees were part of the initial 1982 version of the Treaty, but the Clinton administration succeeded in renegotiating them out of the Treaty just before the latter came into force in 1996 (Pogge, *World Poverty and Human Rights*, 125–6).
54 In the high-income economies, gross national income per capita is $2,226 per month on average (World Bank, *World Development Report 2003*, 235), compared to a monthly average income of about $11.40 for persons living below $2/day and of about $7 for those living below $1/day (note 21).
55 Such scruples are selective (see note 50).

56 See note 21. If we covered this entire shortfall, our share of global income would fall from 80.97 to 80.06 percent, from $25,506 to $25,217 billion (World Bank, *World Development Report 2003*, 235).

57 The WHO Commission on Macroeconomics and Health (chaired by Jeffrey Sachs) has sketched how deaths from poverty-related causes could be reduced by 8 million annually at a cost of $62 billion per year. The Commission proposes that the developed countries pay $27 billion of this cost, leaving $35 billion annually to be contributed by the poor countries (*Economist*, December 22 (2001), 82–3). The high-income countries could afford to pay the full $62 billion, which are under one quarter percent of their aggregate gross national incomes (World Bank, *World Development Report 2003*, 235).

58 UNDP: *Human Development Report 2003*, 290, down from aggregate ODA of $53.7 billion in 2000 (UNDP: *Human Development Report 2002* (New York: Oxford University Press, 2002), p. 202) and $56.4 billion in 1999 (UNDP, *Human Development Report 2001*, 190). The United States has led the decline by reducing ODA from 0.21 to 0.11 percent of GNP in a time of great prosperity culminating in enormous budget surpluses. In coming years, ODA is set to increase in the aftermath of September 11 – the figure for 2001 already includes a special $600 million US disbursement toward stabilizing Pakistan's military dictator.

59 Down from 28 percent in 1990 (UNDP, *Human Development Report 2003*, 290). India, with more poor people than any other country, receives ODA of $1.70 annually for each of its citizens, while dozens of much richer countries receive between $60 and $260 annually per capita (ibid., 290–4).

60 See http://millenniumindicators.un.org/unsd/mi/mi_series_results.asp? rowld=592.

61 "88. Implementation of the Declaration and the Programme of Action in developing countries, in particular in Africa and the least developed countries, will need additional financial resources and more effective development cooperation and assistance. This will require: ... (c) Agreeing on a mutual commitment between interested developed and developing country partners to allocate, on average, 20 percent of ODA and 20 percent of the national budget, respectively, to basic social programmes" (Programme of Action, chapter 5, article 88(c), www.un.org/esa/socdev/wssd/agreements/poach5.htm).

62 See note 43. After the end of the Cold War, the developed countries were able to reduce their military expenditures from 4.1 percent of their combined GDPs in 1985 to 2.2 percent in 1998 (UNDP, *Human Development Report 1998*, 197; UNDP, *Human Development Report 2000*, 217). With their combined GDPs at $25,104 billion in the year 2001 (World Bank, *World Development Report 2003*, 239), their peace dividend in 2001 comes to about $477 billion.

63 Citizens of the high-income countries also give aid through non-governmental organizations. Each year, such aid amounts to about $7 billion, or $7.60 per citizen (ibid. 290).

Index

CPSIA information can be obtained at www.ICGtesting.com
Printed in the USA
BVOW072121221111

276655BV00002B/67/P